I0419963

ANATOMY OF A MIRACLE

SACRILEGE AND REPARATION

By Richard Swiderski

2016

Table of Contents

Introduction

The miracle was new. It was made up of pieces of old miracles: the bleeding host that could fly but not escape the stabbing of the Jew. Later critics would ask why the host didn't flutter away from the tortures before they began. They had forgotten that Christ too could have escaped the torment of the flail and the nails but chose not to for the salvation of all, including the Roman soldiers, or, rather, the Jews, if only they would accept salvation.

The analogy between the host and Christ, his real presence in the body of the Communion wafer, was crucial to the miracle. The marvel packaged an exposition of the doctrine of transubstantiation.

Before, the sight of nature upended by the exercise of divine signmaking would cause the sinners present to see the error of their ways. That certainly was the effect of the host, a consecrated water given to confessed congregants during a Catholic Mass, bleeding and moving on its own in response to doubts and outright attacks. This sight sparked a renewal of faith in the baptized sinners and conversion of the faithless present.

On the Thursday before Easter, 1290, in the Jew's house opposite a church in Paris, the Jew stabbed and tried to boil a host which bled, and flitted, but he was not moved (in most tellings) to renounce his faith and convert. His wife and children (in most tellings), and other members of the Jewish community (when present) accepted instruction and baptism but Jonathas did not. He went to the fire clutching a book he claimed would grant him immunity from the flame. Both Jew and book burned to ash. His resistance unto death was new in several ways, but it still was part of the miracle.

The Jew's motive for conspiring with a vain, impecunious Christian woman to obtain a host then at least drive a knife into it and toss it into a cauldron was the animalistic despising of Christ that had been attributed to Jews with growing emphasis for the previous hundred years. Prior to that Jews were Hebrews, bystanders if that during the Passion of Christ conducted by the Romans into whose hands the Hebrews had delivered Christ.

Urbanization that brought Jewish and Christian communities into closer proximity, social and economic sanctions against the Jews that limited their role in economic life to such trades as moneylending, complete ignorance of Jewish religion all contributed to general distrust of these neighbors. That precipitated in negative characterizations and mass reactions when expectations seemed to be realized. Civil and religious authorities, both exploiting and protecting individual Jews, acted according to their own best interests. Thus everyone in the Jew's vicinity knew why he or she behaved that way and what should be done about it.

The miracle was new also in another motive sometimes tentatively attributed to the Jew: he was subjecting the host to trials to learn how it would respond, and to demonstrate to the idolatrous Christians that they were worshiping a piece of bread. He was a skeptic, a proto-scientist, and like others of those persuasions, was forcibly silenced after being branded a failed magician. Silenced not by God, but by the king's executioner at the behest of the bishop.

This miracle's newness gave it traction that lasted for centuries. It brought together general themes that touched on many of the divisions of medieval, renaissance, reformation, early modern, modern and now post-modern society. It was projected outside of history by being situated at a precise place and time like the Passion of Christ it mimicked, and caused to be further mimicked. All of its ingredients, even the outline of the miracle story itself, were present for years before it supposedly took place yet its full written and ritual formulation did not come until years afterward.

The story of the miracle was so deeply fixed in the mesh of symbols and values that constituted western European Christian society that even questioning historians, Protestant and Catholic, did not fully reject its historicity. The mandate of reparations, services and processions to stay the wrath of God for the sacrilege upon his son, perpetuated the miracle in its architectures. The miracle introduced a transition from older to newer forms of anti-Semitism, from the Jew as Christ killer to the Jew as international capitalist. A miracle all in all.

In the pages that follow I search for the foundations of the miracle, locate is earliest forms and follow its institutions and representations over the hundreds of years that follow. How did it begin, and how did it continue? An academic question, to be sure.

du Maine a perpetuite. ¶ En ce mesme an ¶ premier tout de iuillet fut le miracle du iuif a Paris en sa parroisse de sainct Jehan en greue touchāt l'hostie a corps precieux de Jesuchrist cōsacre dont on fait solennite ou conuent des Billettes a Paris. ¶ Lan

En ce mesme an a premier jour de juillet fut le miracle du iuif a Paris en la parroisse Sainct Jehan en greue touchant l'hostie a corps precieux de Jesuchrist consacre dont on fait solennite ou conuent des Billettes a Paris.

In this same year on the first day of July was the miracle of the Jew at Paris in the parish of Saint Jean-en-Grève concerning the host of the precious body of Jesus Christ consecrated to whom is made the solemnity at the convent of the Billettes in Paris.

La Mer des Histoires 1543: Chap 10

1.
The Jew's House

Intersecting the Bretonnerie
For me full of melancholy
Is found the Rue des Jardins
Where once did dwell the Jews[1]

Count Guillot of Paris wrote a long poem passing along the streets of Paris in his time, the early 14th century. His melancholy arose from the 1290 burning of a Jew (and perhaps his entire family) who lived on the Rue des Jardins. The Place de Grève, a flat public space on the shore of the Seine (Right Bank), and the Rue de Martrai, on this map constructed in the mid-19th century to represent the Paris of Guillot's poem, were the sites of executions. The ovals in the map below encircle the streets of Jewish residence recent and current for Guillot (1300) from the Rue des Jardins on the upper left to the Rue de la Juierie and the Petit Pont on the lower right.

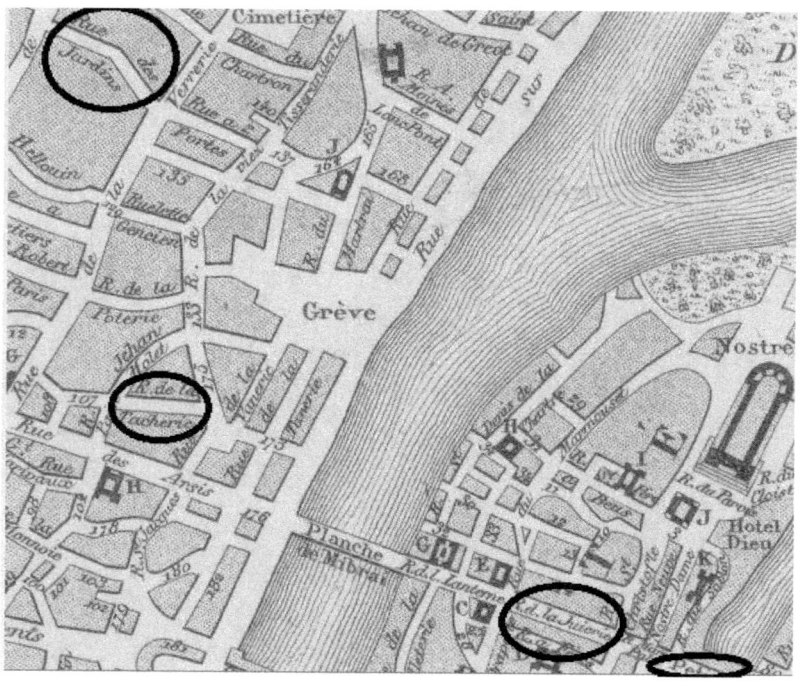

On a map compiled in the 17th century from records to show the arrangement of buildings and streets in Paris in 1223 the Jew's house is not marked, but the Place de Grève (P) and the church of St. Jean-en-Grève (Q) are clearly indicated.[2] From their location it is possible to visualize the position of Rue des Jardins and the house of the Jew in one of the oblongs to the left of the Place de Grève and inside the city wall (squares mark towers and circles mark gates).

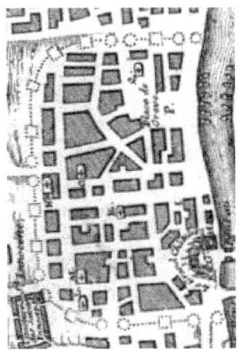

When in the 1387 map of this series the location of the house of the Jew, then the Chapelle des Billettes, is marked in a numbering system (22), it does not seem to be in the correct place.

A 1552 projective map clarifies the relations between the major buildings of the miracle's topography.[3] The Place de Grève is still open to the Seine but now the major building in its space is the Hotel de Ville, the city's administrative headquarters since it was purchased by the provost of merchants for that purpose in 1357 and expanded afterward. St. Jean-en-Grève rises behind it, and two streets to the left is Les Billettes, which marks the building where the Jew lived. There is no map that indicates where the house of the Jew was, only the chapel that replaced it. From the first, the house of the Jew is known by its negation.

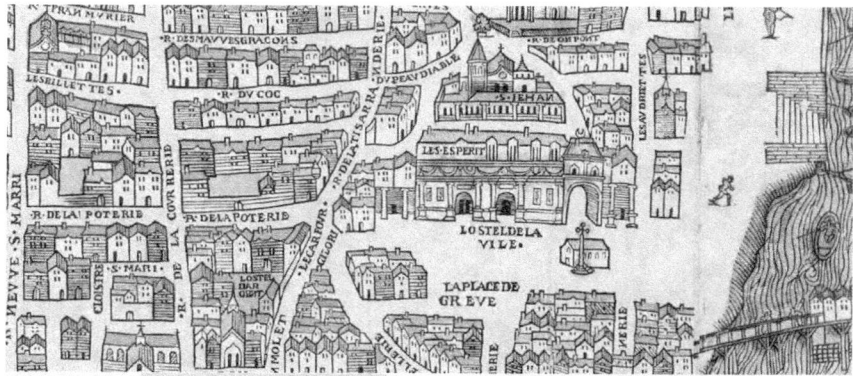

The events at the time of the miracle are read backward from its architectural and institutional structure, which became a firm mainstay of the area for centuries. Where was the house of the Jew in 1290? Was the Chapel of Les Billettes only its ascribed location?

Jews were living in the area inland from the Place de Grève along the Rue des Jardins. Guillot's 19th century editor and the designer of the first map based on his poem, Edgar Mareuse, commented on one of the street names, Le Pet-au-Diable that was applied to the street behind St. Jean-en-Grève after Guillot's time. The inscription "Du Peau Diable" on the 1552 map doesn't make any sense. The mapmakers may have been trying to avoid writing "The Devil's Fart" on their map.

Mareuse thought that the name either expressed local Christians' disdain for the Jews who had a synagogue there, or it referred to a character named Petau who lived on that street. A large boulder, possibly sulfurous, placed near the street, was also known by that name, though it is not clear which came first, the boulder or the synagogue. After the synagogue was gone the street was named Tourniquet-Saint-Jean from the constriction in its right of way.

The 1292 tax roll of Paris compiled by officials under King Philippe le Bel (reigned 1285-1314) listed a total of 126 Jews.[4] They are not identified by name in the street-by-street list but were enumerated separately at the end of the list as a body of distinctly taxable interest. On the Rue des Jardins, where the Jew's house was retrospectively located, there was a man named Peter, "a convert" but no others who might have been Jewish. *"Abraham, fuiz Mosse Marc d'Argent et sa femme"* who lived on Petit-Pont when taxes were collected from them in 1292, probably were Jewish and from the name probably practiced the moneylending trade. Many of the entries in the tax roll give only first name and occupation or place of origin of the listed person.

"The Jews, by turns driven out or received in France, according to the hate or need of the moment…"[5] were once more ordered out of France by the king, at least the English and Gascon Jews were, in 1290.[6] Several English and Gascon persons listed living on streets with Jewish populations (Juiverie, Petit-Pont) in 1292 suggests that the order was not strictly obeyed or enforced.

The "hate or need of the moment" often had to do with the tides of prosperity that carried the Jews away from and toward the nobility and the commoners in cycles. History and fiction across Europe tell of the noble who lives beyond his means at the suffrance of Jewish lenders and pawnbrokers, becomes abusive when he can't pay them back, returns to them when he needs more money. The commoners just pawned and then tried to recover their possessions. The hate-need dialectic between Christians and Jews was as much driven by appropriation-expropriation as it was driven by lending-collecting.

Louis IX (reigned 1226-70), the only French king to be canonized a saint, twice a crusader in the Holy Land, faced the taunts of the Saracens from whom he tried to capture Christian sites, that he was campaigning for those sites while being best friends at home with the people who killed Christ.[7]

Prior to leaving for that first campaign Louis followed the pattern of his predecessors in dispossessing then restoring the Jews. His great piety, and siding with the church in his dynasty's struggle with the barons for control of the state, caused him, unique among the Christian monarchs to whom it was addressed, to respond actively to a missive from Pope Gregory.

Delivered to the Bishop of Paris in 1239 by the excommunicated Jew turned Franciscan friar Nicolas Donin, the pope's letter enjoined the prelate to confiscate all Jewish books by the first Sunday of Lent. In response Louis called for the Jews to defend themselves in a disputation against the charges that the Talmud commanded Jews to kill Gentiles and dishonor agreements with them, and that it contained a number of theological errors.[8] The slanted verdict in the disputation required the Jews of France to turn in all their books. Twenty-four cartloads were burned on the Place de Grève in 1242, to be followed by other burnings.

Louis IX rode to the Crusades in 1248 (in part funded by Jews) having dispossessed the Jews in his realm both materially and spiritually.

From the viewpoint of Christians acting upon Jews, 1290 and the area of the first map were the time and place of great tension. Book burnings and executions of criminals and heretics took place nearby. Louis ordered in 1269 that all Jews wear a yellow badge (*rouelle*) on their clothing (in keeping with the Fourth Lateran Council of 1215). Fines were levied under his successor Philippe le Bel in 1288 after complaints of loud chanting in synagogues.

In 1287 King Edward I of England ordered the expulsion of Jews from his Duchy of Gascony in the southeast of France. All debts to Jewish moneylenders then became payable to the king, who badly needed the money. The 1290 expulsion of English and Gascon Jews from the France of Philippe le Bel was exceeded by the expulsion of all Jews from England in that same year. Jews were suspended between countries where they had dwelt for a long time.

Acted upon, the Jews might be expected to act. The story of the Paris miracle of that year of expulsions and expropriations is how Christians saw a Jew acting in that time and place.

The place where the Jew's house was located was defined by human industry and a Christian cosmology turning secular. The Place de Grève was called by that name from the early years of the formation of the Cité de Paris from the gravel carried ashore by the periodic advance of the river's waters over the edge of that flat space. Boats were regularly moored offshore. They arrived carrying food and goods bartered on the open space, and all the activity associated with that commerce took place in and through that space. The *meuleurs de bois,* the men who measured loads of firewood that regularly arrived, had a chapel dedicated to Sainte Geneviève in the church of Saint Jean-en-Grève.

That church defined one side of the square, and was said to resemble on a much smaller scale the Cathedral of Notre Dame visible across the arm of the Seine on the Ile de la Cité. The church was behind the *Maison des Piliers* constructed by King Philippe Auguste as a residence, which became in the mid-14th century the administrative headquarters of the mercantile body that constituted the government of the city, the *Hôtel de Ville.* The church's growth, spurred by the miracle, would at first exceed the *Maison des Piliers,* which in its new function came to dominate the Place.

The Place de Grève gave a neologism to the French language: *faire la grève,* to go on strike, from the oppositional politics staged there. The ability of the localized names to be generalized to the entire language betokened the centrality of the place to French speakers. Formed of converging symbols, the miracle that took place a few streets away would radiate on waves of signs, and cross readily into other languages.

The agitation that came into focus on the Place de Grève was the struggle for control of urban spaces between religious and secular authorities and the urban populace. The phases of the miracle mirrored the evolution of conflicts from transgression and revolt to execution of the performers-transgressors, which also took place on the Place de Grève. The periphery of the Place de Grève came to be dominated by residential buildings with windows overlooking the square for viewing events there (performances, executions, riots).

In addition to the church of Saint Jean-en-Grève (J, left side, on the first map above), several other churches formed points in the cosmos of the miracle. Saint Gervais (A on the map), of which Saint Jean-en-Grève began as a chapel, remained in the background. Saint Merri (G on the map) was an old church dedicated to St. Peter that became the repository of the remains of Saint Médéric (Merri) in the 8th century and in the 12th century a parish church. It was the site of a Eucharistic miracle. All these churches, including Saint Jacques de la Boucherie (H), contained chapels for saints who were patrons of confraternities, groups of men joined both by trade and residence in the immediate area.

Saint Gervais, for instance, held a chapel for the confraternity of *verriers,* glaziers and painters on glass, and the nearby Rue de la Verrerie was named for its concentration of people in this trade. *Verrerie,* stained glass windows, was a means for the dissemination of the miracle story from the 14th century onward. Likewise there was a Rue de la Tissanderie (weaving), a Rue de la Tanerie (tanning hides) and a Rue de la Boucherie (meat cutting) in the vicinity. If members of the confraternities and trade groups inhabited these streets in the previous centuries, by the time of the 1292 tax records they were more dispersed.

Churches outside of the immediate area but within Paris that partook of the miracle included St. Étienne du Mont and St. Martin des Champs. There were specific connections among these churches, if only that patrons of one were patrons of the others. Saint Étienne du Mont was the site of the remains of Ste. Geneviève, whose votaries had a chapel in Saint Jean-en-Grève. It was the terminus of a major procession bearing the miraculous host.

All of these institutions and the relations among them existed prior to the events that yielded the miraculous host, and made local contributions to its narrative, ceremonial and projective form. In the large sense they formed the walls of the Jew's house.

Notes

[1] Contre val la Bretonnerie/m'en ving plain de mirencolie/trouvai la rue des Jardins/où les Juys maintrent jadis Guillot (1875: 69)
[2] Delamare (1705: t.1, deuxième et troisième plan)
[3] Ville, Cité et Université de Paris, Truschet et Hoyaux (Paris, 1552)
[4] Géraud (1863: 179)
[5] Béraud and Dufey (1828: 365)
[6] Boutaric (1863: 266)
[7] Sauval (1724: 524)
[8] Loeb (1881)

2.
The First Reports

What caused the Paris miracle to be described as it was, happening where it was placed with the persons described? In the absence of contemporary documents, we will never know. The reasons it happened when, where and with whom it did bear symbolic weight outside of the miracle itself. Speculation on its real history based on what is known about the place and time risks constructing another story.

All of the reports of the Paris miracle were written with an eye to its final meaning within the world of Western European Christianity. None is an *arrêt* issued by a parlement in response to a present crime, to achieve the capture of wrongdoers and their punishment. The deed has been done, the outcome registered, and reparation undertaken. Most, but not all reports, give the date as Eastertime, 1290, and the place more or less specifically as a section of Paris, when a place is given.

Lacking the chronological record of such documents as the *Actes du parlement de Paris*, which do not provide an entry for this (or for that matter any other) miracle, assigning priority to the reports is a matter of guesswork. Especially since the reports give the time of the miracle but not the dates when they themselves were set down. How much time elapsed between the miracle event and the record cannot be determined. Several reports were composed close to the time of the miracle.

For the year 1290, the day after Easter, the monk and chronicler Jean de Thilrode entered in his universal history set down 1276-98, a miraculous event that took place in Paris (selection 2-1 following this text). This news reached him at his monastery of Saint-Bavon in Ghent.

"A certain Jew living in Paris had a Christian maid whom he offered ten pounds for a consecrated host."[9] Asking rhetorically "Are not Christians fools to believe in this host?" the Jew had others of his community summoned and together they attacked the host placed on a table with knives, stilettos and other instruments. Their lack of success led the purchaser of the host, whose name Thilrode gives as Johannes, to drive a large knife into it, causing it to break into three pieces and begin to bleed profusely. Many of the Jews present were converted. Johannes continued with his abuse of the host by placing it in a cauldron of boiling water where "from divine grace it was transformed into flesh and blood." Johannes, "the reporter of these events," and his entire family then converted to the Catholic faith.

The information for de Thilrode's chronicle entry must have come originally from Johannes by way of Paris documents.[10] Johannes was the only one present for all of the events. The attack on the host brought to the Jew by a Christian woman in his employ for a cash payment is at first communal and unsuccessful. Then Johannes by himself draws blood and causes it to rupture into a trinity. Still not perfectly awed, he tosses it into boiling water, where its change brings about his and his family's conversion. Johannes wished to dispel foolish Christian faith in the Eucharist. Like other rationalist doubters he is answered with the host's invulnerability, which causes his fellow Jews to convert, and he is further answered with a blood miracle, which spurs his own conversion.

Where the miracle should have been mentioned, it wasn't. Guillaume de Nangis, a monk at the abbey of St. Denis who from 1285 until his death in 1300 had charge of the library, wrote a Latin *Chronicon* from the creation of the world to the year of his death. The earlier years of his chronicle were drawn from the manuscripts of other writers. After 1163 he introduces material not found elsewhere; the period 1285-1300 contains contemporary reports and observations. 1290 and the decade after pass with no mention of the Paris miracle. The 19th century editor of Guillaume's Latin chronicle wrote that the miracle of the Billettes was among the events "of little importance" intercalated into the French translation of the chronicle that became *Les Grandes Chroniques.*[11]

Les Grandes Chroniques de France, the history of the French monarchy from ancient Troy to the 15th century, at first compiled in Latin by the monks at Saint-Denis and then by court officials, turns aside from royal wars and alliances to notice the Paris Jew's 1290 sacrilege (selection 2-2).[12] "*Le bon juif,*" "the good Jew" (the only name given) dwells in the parish of Saint Jean-en-Grève. The Christian woman "vomits out" a host she took during Holy Week and on Good Friday the Jew throws it into boiling water and pierces it, causing it to bleed vermillion. He then takes it out of the water and beats it with a stick. This is proved against him by the bishop Simon Mattifait, who consults with masters of theology and the law, and condemns the Jew to death by burning. The Jew's twelve year-old daughter by his wife Bellatine the bishop has baptized and placed with the *Filles-Dieu de Paris*, a religious community composed of reformed prostitutes with a convent just within the Cité de Paris, near the gate of Saint Denis, and far from the Place de Grève.

The Jew alone is responsible for the violent assault on the host he receives from the Christian woman, who held it in her mouth at Communion and impiously spit it out. On Good Friday, the day of Christ's Passion, the host is boiled until it bleeds the mercurial color of blood, then is beaten. The Bishop (Simon Matifas of Busay, Bishop of Saint-Denis, 1290-1304) in consultation with experts, condemns the Jew to death and sends his daughter to a convent where once-degraded women form a religious order. Conversion is not an acceptable end for the Jew, and it is forced upon his daughter. The fate of his wife, the only named member of his family, is not given.

The *Grandes Chroniques'* telling of the Paris sacrilege is grounded in the Paris terrain and personages of the time. The parish, the bishop and the street where the Jew lives are named though the Jew himself isn't. Once the Jew acts upon the host, the authority of the Bishop to adjudicate breaches of religious law is abruptly asserted with no intervening action. No reason is given for the Jew's attacks on the host, which seem to stem from a raw hostility rather than a wish to disprove the host's assumed invulnerability. His burning at the stake is a heretic's punishment and revenge for his treatment of the host.

"In the given year (1290) there was in Paris a Jew who lent out money in usury, to whom came a commoner woman (*semplice feminella*) to recover her pawned dress…"[13] Giovanni Villani, a Florentine banker who was in Flanders and France from 1300 to 1308, set down a version of the "miracle of the body of Christ" in his *Chroniche* (selection 2-3). Villani represented interests that were replacing Jewish moneylenders as the source of royal finance wherever possible, and had reasons beside religious ones to denounce the Jew.

From the outset sin motivates the actors, the Jew first by usury (*usura*), and after the woman has brought him the host on Easter morning, by gross passion (*per quella cupidigia*) to throw it into boiling water in a kettle. When the water does not consume "the body of Christ" (Villani's only phrase for the host here and elsewhere) he stabs it, and the water becomes vermilion. Cold water also changes color when the host is thrown into it. Christians entering the shop to borrow money see the sacrilege, and the body of Christ leaps into the middle of a table. By the evidence of the Christians the Jew is taken, burned, the body of Christ is received by a priest with great reverence and the Jew's house is made into a church called the Savior of the People.

The bleeding host is central to all of these accounts, and the conditions of its reaching that state remain the same. The context changes to suit the milieu. A monastic chronicler who has converted from Judaism sees it as a revelation that brings about the conversion of the entire Jewish community. The chroniclers of the French monarchy see it as a sign of intractable Jewish disbelief that can only be answered by force, and can be used as an excuse for the king to expel the Jews.

The Florentine banker, who must have known competition from Jewish moneylenders concurs with the low opinion of the Jews, and makes ordinary exchanges extraordinary: the woman's recovery of her coat from the Jew in exchange for the host; water changed into blood; the swift transformation of the Jew's house into a church. For Villani the host is the body of Christ and the Jew replicates the Passion as he tests the sacred body's imperviousness. The enduring host is enshrined by the priest and the Jew's house is converted into a Christian citadel.

The Paris miracle was retold with additions specific to Paris and was adapted to changing social and economic conditions as it spread elsewhere. 17th to 19th century writers, acquiring a historic perspective, set down composite versions of the story which actually were the result of social and economic developments over time. Precisely what happened to occasion the story in the first place may never be known, but a few common points can be recovered from independent records. In Paris the Jew's attack on the host was administratively linked to the cult of Corpus Domini through histories, architecture and artifacts.

Villani's mention that a church was built in place of the Jew's house refers to the papal bull issued by Boniface VIII on August 16, 1295 granting the bishop of Paris permission who delegated the responsibility to a wealthy bourgeois named Regnier Flaming to construct a chapel there. The wording of the papal document, which was repeated in other accounts, suggests the reason for the early focus on the Jew's tossing the host into boiling water: "whereupon indeed water by divine miracle is known to be converted into blood." The stabbed host bled, but its presence in the water caused the water to be miraculously transformed into blood.

These early chronicles, closest to the time of the miracle, gathered elements rather than reported an event. Other chronicles of the same period did not include this miracle. Several of the elements, the sacrilegious Jew, the bleeding host, the Jewish residence converted into a Christian shrine, were reported for other events. The venal Christian woman and the boiled host were unique to this instance. A core had formed; other elements were arriving.

Selections-Texts and Translations

2-1. de Thilrode (1835: 60-61)

Officialis curie parisiensis universis presentia visuris ac audituris cupimus non latere quod quidam Judeus commorans parisius christianam habebat ancillam erga quam hostiam emit pro . x . libras · consecratam ipsa vero hostiam consecratam suo domino presentavit quo facto predictam hostiam posuit in mensam ac alios Judeos fecit

convocari · dicens numquid non sunt stulti christiani in hanc hostiam credentes · accipientes cultellos et stilos ac instrumenta alia hostiam delere volebant quod facere non potuerunt tandem quidam ex ipsis magnum arripiens cultellum hostiam percussit et in tres partes hostia se divisit et continuo sanguis exivit quo miraculo facto multi sunt conversi · Insuper hostia ponebatur in caldario pleno aqua ut bulliretur et destrueretur · Hostia vero ex divina gratia in carnem et sanguinem se mutavit hiis miraculis visis Johannes exhibitor presentium cum omni familia sua ad fidem catholicam est conversus hec acta sunt . Anno domini - M.°CC.° nonagesimo in postero die resurrectionis domini ·

> Annus millenus ac ducentenus ab ortu .
> salvatoris erat · quinquagenus quoque trinus ·
> quando per ollandos flandria succubuit .

In the presence of all official Paris at the court, which seeing and hearing we do not wish to conceal, a certain Paris Jew had a Christian maid who sold a host for ten livres. She truly presented the consecrated host to her lord who thereupon placed the host upon a table and had other Jews summoned, saying, "Now are not Christians stupid believing in this host?" Gathering knives and stilettos they wished to destroy the host but were not able, then one among them grasping a large knife struck the host and the host divided itself into three parts and emitted blood copiously by which miracle done many were converted. Moreover the host was placed in a cauldron full of water to boil and dissolve it. The host truly from divine grace was transformed into flesh and blood by these miracles. Johannes the party responsible was converted together with his entire family to the Catholic faith. This happened so in the year of the Lord 1290 in the latter day of the resurrection of the Lord.

2-2. *Les Grandes Chroniques.* Paris, ed. (1837: 100)

Charles les contes d'Anjou et au meisme a perpetuite teint.

(1) En ice meisme an, en la kalande de juignet, il ot un juif à Paris en la paroisse de Saint-Jehan en Grève (2), lequel fit tant par devers une femme crestienne que elle li aporta le corps de Jhésucrist en une oeste (3) sacrée, laquelle elle avoit reçue en la sepmaine peneuse en la avommichant, et la bailla au juif. Quant le juif l'ot par devers soy, si mist ladite oeste en plaine chaudière de yaue chaude, le jour du vendredi aouré ; et quant ladite oeste fu en l'yaue boullant, il la commença à poindre de son coutel, et lors devint l'yaue aussi comme toute vermeille. Et après ce , il osta ladite oeste de la chaudière, et la commença à batre d'une verge : laquelle chose fu toute prouvée contre le juif par l'évesque Symon Matiffait. Si avint que du conseil et de l'assentement des preudeshommes qui à Paris estoient régens en théologie et en décret, ledit juif fu condamné à mourir et fu ars devant tout le peuple ; et estoit appellé Le bon juif, et sa femme avoit à non Bellatine, laquelle avoit une fille à l'aage de douze ans ou environ, que ledit évesque Simon fist baptisier ; et la fist demourer avec les Filles-Dieu à Paris.

In the same year, in the month of July, there was a Jew in Paris in the parish of St. Jean-en-Grève, who did so bargain with a Christian woman that she brought him the body of Jesus Christ in the blessed host which she had received in Holy Week by vomiting it out and dispensed it to the Jew. As soon as the Jew had it to himself he placed said host in a cauldron full of warm water the day of Holy Thursday. And when the said host was in the boiling water, he started to pierce it with a knife, and then also the water became all as vermillion. And after that he removed said host from the cauldron, and began to beat it with a flail: which matter was proved against the Jew by the Bishop Symon Mattifait. Thus after the counsel and assent of the gentlemen who were regents in theology in Paris and by decree said Jew was condemned to death and was burned before all the people. And he was called "the good Jew" and his wife was by name Bellatine, who had a daughter of the age of twelve years or about, who the said Bishop Simon had baptized and made her live with the Filles-Dieu in Paris.

2-3. Villani (1537: 94)

D'uno miracolo che auuenne in Parigi del corpo di Christo.   Cap.   c.xxxvi.

El detto anno, essendo in Parigi uno giudeo che prestaua d'usura, alquale uenédo una semplice feminella per suo pegno, il giudeo le disse, se tu mi rechi il corpo del nostro Christo io ti rédero il tuo pegno sanza denari, la feminella il promisse, & la mattina della pasqua andandosi a comunicare ritenne in bocca il sacramento del corpo di Christo, & recollo al detto giudeo, per quella cupidigia, ilquale giudeo messa una padella al fuoco con acqua bogliente ui gittò dentro il corpo di Christo, et non potendolo in quella consumare cõ uno coltello il feri piu uolte, ilquale fece abõ deuidemente sanguae, onde tutta l'acqua diuenne uermiglia, et di quella il trasse & nascofelo in aqua freda & similemente diuenne uermiglia, in quelli suoi segni s'accorsero christiani per impermutare danari, saccorsero del sacrilegio del giudeo, faltrando il corpo di Christo per se medesimo in so una tauola, & cio conosciuto per li christiani, il giudeo fu preso & arsiy, & il corpo santo di Christo con grande reueréza per lo sacerdote fur riccolto, & della casa doue auuenne il miracolo si fece una chiesa, laquale si chiama il Saluatore della gente.

Chapter 136. A miracle of the body of Christ that happened in Paris. In the said year there was in Paris a Jew who made loans on interest, to whom came a simple little woman to redeem her pledge. The Jew said to her, "If you bring me the body of your Christ I will return your pledge to you without payment." The woman promised to, and the morning of Easter, going to communion, retained the sacrament of the body of Christ in her mouth, and brought it to the Jew's shop. With that rapacity the Jew put a vessel on the fire with boiling water and threw in the body of Christ, and not being able to consume it in that vessel struck it many blows with a knife, which made blood abundantly, so that all the water turned vermilion, and he took it from that vessel and in cold water likewise became vermilion. At which time Christians arriving to borrow money noticed the sacrilege of the Jew and the body of Christ leaping by itself over a table. And made known by the Christians the Jew was taken and burned, and the body of Christ was received with great reverence by the priest, and a church was made of the house where the miracle occurred which is called the Savior of the people.

Notes

[9] de Thilrode (1835: 60-61)
[10] Robert (1881: 220n69)
> 69. **1290**, Pâques. — Relation du sacrilège et du miracle de l'église des Billettes. — *Magna quidem fuerunt beneficia* (Duchesne, 35, fol. 123 ; Fontette, 32, nº 39).

[11] Géraud (1843: xvfn1)
[12] Paris, ed. (1837: 100)
[13] Villani (1537: 94 (Book 7, chapter 136))

3.
Elements of the Miracle

The miracle, itself designated by different names, was preserved and disseminated as an axis of names and events conveyed in the midst of changing beliefs and terrains. The event in that place and at that time was the precipitation of existing themes into a narrative within an arrangement of urban space and human groups. An emergent ideology made a cosmos out of part of a city. Though the miracle lacked an identifiable narrator or reporter, and did not appear in chronicles of the time it was said to have occurred, it seemed authentic from the unique combination of elements achieved.

After outlining the miracle in the first notices, I will present the elements brought together in the mature tellings to form the body of the miracle. Successive chapters will examine the institutional form of these elements as they played out in time and affected subsequent formulations of the miracle, some of which no longer were connected to the specifics of place while perpetuating the cosmology.

A key text of the fully formulated miracle narrative is from a Latin manuscript (1322) in the Bibliothèque Nationale de France, transcribed and published in a 19th century journal devoted to making historic manuscript texts available to scholars.[14] It is the earliest text to contain most of the elements that formed the miracle story widely reported as historical. The following outline summarizes this story and its variants. The original text with translation is the first selection in the Appendix to this book (A-1).

The date of 1290 is given in the manuscript and is usually cited, though other dates are given in a few sources, but the Eastertime period of occurrence is essential to all accounts of the miracle. It may be mapped onto the days of Easter week, which are a culmination of Lent in the Passion, Crucifixion and Resurrection of Christ on Easter Sunday.

The location of the miracle most often is Paris, by which is meant the Cité de Paris, and that portion of the old walled city that later was designated the Right Bank of the Seine and much later the 4th Arrondisement. The Jew's house itself the center of the action is pinpointed on the city map only after a chapel is created that circularly defines the location of the Jew's house.

The question of what actually occurred in the house that became the chapel is the intriguingly unresolved mystery of the miracle. Did a Jew or someone identified as a Jew live there, and did he act in a way that caused him to be accused of the desecration? All answers are in retrospect; no sources set the scene without leading up to the miracle.

The churches of Saint Jean-en-Grève and Saint Merry are named. Other prominent churches such as Saint Gervais and Sainte Croix de la Bretonnerie are less frequently included.

The Jew's business conducted out of his house is that of a moneylender offering secured loans at interest, described as usury. The Paris of the late 13th century abounded in Christian moneylenders, called "lombards." The two individuals designated "usurier" in the 1292 tax census were not Jewish.

A Christian woman has left with the Jew her finest garment, one she wants to wear on Easter, as collateral for a loan occasionally specified as 30 pieces of gold, the amount paid to Judas for betraying Christ. No reason is given why she chose the Jew over other moneylenders. The penniless owner going to great lengths to recover a pawned possession is a well-established dramatic theme

The Jew's greed and the woman's vanity provide the impetus. To release the garment the Jew offers the woman a trade: bring me the host you receive at Eastertime Communion and I will return your possession and forgive the loan. The motives of the two arise from their fixed characters. The woman's vanity turns upon the greed projected into her by the Jew's offer. Why does the Jew want the host?

The characterological mind frame of the miracle story's intended audience had access to several reasons for the Jew's offer. First, Jews were not known to make offers to their own disadvantage. What he seeks to gain is not monetary, but probatory, a quest for a sectarian triumph. He wishes to possess the host to have the opportunity to disprove that it is godly, that it is anything more than a material object. This is consistent with medieval Jewish dismissal of Christian worship as idolatry.[15] The Jew's names for the host reflects his belief about Christian beliefs: "your god," "idol," or "bread," among others. The Latin narrative's names for the host, if it isn't "host" throughout, are reverential: "the body of Christ," *digne personne* ("worthy person"). Christian acceptance of the host as a "person" was both being promoted and anticipated in the narrative.

The Jew simply may be enraged against Christians and their beliefs and lashes out against what is dear to them. Tales of Jews carrying out programs of desecration upon Christian religious objects such as statues and crucifixes, and ritual murders of the Christians themselves, were the background of the miracle. The fiction of procuring Christian blood for imagined Jewish ritual practices, the blood libel, is not part of the tradition of this story.

The Jew has a name, Jonathas, Jonathan, Jacob, or Johannes if one is given; the "evil" Christian woman never does. The Jew may have a family, a wife and children, at the very least a daughter, some of whom may have names.

The Christian woman agrees to the Jew's proposal. She receives the host as usual, at Mass in Holy Communion. Where any attention is given to how the woman procures the host, she accepts it on her tongue, conceals it in her mouth, and later spits it out into a cloth, which she presents to the Jew, who has no compunctions about handling it. The woman has received the host without devotion, and she does not absorb it because she is not worthy of its gift. This may or may not be made explicit. She recovers her clothing and leaves the Jew's shop. Her eventual downfall is annexed to the miracle story in the later dramatic and painted representations. In the early versions she disappears with her gown.

The Christian woman is sometimes a maid in the Jew's household. Like many Christians she has borrowed money from the Jew. The ledgers that stand on shelves in visual representations of the Jew's shop contain names and sums, and are themselves an object of desire. The woman's method of resolving her debt and recovering her possessions is all the more rebarbative to those who wouldn't consider dishonestly receiving and selling the host to resolve a debt. This is one of those trades, like money for sex, widely condemned but carried on in secret, and disgraceful when revealed.

The Jew either makes his family witness at least the beginning of his assault on the host, or he goes about it entirely by himself. The role of his wife, named or not, may be that of a passive bystander, or an active opponent of his receiving the host and attacking it. The children, a girl and at least one boy, are passive observers at this point. In no version of the miracle does the Jew try to make a show of his deeds for the Christian public.

The Jewish community, in some versions summoned and taking part at least in the first phases of abuse, are quickly converted to Christianity by the spectacle of the host's invulnerable bleeding. de Thilrode's and Villani's chronicles, quoted in the last chapter, have the Jewish community as a whole setting upon the host, which forms the basis of the Brussels variant of the miracle narrative developed in the late 14th century.

The Jew's deeds at the very least include stabbing with a sharp knife the host placed on a table, and to his chagrin drawing streams of blood, or exactly three drops of blood. The Jew is undeterred by this, though his family flees. The words used for the first instrument connote a sharp-pointed short-bladed possibly folding knife (*canif, canivet, cultellum pennarium*) that was carried by people for everyday needs, for instance cutting bread. The host splits into three or five pieces while remaining integral.

The Jew may voice his intent to shatter the host, that is, pulverize it, as might be expected of a piece of dried bread or a wafer set upon with sharp instruments. It does not disintegrate or dissolve, a primary feature of this and other Eucharistic miracles. It maintains physical wholeness through symbolic wholeness.

Enraged by the host's invulnerability and/or its bleeding, the Jew switches to other tools and actions. He uses a hammer to transfix the host with nails to an upright post and then pierces it with a hunting spear. At this point the Jew's wife, appalled and terrified by the proceedings and urging the Jew to desist, removes herself and the children from the scene of abuse. In some texts the Jew's frenzy can seem as much like domestic abuse as sacrilege, as he becomes wrapped up in the fury of his assault.

The sequence of abuse, each step of which has sent forth streams of blood, changes means when the Jew tosses the host into a pot of boiling water, which turns blood red. In brief versions, because of a naming tradition, this may be the only act included. A vessel of cold water follows, with the same outcome. The blood and water recall the two fluids that issue from the crucified Christ's wound when he is pierced by a centurion's lance. The host always remains whole, and stained by blood.

The Jew might just throw the host into the fire, from which it escapes unconsumed. In one scenario the Jew transfixes the host while it is in the water where it bleeds anew. In most tellings the host transforms the water into blood without itself disintegrating. Some versions needed to resort to further piercing to explain the blood in the water.

Two more prodigies follow. The host flies out of the cauldron and through the air, and a cross with Christ crucified appears above the boiling water. In its most extended form, the Jew's attacks parallel step by step the sequence of Christ's Passion, from the piercing with the crown of thorns, the scourging at the pillar to the crucifixion manifest at the end. This emphasizes the transubstantiation of the host into Christ's body and evokes the culpability of the Jew and his people for subjecting Christ (the host) to these tortures. It makes the Jews the active agents of deeds the Roman soldiers performed in the gospel account, encapsulating the historic transition from Hebrews to Jews.

The appearance of the Christ crucified drives the Jew from the interior room where all the violent acts have been carried out, and into a hiding place. An underground cell is sometimes indicated, and actually was the place where the relics were exhibited in the chapel of the miracles made from the Jew's house.

The miracle becomes known to the Christian community outside in one of two ways, which distinguish two miracle narratives. Either Christians enter the Jew's house seeking loans and witness the blood evidence of mayhem, or the Jew's son boasts to the children of families going to Easter morning services in a neighboring church that they need not continue since his father has killed their god. The church they are planning to attend is given in the Parisian recensions of the miracle as Ste. Croix de la Bretonnerie, located near the Jew's house.

Alerted by the child's words, a goodly Christian woman (Martine, sometimes) enters the Jew's house seeking fire for her stove. The host flies into her tinder box. Or she enters the house holding a wooden bowl, into which the host quickly guides itself.

In one striking variant, from an old French manuscript text translated in the Appendix to this book (A-3), the Jew attempts to bribe the Christian woman to secure her silence.

The woman carries the host in its receptacle to the nearby church of St. Jean-en-Grève, if the church is named. The parish priest receives it and places it on the altar, or it flies from the receptacle to the altar. Or the priest or a bishop goes to the Jew's house and himself receives the flying host. At this point in the miracle narrative the fixed location of the host in the present-day church may be cited as proof of the events. The goodly Christian woman is in some versions miraculously detained in the church until she relates to the gathering crowd how the host came to her.

After or before the recovery of the host a crowd enters the house and brings the Jew to justice. He (and his family) are taken before the bishop, the only distinctive historic character named, and interrogated by the bishop and his councilors. The Jew is offered the alternative of conversion to Christianity or death. His wife and children are most likely to accept conversion, or be forcibly converted. One daughter may be baptized and given to the religious order, the *Filles de Dieu*. Only in one picturing of the miracle is the entire family burned at the stake. The task of burning the condemned falls to the secular authorities at the behest of the prelate and his court.

If the Jew remains intransigent and is condemned to the fire, he asks that a book be brought from his house. He is confident that the book will protect him from burning. Both he and the book are reduced to ashes, a recollection of the burning of the Talmud.

If the narrative continues after this it is to tell of the seizure of the Jew's house and its conversion into a chapel through the largesse of a Christian layman, Renier Flemane (Rayner Flaming, etc). A religious order is brought from their house in Chalons to serve as caretakers of the shrine and its relics. An annual feast day and procession are decreed to be celebrated in reparation.

In written texts the miracle story can be as brief as a few lines, summarized as "the Jew-the theft of the host-the abuse of the host and miraculous response-the Jew's punishment."[16]Additions to that line are either enhancements meant to emphasize one or another of the basic elements for communal relevance or to introduce features of the miracle's institutionalization.

The basic texts were in Latin and vernacular languages, especially French and Italian. The most extended texts in Latin were not translated into vernacular languages until the 18th century. The difference between the briefest texts and the longest ones is the difference between the story itself and the circumstances and purposes of its perpetuation. Oral transmission can only be inferred from the written record, which does not record one person relating the story to another but treats it as an eternal truth, a fixture of universal history.

In written and visual forms the miracle was adapted to the aims of its purveyors who included, transformed and excluded elements of the story. If it were one of the hundreds of other Eucharistic miracle stories spreading from specific locales it would not be recognizable in its transformations. The core of the Paris miracle is formed of unique elements that identified it from one transformation to another, even if Paris was not named as the locus. The Paris elements are innovations in the new history of Eucharistic miracles. Their combination formed a center around which new versions could be built.

The host made to bleed by a Jew who attacks it with implements, the burned-boiled host and the intransigence of the Jew are the two new elements that appear with the 1290 Paris miracle story. Thilrode differs from the *Grandes Chroniques* and Villani, in having the Jew accept conversion. For all three this is the basic string of events.

The action of a person who penetrates the host and causes it to bleed was new with this miracle, the imagery most concisely taking the shape of the Jew driving the long blade of a knife directly into the host laid flat on a surface. Eucharistic miracles from the time of Pope Gregory the Great (590-604) were visions of a bleeding, fleshly host appearing to a priest who had doubts that the host is the body of Christ. The maturation of the dogma of transubstantiation with the Lateran Council of 1215 increased the urgency and variety of these visions. The host became the body of Christ when consecrated during the Mass while retaining the external appearance, the Aristotelian accident, of a wafer.

Dialogus miraculorum (1219-23) by the Cistercian monk and chronicler Caesarius of Heisterbach contains a section (Distinctio 9) on miracles of the Blessed Sacrament. The author begins on a note of caution.[17]

> Speaking with you on the sacrament, the body and blood of Christ, I attend to that with fear because where faith alone is at work, and the judgment of reason is excluded, the discussion is not without danger.

The twenty five Eucharistic miracles then described are mostly without comment from the two figures in dialogue on these occurrences. This tension between faith and reason is felt through the history of Eucharistic miracles where blood is shed. The potential for unreason presses attempts at resolution all the way through.

Some of the elements of the Paris miracle are present in Caesarius' instances. The hosts bleed, spontaneously in the sight of a priest (9:17, 9:18) or a doubting layman (9:19), and they survive intact the burning of a church (9:16) or a shipwreck (9:13), making their way to another vessel still afloat. They exercise an influence on animals or humans in their vicinity. They cause bees to construct a palace of wax (9:8) and are not touched by gnawing rodents (9:11). A wayward priest who takes the host in his mouth in the hope of enhancing his appeal to a woman finds himself unable to leave the church (9:6). The pyx (ceremonial vessel) containing hosts Albigensian heretics toss into the river rises above the waves (9:12).

The bleeding, durable and fluttering host of the Paris miracle is present in these brief histories, composed shortly after the Lateran council Many of them identify a specific town or location where the miracle took place, but do not give personal names, only the social station, of the protagonists, who generally are men. The only violence threatening the hosts is from natural forces or animals, who are deterred from damaging them. Volitional malice is confined to the Albigenses, members of a dualist sect in the south of France (Languedoc) and under attack by a crusade during the period Caesarius was writing the *Dialogus*. Caesarius authored a chronicle of this Crusade, which annihilated the heretics and advanced the interests of the French crown in the region. Even the Albigenses do not assault the host directly.

Proceeding from this collection of Eucharistic miracles, three further elements are needed to form the Paris miracle: the Jew, the penetrative violence against the body of the host, and the Jew's refusal to convert. If the body is human then both elements are supplied by a mythology pervading Europe and the Near East from antiquity onward: the blood libel against the Jews. This was a libel because its inventors and transmitters asserted in print as fact that Jews crave Christian blood for quasi-religious purposes. Jewish groups and individuals were reputed to carry out bloodletting murders of Christians, especially of children.

This belief and writings took on concrete form with accusations in specific places. Ritual murder accusations preceded communal attacks on Jewish residents from the mid-12th century onward in England, France, Germany and elsewhere in Europe. A child disappeared, his (usually) mutilated remains were discovered and his death was blamed on the local Jewry. In some cases from the time of the year the death was associated with the imagined use of human blood to make unleavened bread (*matzot*) for Passover. The bleeding bread of the Eucharistic miracle inverts this making-bread-from-blood accusation.

Another book of miracles collected by Caesarius contained the story of a Christian schoolboy who continuously sang the Salve Regina to the great annoyance of the Jews in his town. They made him captive, and when he did not accede to their demands that he cease his innocent singing, they cut off his tongue, sliced him into pieces and buried him in lime.[18] After officials located his remains, the Virgin Mary restored and resurrected him, which so astounded the Jews that they accepted baptism. Whether their aim was draining his blood or just silencing him, the Jews cut their victim. They might repeat the tortures of Christ's Passion, as they did with Little "Saint" Hugh of Lincoln in 1255.

Secular and religious authorities generally did not sanction ritual murder accusations against Jews. Any label of sainthood or martyrdom for the victims was popular in its making. For the sake of keeping public order, and to suppress the widespread looting and robbery that might follow the spontaneous appropriation of Jewish property, sheriffs, provosts and bishops sometimes intervened to protect the accused Jews until a formal weighing of the evidence could take place.

They were less likely to fend off another accusation leveled against the Jews: host desecration. Jews might be designated the thieves when hosts and their containers disappeared from churches. The belief that the consecrated wafers were useful for love magic and for enhancing fortune was directed against members of the one group (before there were Protestants) who discounted transubstantiation and seemed bent on openly disproving the sacramentality of the host. When hosts went missing a blameworthy malefactor had to be found. Sometimes, however, there were no Jews to fasten it upon.

The sheriff placed the Jews of the community under protective custody after the body of 12 year-old William of Norwich was discovered in 1144. This was the first of a series of murders of boys in different English towns over the following decades attributed to blood-seeking Jews. Deliberate attempts by local clergy to create profitable cults, identification of Jews with the upper classes who shielded them from the resentful peasantry and xenophobia stirred up by crusades made Jews the target of robbery and murder by mobs as the century wore on.

On the continent Holy Roman Emperor Frederick II Hohenstaufen addressed the upheaval of vengeance-seeking crowds spreading another rumor of Jews draining blood from Christian children, this time for magical purposes, in Fulda (1235). Frederick announced that if the allegations could be proven he would kill all the Jews in the empire, but if not, anyone molesting Jews would be treated as a criminal. A council of Jewish converts to Christianity, considered the most reliable judges of interfaith matters, in 1243 proclaimed that there was no proof of ritual murders by Jews. The blood libel stirrings were revolts against an economy of which the Jews were the most vulnerable agents. The accusations continued, and even were encouraged by the gentry's perceived alliance with the Jews.

The popes took a shifting position on Christian communal actions against the Jews. From Pope Calixtus II in the 9th century a line of popes endorsed and reissued with their own modifications an encyclical titled *Sicut Judaeis* from its words, "Thus to the Jews." This document enjoined prelates and the faithful not to force Jews (and Muslims) to convert to Christianity, and interdicted killing, causing injury and taking property.

Pope Innocent IV exhibited the spectrum of papal strictures concerning the Jews in his letters to monarchs and archbishops over the years. On May 9, 1244 he asked and urged King Louis IX of France to have consumed by fire the book called the Talmud greater in size than the Bible and full of blasphemies against God, Christ and the Virgin Mary, "execrable fables, erroneous abuses and unheard of follies," condemned by the Paris chancellery and the doctors of the university.[19] Jewish servants and nurses employed by Christians must not have it in their possession. Pope Innocent IV perpetuated the policy of his predecessor Gregory IX.

In 1247 he was met with the argument from a delegation of Jews and Christians that Talmud burnings were in violation of the church's tolerance, and rescinded his trial and burning order in favor of censorship only.[20]

A pair of letters sent to the Archbishop of Vienne in Provence from the pope's temporary station in Lyon on May 28, 1247 air the complaint brought to the Holy See by Jews from the town of Valreas in Provence. The pope may have garnered more detail from the proximity of his station to the site of the atrocities. The death of a young girl found in a ditch with a cross attached to her was blamed on the Jews, whom the local lord Draconetus subjected to tortures. "...some of them burned, others of the men their testicles torn off, of the women their breasts excised, still others afflicted with various other punishments."[21] The pope also named bishops who connived to imprison and torture the Jews. In the second letter to the Archbishop sent on the same day he instanced the outlandish jealousy and despicable cruelty that coupled with greed for things and blood lust contrary to the meekness prescribed by the Catholic religion led Christians to despoil, injure and kill Jews all without judgment.[22] He required that those being held be released.

Pope Innocent IV only refers to the crucified young girl who was discovered, not to the assertion that that Jews sought her blood for nefarious purposes. In this case the nobility and the prelates were the instigators of the assault on the Jews. They were driven by a wish to take the Jews' possessions.

The Pope's next letter, addressed to the archbishops and bishops of Germany on July 7, 1248 from Lyon, is broader by far. Some seculars as well as chief ecclesiasts and other powers of Germany (Alemannia) have against good conduct falsely imputed that Jews during the solemnity of Easter commune upon the heart of a slaughtered boy.[23] They believe they are enforcing the law but manifestly are acting contrary to the law. They must show themselves favorable and benign to the Jews and not molest them. The same letter was to be sent to the archbishops and bishops of France.

The Pope denounces a range of accusers secular and religious, and rejects as false the apparently widespread belief that Jews seek out Christian children to kill at Eastertime. Again he makes no mention of the Jews taking blood, but instead uses the language of Communion, of the Paschal meal which Christianity and Judaism share, but which has been perverted into cannibalism by the accusation against Jews. Following that is the mild enjoinder not to molest the Jews.

Blood libels and the popular reaction continued unabated in Germany and France after these letters, and the Pope issued no more instructions on the matter. His next intervention concerning the Jews was in answer to a highly localized complaint. The clergy at the cathedral on the island village of Maguelone (Languedoc-Roussillon), at the time a prosperous salt-producing area, protested to the Pope that the Jews in the town wore large enveloping capes so similar to those of the clergy that pilgrims and new arrivals in the town mistook the Jews for clergy. The Pope's July 7, 1248 letter from Assisi ordered that the Jews adopt a common fashion in capes that distinguished them from clerics and laity.[24] He was no more specific than that. His mandate did add one more instance to the history of Jews being forced to adopt clothing and badges that set them apart from the rest of the population.

His final word on a population of Jews came from Assisi on July 23, 1253, another missive to the Archbishop of Vienne. The efforts to convert the Jews in his archdiocese had come at great expense and scandal, and threatened grave danger to the Christians. Pope Innocent authorized the Archbishop to expel the Jews, especially those who do not observe the provisions of the Holy See concerning them. Christians, including royal officials, who oppose this initiative should be countered with ecclesiastical prerogative.

Pope Innocent IV at first embraced his predecessors' campaign against the Talmud, then was persuaded on the broader principles of Christianity to relinquish at least the forced destruction of the book (and its possessors). He generated his own version of the longstanding papal defense of the Jews, urging tolerance in response to blood libels.

He then moved in the direction of Jewish exclusion and finally expulsion from the area where he had denied capital charges and called for tolerance. He alternately resisted church and secular officials' charges against the Jews and tried to disqualify officials from supporting the Jews against expulsion. All the while he applied contradictory principles of the church's approach to the Jews developed by previous popes: the Jews as intransigent refusers of the grace of conversion; the Jews as believers in the same God who must be tolerated and converted by persuasion.

Pope Gregory X in 1272 continued the approach-avoidance by turning the encyclical of protection directly toward the blood libel. After deploring the Jews' intransigence in matters of faith, he recognized that Christians plotted against the Jews by abducting Christian children and trying to extort money from the Jews by holding over them the threat of a blood libel accusation.[25]

This history of papal give and take about the Jews was an element of the 1290 Paris miracle. It was the year of the first European national expulsion of Jews as a people, by England. Thousands of Jews fled for their lives across the channel having lost their property. For the most part they did not settle in France. Their movement did create a pressure, and in certain minds a sense of a possibility.

The blood libel was a useful device to dispossess Jews while avoiding wholesale expulsion. That would require having a Christian child disappear in a manner that could be blamed on Jews. Papal and royal disapproval of such machinations would preclude the attempt.

The 1290 Paris miracle was a compromise that allowed the authorities to participate in an anti-Jewish movement that remade the blood libel into a more acceptable instrument. It included Eucharistic miracle elements and blood libel elements substituting the child-like host for the Christian child of so many martyrdoms. Unlike a child, the host could bleed copiously through the Passion all the way to the crucifixion. The Jew could be forced to convert or be burned at the stake, his house turned into a chapel and his implements confiscated as relics. The host itself would become a relic and lasting evidence for the tricky dogma of transubstantiation.

Elements critical to the Paris miracle, the torture/desecration of the host by the Jew and its boiling, allowed the extension of the blood libel and the Passion of Christ into domestic space without requiring the involvement of a child and without courting official resistance. The instruments of the torture replicated the Passion merged with the blood libel without challenging papal and official disapproval while fomenting the creation of temples of the miracle on the real terrain of Paris. The Jew's house was confiscated and the satellite church of St. Jean-en-Grève gained an identity. The miracle story and its artifacts were initially so compelling, so much a precipitation of historic contradictions held in check, that no real events could be discovered behind them.

Paris had its own blood libel legend in communion with all the others and ready to spread.

Two separate credos are brought into convergence in the basic story: the hostility of Jews to Christian belief and worship and the dogma of transubstantiation. They are linked through the magical invulnerability to damage. The Jew's success in procuring a consecrated host is the result of stereotypical economic relations between Jews and Christians, but the outcome is determined by the difference in belief as Christians see it, between those who deny the truth and those who accept it.

The Jew is forced to convert, to accept Christian belief, or is immolated as a heretic. The Christian woman who obtains the host for him is vulnerable to his blandishments not because she is a disbeliever or has doubts about Christian doctrine. She is a sinner who temporarily has placed material gain before faith and can be forgiven if she repents. The Jew is offered the same status.

The refusal of the Jew to convert and his burning added an element to the construction, that the Jew might be the martyr.

The Eucharistic miracles that took place after the definitive statement of transubstantiation doctrine are all manifestations of wrestling with the doctrine, of priest and congregant seeing the host bleed when they are in doubt. The Jew has no doubts; he does not understand, perhaps he cannot. The Jew tests the host to determine if it is a god as he thinks the Christians must believe. By bleeding and not disintegrating when he knifes and subjects it to the other tortures, the host evinces the dual nature of a Christian sacramental. It is the body of Christ in bleeding when pierced and enduring the onslaught. Outwardly, in the accident of appearance, it is still a wafer, but its essence is Christ's body. The Jew has inadvertently proven transubstantiation by his assault.

Boiling the host in hot water is added to the instrumental tortures of Christ's Passion. After the knifing it is the one step of the Jew's domestic rage to be described in texts if the others are left out, and it is the most likely to be represented visually. The water to turns to blood and the crucifixion, the final stage of the Passion, appears in the billowing steam. Visions in water and smoke were credible and persuasive. The phrase "boiled God" with its overtones of risk and triumph became a tag for this miracle in particular.

Jews were forcibly converted or harshly punished after outraging the populace over a rumored act. A repertory of misdeeds was attributed to Jews (as to others throughout history) to justify verbal and physical antagonism against them by individuals and collectives. These were projections of Christian anxieties about Jews and others like them calling for prosecution and containment.

Moneylending was denounced by Christian leaders from early in the history of the church, but there were Christian moneylenders, the Lombards and Florentines from Italy and the military order the Knights Templar, who were at times castigated by ecclesiastical and secular authorities. It was necessary to find something uniquely odious about Jewish moneylending and not merely the high rate of interest required to protect the lenders from default. By corrupting a Christian woman to transport a host into his hands using the security on a loan, the Jew was guilty of a uniquely sinful form of usury.

And of having the host transported into his hands. The woman who procured the host, where her technique is described at all, carried it in her mouth until she could spit it out into a cloth. Only the consecrated fingers of a priest were allowed to make physical contact with the host (there are exceptions today). The Jew began his desecration by touching the host. The good Christian woman who rescues the host at the end of its ordeal never touches it. The host glides into her wooden bowl or tinderbox and then into the priest's fingers or onto the altar.

A further indictment of the Jew, qualifying him for the punishment of a heretic, is his assurance that his book will protect him. The Christians confidently bring it to him, and it becomes ashes with him. The quantities of Jewish books readily burned on public squares in 1242-44 and especially on the Place de Grève were evidence that the books were not fireproof.

The only positive belief attributed to the Jew would make him further a candidate for immolation. He is a magician who places faith in a false idol, his magic book. Unable to identify idols that Jews worshiped, Christians targeted the books that certainly were present in Jewish households and places of worship, a source of suspicion for a population whose literacy in the liturgical language depended upon priests. The Jew's expectations of his book did not reflect Jewish belief but were another projection of Christian beliefs about Jews.[26]

This applies equally to the understanding of the Jewish community in the miracle narratives. If other non-family Jews appear at all they come in answer to the Jew's summons to support his outrages, and they are made to answer for them collectively, at least by conversion upon witnessing the miracle. The community like the faith itself is fabricated to meet the needs of the narrative.

The only Jewish women present are the Jew's wife and possibly his daughter. They do not stand as much in contrast to Christians in general and to Christian women as do the Jewish men.[27] All the Christian men in the miracle narrative are church and secular officials, or members of a mob. The women have no official position but function as decisive movers of events because they can travel between the interior of the Jew's house and the Christian city outside. The first Christian woman is a creditor of the Jew and possibly a domestic in his employ; the second Christian woman enters the house on a pretext she might use to enter any house, to ask for fire.

All the elements of the miracle are composed to make a social and cultural picture credible for a lay Christian of the late 13th century. The miracle was not confined to that time and place, which was true of all miracles. What caused this one to stand out and last beyond its time and place of occurrence was its melding of anti-Jewish sentiments and transubstantiation doctrine into a drama that made both seem natural. This success, and its ultimate failure, were built by making the miracle architectural and ceremonial in a loose celebration of its elements.

The Jewish view of the events, or interpretation of the miracle story, was not set down in written form in any of the languages used by Jews. The story is exemplary of relations between Christians and the northern French Jewish community in that it centers on an individual Jew and not the entire community. Where other Jews as members of a community are present in a version of the miracle it is probably one developed in another country.

Political leaders in France did not usually extend the treatment of an individual to all the Jewish residents of a town as they did elsewhere.[28] This did not exempt Jews from atrocities in French cities and towns. The individual focus, historian Ivar Marcus contends, was the result of the French Jewish community not having a strong identity of their own compared with other Jewish communities. Despite the powerful presence of Rashi and his school from the 12th century onward, there was no sense of a community founder and no common language apart from those used elsewhere.

Stories of host desecration by Jews abounded in Europe from the late 13th century to the late 15th century, and there were a few where the building where the desecration was consummated was seized and made into a Christian shrine. Nowhere but in Paris was the desecration entirely the work of an individual acting out a pattern of abuse preserved in its location, relics and by ceremonial commemoration. The house of the Jew was the house of the miracle looking backwards.

Today the *Memorial du Martyr Juif Inconnu, The Memorial of the Unknown Jewish Martyr*, a monument containing the ashes of victims from World War II concentration camps and the Warsaw Ghetto, is located at 17 Rue Geoffroy l'Asnier in the 4th Arrondissement of Paris. It is in the same general area of the Jew's house but not nearby, in the same way that martyrdom comes close to applying to the individual Jew of the miracle. This hovering on the brink of identification anticipated the quest to individualize ashes rendered impersonal by atrocity. That also is an element of the miracle story not visible to its consumers.

As the burning of the Jew entered into the field of visual representation, the danger that it might be mistaken for a Christian martyrdom became pronounced.

Notes

[14] De miraculo hostiae a Judaeo Parisiis anno Domini M. CC. XC multis ignominis affectae, *Recueil des historiens des Gaules et de la France* 22(1865): 32-33 and Lenoir (1893: 217-18n1). Also in S. René (1725: 2,148). See Appendix for text and translation.
[15] Stow (2006: 22-23)
[16] Dahan (1999: 228) summarized the canonical story down in six episodes.
[17] Caesarius of Heisterbach (1851: 164)
[18] Meister (1901: 189-91)
[19] Berger (1884: 1,115: 682)
[20] Chazan (1980: 231-35) Translations of Pope Innocent IV's letters
[21] Berger (1884: 1,420-21: 2813)
[22] Berger (1884: 1, 424: 2838)
[23] Berger (1884: 1, 463: 3077)
[24] Berger (1887: 2, 3: 4123)
[25] Letter against the Blood Libel. http://legacy.fordham.edu/halsall/source/g10-jews.asp
[26] Einbinder (2002: 4)
[27] Rubin (2006)
[28] Marcus (2014: 109)

4.
Appearances

Once the miracle became a known narrative formed of certain fixed elements and a few others added and lost from one iteration to the next the miracle as a whole could be fit into schemes of time and values. From the first notices it was an event in histories and scholarly compilations: Paris history, French history, Christian church history, cosmography, Bible commentary and the history of the Jews. Over time it has become the exclusive property of the latter.

Its role in each of these depended upon the author's general intent, sources drawn upon, and expected audience. At first its presence in chronicles is a measure of its spread by oral communication, which eventually was encompassed by the written, ritual and visual forms. It was called common knowledge in Paris as late as the mid-19th century. Examining appearances of the miracle takes into account differences between a source inscription and the one being examined.

The miracle narrative also appeared widely in compilations made outside of France and Belgium from the mid-15th century onward. The Paris and French histories included it as a Paris event with wide implications. It does not appear in Paris histories after the late 19th century; it does appear in guidebooks to this day.

Works whose authors were not concerned with placing the miracle in Paris history found reason to position it in the unfolding of God's plan for the world since the creation, or as an example of a dispensation granted to humanity in general. Like the Paris histories these writings often served as the basis for the inclusion of the miracle in other works. Its mutations from one work to another disclose variations in perspective. Excerpts from nine of these instances, dating from the 15th to the 17th centuries, five in Latin, four in French, are given with translations at the end of this chapter. This is by no means an exhaustive compendium.

Antonio Pierozzi, or Forcigliano (1389-1459) was a Dominican, a member of the Order of Preachers, in his written moral theology and history sought to exemplify the actions of God in the world of experience. He offered suggestions for the improvement of human economy to benefit all, and might be considered a forerunner of Christian Socialism. He ruled as Archbishop of Florence in his later years and was canonized in 1523 as St. Antoninus by a pope who sympathized with his advocacy of church reform.

The three parts of his *Chronicon*, composed between 1440 and 1459, based on a series of Lenten sermons he gave in the 1420's,[29] follow the course of human events from the Creation to the year of his death. It first appeared in print in 1484, and afterward in at least ten editions mostly from French and German printers. It was useful to preachers and confessors for the many instances it provided of divine will intersecting with human actions. In some surviving copies specific sections are marked out with ink lines, including the account of the Paris miracle, in the same year as family turmoil in Florence described in the passages immediately before the miracle.

Antoninus derived his account of the miracle (selection 4-1) directly from Villani's chronicle of the previous century (2-3): the words match, Italian to Latin, but not the sentiment. The Jew lent the money to the woman at interest (*usuria*) and with a pledge (*pignorus*) in both texts, and the Jew is quoted in both saying that he will accept the host in payment for her loan and will grant her the pledged clothing in exchange. She takes the host at Communion, and removes it from her mouth to give to the Jew. Antoninus here adds to Villani's plain statement that she is motivated by greed, loving money more than her soul.

Antoninus also makes a point about the nature of her sacrilegious Communion. She does not absorb the host as would a communicant who is free of sin, and is not purified by taking the sacrament. Villani's *semplice feminella*, a simple little woman who acts according to her vanity, is for Antoninus, who commented in his writings on the excesses of women's dress, a *mulier*, a woman, who puts her soul in peril and does not notice that she is able to transport the host because she is not in the state of grace that would allow her to assimilate it.

The Jew immediately subjects the host to boiling water in a vessel-*padella* in Villani's Italian and *patella* in Antoninus' Latin, a word used in no other miracle account-and when it doesn't disintegrate stabs it with a knife (Villani) or a sword (Antoninus) causing it to bleed and redden the water, then put it in cold water, which it likewise causes to become bloodied. Both accounts agree that Christians then enter the house seeking a loan, see the sacrilege, the host leaps up over a table (*tabula, tavola*), the Jew is taken and burned and the host is received by a priest. The Jew's house is made into a church, the church of the Salvation (Villani)… of the Billettes (Antoninus).

Antoninus makes Villani's tale of the simple woman, the Jew and the stolen host into a paradigm of sinfulness and the sacrament. The Jew is engaged in moneylending at interest on pledges, a practice officially disapproved by the Church but permitted, almost required, of Jews, who were barred from any trade in which they might compete with guilds. Villani and Antoninus are united in seeing moneylending as the main field of contact between Christians and Jews. Villani's woman accepts the Jew's offer and brings him the host because she is a gullible fool. For Antoninus she is by nature a woman like any other, who willingly agrees to do as the Jew asks and has put her soul in peril of damnation by placing her dress and money over her own salvation. The miracle story has become a parable of the material effects of the deadly sin of greed upon the soul.

The deposed Doge of Genoa, Battista Fregoso, also known as Fulgosius (1453-1504) brought with him on his exile to Lyon a manuscript of a book he had composed in Italian, in imitation of the *Factorum dictorumque memorabilium libri IX* of the Roman author Valerius Maximus.[30] Valerius' book was a collection of anecdotes intended to illustrate virtues in the lives of powerful men. Fregoso's version was translated into Latin by the Italian ambassador to the French court, and printed in Milan in 1508, after Battista's death. The Latin gave the text currency in humanist circles within and outside of Italy.

Fregoso extended Valerius' first book on religion with a "more recent" section that added Christian instances to the display of classical virtues. The Paris miracle (selection 4-2) appears in a subsection titled "Marvels of the blood of the Redeemer." Fregoso's Latin is nothing like Valerius' convoluted language, and is more in the mode of concise writing favored during the Republic and early Empire.

The influence of Villani cannot be detected in the diction as it can be in St. Antoninus' text, but this may be due to the translation into Latin not taking Villani's Italian into account, which Fregoso may have done in his Italian original. The "Parisians" rather than "Paris" are the subject of the miracle, as in both the earlier texts, and the woman is *inopis muliercula*, a diminutive, slighting expression for a poor maid or serving woman, parallel to Villani's language in sentiment, but not verbiage. The Jew has the woman's clothing *oppignaturam*, in pledge, invoking *pignuris* but not *usuria* of both the other authors. The host is abruptly obtained by the Jew with no reference to Communion or the oral means of carrying the host.

The Jew does not throw the host into a *patella* with boiling water but into a *sartago*, a frying pan, over a fire, and sees that it does not change form or color, as a piece of bread would under those conditions. He stabs it with a sword, it bleeds, and there is no further test to follow. The Jew is not taken and burned. The host is indestructible but it does not dance before it is transferred to a place dedicated to it, the name of which refers to the boiling though the host wasn't boiled in this version. The Jew's house becomes a church for all three writers, but only Fregoso has the host and sword relics on view there.

sartago Clarke (1832: 304)

The *sartago* was a Roman cooking vessel in which meat and whatever else was available were tossed to fry over an open flame. The name also signified a jumble or a hodgepodge, and was often used figuratively, as in *sartago loquendi*, confused speech. For it to replace the pot of boiling water lightens the miracle despite the stabbing and bleeding. The sword and the bloodied host are relics. A joyous pilgrimage is in the offing.

The other instances of host-blood miracles in Fregoso's collection are similarly cursory, expositional, and grounded in their relics. His book went through many editions in its Latin translation, but the details pared away, and the new ones introduced, were not carried over to other retellings of the Paris miracle, including those that specifically cited Fregoso.

It did share the barest outline with other authors' Paris miracle: the poor Paris woman who wants to redeem her clothing under pledge to a Jew at Eastertime; the agreement to deliver the host in exchange for the clothing; the indestructible host over fire struck by a sharp instrument and bleeding; the Christians entering the Jew's shop and discovering the host; the Jew's house converted into a church. This outline is the international humanist form of the miracle that permitted it to be transmitted across languages and national boundaries among the members of a Christian elite literate in Latin.

Johannes Vergenhans (c.1425-1510) signaled his membership in this elite by Latinizing his name, not by giving it a Latin syllabification like Fregoso/Fulgosius but by translating it from the German word for "ferryman" to Nauclerus, meaning "ship's master." Nauclerus was a Catholic priest and doctor of canon law from a family in service to a Swabian noble family, who obtained patronage positions for him. He lectured in Basel, Switzerland, worked in the papal chancery in Rome and ultimately became a professor and rector of the newly founded university in Tübingen.

30

His major work, *Chronica*, was first printed in 1516, well after the author's death. Erasmus contributed a commendatory letter to the preface, in which he excused the lack of style in Nauclerus' Latin. The *Chronica* is a universal history from Adam to 1500 divided into generations since the first man, marked by the year of the current pope and the name of the Holy Roman Emperor at the time. Nauclerus added more recent Latin histories, especially Antoninus, to the Bible and the usual classical authorities. The year 1290, the beginning of the 44th generation, was first distinguished by an *insigne miraculum*, a signal or emblematic miracle, a miracle ranking on the order of the virgin birth (4-3).

The text does not bear the verbal traces of derivation from Antoninus. Nauclerus uses the same outline and excises the Florentine bishop's moralizing. The woman has borrowed money from the Jew "on her clothing," without explicit usury or pledge, and she wishes to be granted her dress for Easter day, to which request the Jew is quoted making his proposition, accepted by the woman "overcome by greed." The host is boiled and bleeds when struck, and the interloping Christians put out the alarm. The Jew is captured and burned, the host is enshrined and the Jew's house is made into a church.

All the phases of the international humanist form of the miracle are present, with the major exception of leaving out the host's first instance of indestructibility. Fregoso's circumscribed account includes explicit mention of host's survival of the fire, as do both Villani's and Antoninus' in a few words. The host's retaining its shape in fire exhibits the enduring essence of Christ's body, a doctrinal point which would not have escaped a canon lawyer like Nauclerus. The Jew is driven to his further acts by the failure of the seemingly frail host to disintegrate in boiling water. If that is absent his rage seems motivated by hostility alone. The indestructibility of the host, strongly asserted and not asserted at all, is the most marked phase of the miracle in the international humanist form. The vision of the host outlasting both damage and bleeding, found in few other miracles, may have put too much pressure on transubstantiation doctrine, and Nauclerus demurred in his recounting.

The 1544 German-language *Cosmographia* by the German Franciscan turned Lutheran, Sebastian Münster (1488-1552), does not include the Paris miracle at all. Münster followed Nauclerus by several decades, teaching at the University of Basel after it had become Protestant. His academic specialty was the Hebrew language, and in addition to Hebrew grammars and a trilingual Hebrew dictionary, he published a Hebrew text of the Gospel of Matthew given to him by Spanish Jews he converted to Protestant Christianity. 1290 in Münster's original text is the year Philippe le Bel warred against the Flemings and killed many of them.[31]

The miracle does appear in François de Belleforest's 1575 French version of the *Cosmographia* (4-4). The prolific translator of writings from other European languages into French translated the German text with emendations, and entirely new sections, including one on the churches of Paris, which contains the miracle as the founding story of the church of the Billettes.

Belleforest's miracle eschews the international humanist version for the French national one of the *Grandes Chroniques*. It is almost an exact replica of the text that appeared in Gilles Corrozet's 1550 antiquarian history.[32] Corrozet's in turn was based on the Paris tradition beginning with the 1322 Latin text of the Billettes cartulaire (in the Appendix; discussed in the Elements chapter).

Corrozet's was an original summation of the earlier text; Belleforest's was plagiarism, observable in other parts of his *Cosmographie*.[33]

In contrast with the international humanist version this tradition does not elaborate how the bad Christian woman obtained her loan: no interest or pledge, no clothing, only surety (*gages*). The Jew first stabs the host, which bleeds, tosses it directly into the fire only to have it flit away, then into boiling water with more bleeding, followed by the apparition of the crucified Christ. The Jew's son tells the Christians about the miracle, leading immediately to the Jew's arrest and burning.

The Paris texts name officials and places, from St. Merry, where the woman receives the host, to St. Jean-en-Grève, where it is enshrined, and Philippe le Bel and Jeanne his queen, who found the chapel in the Jew's house and bring the religious from Rogney to staff it. The knife is shown annually on the Sunday after Easter, at the Billettes chapel and monastery.

With a few differences in spelling, the language is identical between Corrozet and Belleforest: the woman is "poor but wicked" *("pauvre mais mechante")*; the Jew is "like a second Judas," *("comme un second Iudas")* and "the accursed Hebrew" *("le maudit Hebrieu")*; the king and queen "cause to be purchased" *("feirent achepter")* the house of the Jew. The changes and additions Belleforest introduced to Corrozet's text stand out.

Where Corrozet later in the text describes the Jew's actions as a "tyranny," Belleforest has him making mock of Christianity. "And it is a wonder of the crowd of people rushing to see what they have seen many times, so great is the devotion of the citizens of Paris" is an addition to the text where the knife relic is said to be shown. "Quasimodo," Belleforest adds to the expression *"Pasques closes"* that Corrozet uses, because that phrase might not be so widely understood to name the Sunday after Easter.

Corrozet had educated himself to become a bookseller, a status not easily attained or sustained in 16th century Paris. His first book he wrote and published himself, and sold from his shop in the Palace, was a listing of the streets and neighborhoods of Paris (1532). He was still issuing editions of the book when he issued the first edition of his *Antiquitez, histoires,* in 1550. The 19th century bibliophile who edited a reprint of the earlier book speculated that Corrozet served as a guide to visitors to Paris.[34] That would explain the street by street survey, followed by the much more richly detailed guide book, which also went through many editions. Corrozet's version of the miracle is made for pilgrims seeking out churches with stories, and the relics they contain.

Belleforest's French-German cosmography was not just a translation but a positioning of France more centrally in the world Münster arranged. France was "a little too summarily treated in the original work,"[35] which deficiency the highly prolific Belleforest set about to remedy. The church of the Billettes is still Corrozet's pilgrimage site, but now the Jew is a villain to all Christians, and the Parisians set an example of zealous devotion by flocking to the church for repeat viewings of the knife relic.

Even if Belleforest's changes are the work of a plagiarist trying to distinguish his work from the original, they still march with the author's attempts to win favor with French-speaking purchasers and readers. The low esteem in which the others held his work in general was based on an evaluation of his honesty and the quality of his writing, not buffered any sense of national or local solidarity he sought by his Gallicizing gestures.[36]

Cesare Baronio (1538-1607) began to write his *Annales Ecclesiastici* at the urging of Philip Neri, to counter the *Magdeburg Centuries*, a history of the Catholic Church by a group of Protestant scholars who questioned the relationship of the church's development during the middle ages to the word of Christ. Baronio was a doctor of canon law and teacher who had long been a lecturer on church doctrine and history when Neri made his request. Baronio eventually was made a cardinal, had a serious chance of being elected pope, and also was a member of Neri's Congregation of the Oratory, succeeding the founder as head of the Congregation.

Like the Protestant work it was meant to challenge, Baronio's twelve volume history covered the first thirteen centuries of the church's history, but unlike the earlier work, it was in the archaic form of annals, a year by year history. The final volume, published the year after the author's death, completed the thirteenth century, and for the end of the year 1290 turns to the "prodigy the Divine Numen sent to the Parisians to expunge their perfidy" (4-5). Baronio then quotes in full St. Antoninus' chapter on the miracle with acknowledgment of the source.

The introduction is a pointed reference to the feud between Pope Boniface VIII and Philippe le Bel, heir and promoter of a French monarchy becoming a bureaucratic state. This would lead to the French captivity of the papacy itself, in Avignon from 1307 and, an event in which Baronio had a role, the assumption of the throne of France by Henri IV who converted from Calvinism to Catholicism to make himself more acceptable to those perfidious Parisians, who later assassinated him. These events took place long after the 1290 date of the miracle, but seemed to Baronio to be consistent with Parisian character defects calling for divine correction.

The inclusion of the miracle toward the end of Baronio's history was a corrective to the Protestant history, *Ecclesiastica historia…* called *Magdeburg Centuries* after the city where its authors lived, and after the novel technique of dividing the books into centuries subdivided into topical sections (doctrine, prominent figures, martyrs, and so on) each of which proceeded chronologically. There was a separate section on miracles, which also were discussed in other sections. The final volume of the Protestant *Ecclesiastica historia…* (1574), which covered the 13th century, contains no trace of the Paris miracle. There are miracles of Communion bread turning into flesh and wine turning into blood, and the year 1290, Generation 44 in Nauclerus' chronicle, is referenced, but no Jew ever tempts a Christian woman into providing a host for his abuse.[37]

Baronio's inclusion of a direct quote from St. Antoninus' annals is a reassertion of that form of history, year by year, against the topical centuries approach, and of transubstantiation and the real presence that the miracle serves. Henri de Sponde (1568-1643) composed a continuation of Baronio's annals in the same year by year form. de Sponde, or Spondanus, was a convert from Calvinism who was ordained a Catholic priest, became rector of the French national church in Rome and eventually the bishop of Pamiers. His history was titled *Ecclesiasticorum Annalorum Eminentis Cardinalis Caesaris Baronii Continuatio* (1612), but it began in 1197, not at the 1300 end date of Baronio's annals. This gave de Sponde the opportunity to review and revise entries in the overlapping history, and add weight to the rejection of the Protestant reading of ecclesiastical history.

de Sponde introduces each of his date entries with the year since the birth of Christ, the year of the reign of the current pope, of the Holy Roman Emperor and of the Byzantine Emperor, thus positioning it in the universal and immediate polity of Christendom. He lists each of these for the year 1290, and immediately launches into an account of the Paris miracle (4-6), which situates it in the whole of Christian history.

The entry for the miracle does not replicate Baronio's quotation of Antoninus. de Sponde does cite the cardinal-saint's annals, as well as de Nangis, Villani, the section on the miracle in the *Fortalitium Fidei*, and the archival documents that form the basis of Séguier's 1604 *Histoire miraculeuse*...The result is a mixture of the international humanist and the French national traditions of the miracle.

The woman has borrowed money from the Jew under interest and pledge of her clothing. She takes Communion and hides the host in a napkin. The Jew immediately retreats to an underground cell where he throws the host into boiling water then stabs it. The copious blood reddens the water. He is discovered by visiting Christians, taken captive and burned because the host is seen rising from the water and coming to rest in a bowl. The house of the Jew is made into a temple adjoining the monastery of the Billettes, and the host is enshrined in St. Jean. The Jew's underground cell is now a chapel where the water vessel, knife and bowl relics are visited.

Though there is no written testimony to this effect, it is possible that the flying host and the apparition of the crucifix in steam were illusions performed for pilgrims in that enclosed cell. Projection of a figure on a translucent sheet into steam had long been practiced, and it was well known that roiling clouds of steam can carry aloft light pieces such as wafers.

This version of the miracle emphasizes the institutions created or enhanced by the miracle and the relics that pilgrims can view there. In this it is like the French national and pilgrimage-oriented story Belleforest made from Münster's original. The references to interest and pledge, the revelation to visiting Christians and the single act of abuse, tossing the host into boiling water and stabbing it, place it in the frame of the international humanist tradition.

This hybrid was the work of a French convert to Catholicism who was the ecclesiastical officer of the French national church in Rome. de Sponde was the godson of Henri I de Navarre, the Protestant heir to the French throne who was allowed to enter Paris to claim his heritage only after he converted to Catholicism himself. He revised and extended the annals of Baronio, who had been the pope's confessor at the time Henri IV petitioned to have the ban of excommunication removed and be admitted into the Catholic Church. At the urging of Philip Neri, Baronio withheld confession from the pope until he agreed to remove the ban and accept the king into the Church.[38] de Sponde acted upon Baronio's legacy and replaced Antoninus' miracle with a composite to reflect the restoration of the Catholic writ in an environment of conversion from Protestantism.

de Sponde's adaptation of the miracle to contemporary church politics-ecclesiastical history-at the beginning of the 17th century anticipated further adaptations during the following centuries often drawing upon or at least citing the authority of these antecedents. This was parallel to and sometimes interdigitated with the French national miracle tradition in the works of Paris historians and guidebook writers.

Before de Sponde's volumes were issued, Ferre de Locre, in a 1608 Latin devotional manual to the Virgin Mary, summarized the miracle as the cause for the founding of the Billettes chapel (4-

7). The details of the Jew's bargain with the woman, her procurement of the host, its mistreatment by the Jew, its recovery and enshrinement, and the manner of the Jew's apprehension and punishment, are all left aside, giving way to the conversion of the Jew's house and the establishment of the temple.

The preacher Jacques Marchand (4-8) quotes Fregoso's miracle account in his compilation of sermons and cathetical instructions, *Hortus pastorum* (1638). Marchand probably was aware of the other versions of the miracle but chose Fregoso's for the abrupt drama of the unchanging fried host bleeding when struck, suited to the oral stylings of the sermon. Fregoso also devoted a portion of his attention to the transformation of the Jew's house and the relics present, which carried the sermon's urgings to pilgrimage for Marchand. There were miracle texts available for different purposes.

Thoma le Blanc (4-9) chose Antoninus and de Sponde for his miracle references when he included the story in an analysis of the Psalms of David (1698). The Jesuit theologian reduced the story to two sentences yet included a detail missing from both of his cited sources. Here the Jew intended to cut the host into pieces but he did not succeed, and it bled. Both Antoninus and de Sponde have the Jew tossing it into the boiling water with the intent of dissolving it rather than breaking it into pieces. le Blanc gives primary emphasis to its indestructability followed by bleeding. Like the others he has the Jew's house transformed into a temple housing the relics, and he adds St. Jean as the site of the host's resting place.

These 17th century Latin citations of the miracle each for a specific purpose focus on the rudiments, the bleeding manifestation and the shrines where the objects might be seen. They all depend on citations whether they quote them exactly or just attach their authority. They resemble the other traditions being taken as history in France only in the presentday visitable sites of the miracle to which they all cling.

Selections-Texts and Translations

4-1. St. Antoninus of Florence *Historiarum Domini Antonini Archipraesum Florentini Chronica Partibus Tribus ab initio mundi ad MCCCLX.* Lyon: Aegidius et Iacobus Huegetan Fratres, 1543. Vol. 3, fo. LXXVII, Capitulum V.

In this same year an important miracle happened in Paris concerning the Eucharist. A certain Jew loaned a woman a sum of money at interest with her clothing under pledge. In order to be able to dress herself for Easter as the time approached she went to the Jew to redeem her tunic. The perfidious Jew made bold to tell the woman, "If you bring me the body of Christ as is said to be in the consecrated host, I will restore your clothing to you without any payment." The woman, overcome by greed, loving money more than her soul, promised it to him. On Easter Day going to Communion she retained the sacrament in her mouth neither absorbing it nor taking it as purification she left the church and brought it to the Jew. He with most perfidious sacrilege placed the sacrament in a vessel over a fire with boiling water, and when it lasted there seizing a sword struck the host many times and blood poured out. The water was reddened in color. Removing it from the pot he put the host in cold water which reddened entirely. Christians intending to borrow from him at interest entering his house discovered the most grave sacrilege of the Jew. The host nonetheless by itself rose over a certain table. Thereupon the Jew, captured and having confessed the crime, was burned. The sacrament reverently received by the priests with much devotion, faith and honor was borne to the church. From the house of the Jew was made a church called the church of the salvation of the Billettes.

4-2. Baptista Fregoso, *Factorum et dictorum memorabilium libri IX*. Cologne: Arnold Mylius Birckmann 1604: 50-51 (1508) Book 1, Chapter 6. De miraculis. De sanguine redemptoris miranda (Marvels on the blood of the redeemer)

> Salutis anno ducentesimo nonagesimo supra mille, in
> Parisiorum vrbe quidam Iudęus, per inopem mulierculam,
> cui vestem quam ab ea oppigneratam habebat, se gratis re-
> stiturum promiserat, Christianam hostiam in paschate
> assecutus: cum accenso igne in sartagine vellet assare, vt
> perspexit eam non mutare formam nec colorem, gladio
> eam pupugit, ex qua confestim sanguis manauit, re autem
> detecta, superuenientibus Christianis, hostia in loco ei di-
> cato restituta, Iudæi domus in templum conuersa est, quæ
> etiam nunc Saluatoris bullientis nomine compellatur, vbi
> hostia gladiusque etiam nunc ostenduntur. Temporibus
> nostris, eo bello quod Carolus octauus Gallorum rex ges-
> sit aduersus Annam eius Galliæ partis, quæ Britannia di-
> citur ducem, quam postea in matrimonio coniunctam ha-

(De sanguine redemptoris miranda)

In the year of grace two hundred and ninety over a thousand, in the city of Paris a certain Jew, for a poor working woman, whose clothing he had under pledge to repay (*vestem ab ea oppigneratam*), promised to restore it without fee, if she abstracted the Christian host at Easter. When he tried to bake it in a pan over a raised fire, as he noticed it changed neither form nor color, he struck it with a sword, from which blood suddenly emerged. The matter being detected by arriving Christians, the host restored to a place dedicated to it, the house of the Jew converted into a temple, which now is called by the name of the Boiled Savior, where the host and the sword now are shown.

4-3.   Johannes Nauclerus, Chronica D. Iohannis Naucleri. Cologne: Arnoldus Quentelius. (1614: 2,975) original 1516 Generatio XLIII

ANNO Domini 1290. sub Nicolao quarto anno eius tertio Rudolpho rege Rom. existente, incepit 44. generatio. Eo autem anno insigne miraculum accidit Parisijs, nam cùm quidam Iudæus mutuasset cuidam mulieri super veste pecuniam ante festum Paschæ, mulier carens bona veste, periuit à Iudæo, vt vestem sibi per diem concederet. Ad quæ Iudæus: Porta, inquit, mihi Corpus Christi, quod dicitis esse in hostia, & ego tibi vestem gratis restituam. Mulier cupiditate deuicta, sumens Sacramentum & secretò extrahens ab ore, Iudæo præsentauit: qui vestem ei restituit, & Sacramentum in patellam cum aqua misit. Verùm in aqua bullienti cùm Sacramentum illæsum mansisset, ille gladio percussit Hostiam, moxque sanguis exiuit, quo aqua tincta est & rubea effecta. Christianis autem superuenientibus, & ad vsuram petentibus, Hostia euolauit super tabulam in eorum conspectu. Captus est Iudæus, & pro confesso scelere combustus, indeque Sacramentum cum processione ductum est ad Ecclesiam, & ex domo Iudæi fabricata est Ecclesia Saluatoris. Circa initium istius gene-

Iudæi Parisiensis crudele scelus.

In the year of the Lord 1290, under Nicolas the fourth in his third year, Rudolph the Roman king, began the 44th generation. In this year a signal miracle happened in Paris. When a certain Jew loaned a certain woman money on her clothing before the feast of Easter, the woman wishing good clothing petitioned the Jew to grant her the clothing for the day. To which the Jew: "Bring to me," he said, "the Body of Christ, which is said to be in the host, and I will restore your clothing to you for free. The woman, overcome by greed, taking the Sacrament and secretly removing it from her mouth, presented it to the Jew, who restored her clothing to her, and put the Sacrament into a pot with water. Truly when he placed the Sacrament in boiling water, he struck it with a sword and immediately blood emerged, colored and reddened the water. When Christians arrived seeking a loan, the Host rose over the table in their view. The Jew was captured and, on the confession of the crime, was burned and the Sacrament with a procession was brought to the church and from the house of the Jew the Church of Salvation was made.

4-4.   Sebastian Münster/François de Belleforest. *La Cosmographie Universelle de tout le monde.* Paris: Michel Sonnius 1575: 223-24 Eglises de Paris. In orig Münster *Cosmographia Schreibung Aller Lander.* Basel: Heinrich Petri 1544 no churches of Paris section, lxxxvii 1290 wars of King of France against Flemings

In the reign of Philippe le Bel, being in Rome Pope Nicolas 4, that is in the year of our Lord 1290, was built the Church of the Billettes, for the occasion as follows. A Jew having loaned money on surety to a poor but wicked woman in Paris, arranged trade with this miserable woman that she would bring to him the Blessed Sacrament that she would receive the day of Easter. She did not fail, thus going to St. Merry, comes to blessed Communion and like a second Judas, she brought the Host to the infidel merchant, who suddenly set upon the precious body of our Lord with strikes of a knife and although it be impossible, so is it that the blessed Host poured out blood in great abundance. This did not prevent the accursed Hebrew from throwing it into the fire, from which it left with no wound and took to flitting about the room. The frantic Jew seized it and threw it into a cauldron of boiling water, and suddenly this water all was changed into to the color of blood. And as soon as the Host miraculously arose and appeared clearly and visibly what was hidden under the bread, that is the form and figure of our Lord Jesus Christ crucified, and not without great astonishment of the Jew who without converting retired all in despair to his chamber. This crime so detestable was discovered by a son of the Jew who told it to the children of the Christians not thinking it would mean the ruin of his father. This caused the lodging of the criminal to be entered, the host found and brought to St. Jean-en-Grève, the Jew was taken and burned alive according to the gravity of his crime. After this when King Philippe le Bel and Madame Jeanne were informed of the truth of the crime, caused to be purchased the house of the Jew where they founded a Church, which they gave to the religious and hermits of the hospital Notre Dame, whom they caused to come from a place on the riverbank of Rogney in the Diocese of Châlons so that they serve God and make a memory of this miracle in the same place where the Jew set about mocking the Christian religion. In this church you see an underground in which this abominable crime was perpetrated and in which the knife with which the Jew made the blows is shown each year on the day of Quasimodo or Eastertime. And it is a wonder of the crowd of people rushing to see what they have seen many times, so great is the devotion of the citizens of Paris who call this Church and the Billettes and the monastery of humility Notre Dame.

4-5.	Cesare Baronio *Annales Ecclesiastici denovo excusi et ad nostra usque tempora perducti*, Tomus Vigesimus Tertius, 1286-1312, Augustin Theiner, ed. Bar-le-Duc: Ludovic Guerin (1871:88-89) orig 1588-1607

54. *Miraculum circa Eucharistiam Parisiis.* — Absolvamus hunc annum celeberrimo prodigio, quod divinum Numen Parisiis ad expugnandam eorum perfidiam, qui sanctissimi Sacramenti detrahunt dignitati, edidit, dignissimamque admiratione historiam a sancto Antonio [1], audiamus : « Eodem, inquit, anno, insigne miraculum accidit Parisiis circa Eucharistiam : nam cum quidam Judæus mutuasset sub usuris cuidam mulieri certam quantitatem pecuniæ super pignus cujusdam vestimenti sui, illa, ut ea posset vestiri in Paschate de propinquo advenienti, accessit ad Judæum ad concedendam tunicam suam. Sed perfidus Judæus ausus est dicere mulieri : Si tu portas mihi corpus Christi, quod dicitis esse in hostia consecrata, ego tibi restituam vestem sine aliqua pecunia. At mulier cupiditate devicta, plus amans pecuniam quam animam, hoc ei promisit. Unde die Paschalis accedens ad communionem, in ore retinuit Sacramentum, non glutiens, nec purificationem sumens; sed recedens ab Ecclesia Judæo detulit. Qui, ut perfidissimus et sacrilegus, posuit Sacramentum in patella super ignem cum aqua bullienti : et cum Sacramentum illæsum perma-

[1] S. Anton. III. p. tit. xx. c. 5. § 3. Jo. Villan. l. VII. c. 14. Naucler. gen. 44 et alii.

NICOLAI IV ANNUS 4. — CHRISTI 1291.	89

neret, ille gladium accipiens, pluries percussit hostiam ; indeque sanguis exivit, quo aqua tincta effecta est rubea tota. Extrahens autem de patella, misit hostiam illam in aquam frigidam, quæ etiam tota effecta est rubea. Christiani autem pervenientes, ut acciperent ab eo sub usuris, et domum intrantes ejus, perpenderunt sacrilegium maximum Judæi : hostia nempe per seipsam evolavit super quamdam tabulam. Captus ergo Judæus, confesso scelere, combustus est, et Sacramentum reverenter acceptum a sacerdotibus cum multa devotione fidelium et honore deportatum est ad Ecclesiam, et ex domo Judæi fabricata est Ecclesia, et vocatur Ecclesia Salvatoris Delbolgente ».

Miracle on the Eucharist among Parisians. We complete this year with the most celebrated prodigy, which the Divine Numen sent to the Parisians to expunge their perfidy which the most Blessed Sacraments diminish in their dignity, and let us hear the most dignified history from St. Anthony: (quoted from St. Antoninus above)

4-6. Henri de Sponde (Spondanus) *Annalium Ecclesiasticorum Eminentis Cardinalis Caesaris Baronii continuatio ab anno M.C.XCVII.* Lyon: Fratres Anissonii et Ioah. Posuel. 1678: 416.

IESU CHRISTI
ANN. 1290.
NICOL. IV.
ANN. 3.
RUDOLPHI
ANN. 17.
ANDRONICI
ANN. 8.

I.

MIRACULUM DE EUCHARISTIA LUTETIÆ.

ANno Christi millesimo ducentesimo nonagesimo, Indictione tertiâ, insigne miraculum accidit Parisiis circa sanctissimam Euchariſtiam. Cùm enim quidam Iudæus Christianæ mulieri sub usuris & pignore vestis certam pecuniæ quantitatem mutuò dediſset, eâque adveniente Paschate veſtem repeteret in solemnitate induen-

mo octogesimo quinto vel sexto eum contigiſse scribant. Sed ab Anglis ſtant cetera eius temporis monumenta, de quibus dicetur. Obiit autem, cùm poſt omnem prolem amiſſam, novæ suscipiendæ spe uxore recèns ductâ, iuveniliter equum agitare volens, eiectus in terram pronus confractâ infeliciter cervice repentè exanimatus est: poſtquàm regnâſset non tantùm annos triginta septem, ut Scoti ponunt, verùm quadraginta unum, quot numerantur ab anno 1249.quo regnare cœpit ad hunc 1290. Inter salubres leges ab eo conditas reperitur Magiſtratibus imperâſse, ut otiosos qui nec artem scirent, nec patrimonium haberent, severè compescerent; quòd omnium scelerum ac flagitiorum ex otio, velut fonte, primordia dimanare existimaret. Cúmque vel navigandi inscitiâ, vel temerè se mari cô-

ſtem repeteret in solemnitate induendam; perfido Iudæo sine pretio restituere offerente, dummodò mulier CorpusChriſti quod sumptura eſset ad eum deferret; promisit misera, & ore reservatam Euchariſtiam, sudarióque involutam Iudæo tradidit. Quam sacrilegus in subterraneâ cellâ domûs suæ super ignem in aquâ bulliente ponens, illæsam permanentem pluribus cultri ictibus pupugit, unde copiosus sanguis effluxit qui totam aquam rubram fecit. Re à Christianis fortè detectâ, ipsa sacra Euchariſtia in evidentiorem sceleris manifeſtationem ex vase aquæ evolans trabi superpositæ insedit. Captus Iudæus igne combustus est, sacratiſſima Hoſtia solemniter in ecclesiam parochialem S. Ioannis delata; ubi hactenùs illæsa & integra conservatur: domus Iudæi in templum conversa, addito cœnobio Fratrum *Charitatis Beatæ Mariæ* sub Regulâ S. Auguſtini, quod vulgò *Billetarum* vocant, ab aquâ sive à

vigandi inscitiâ, vel temerè se mari committentium avaritiâ multa fierent naufragia, & ad hæc accedente piratarum violentiâ, mercatorum ordo propè ad inopiam redactus eſset, quæſtûs causâ suos navigare vetuit. Quòd inſtitutum cùm propè annum duraſset, ac multorum sermonibus tamquam publicè noxium reprehenderetur; tandem peregrinarum mercium brevi tanta vis invecta eſt, ut non solùm rerum copia, sed pretij vilitas memoriam superiorum temporum superaret. Verùm ut hic quoque mercatorum ordini consuleretur, vetuit quemquàm à peregrinis invecta emere præter mercatores; ceteros autem quod cuique usui eſset ab illis redimere.

Narrant iidem auctores g, insignem quemdam ariolum (cui nomen *Thomæ Leirmondo*, habito Anglis & Scotis vati, eò quòd res futuras prædicere solitus eſset, licèt verbis obscurioribus; qui & sermone patrio vaticinales ryth-

III.

lib. 1 confid.
9.5.6. De
hac nullare
vide infr.
an. 1195.
XVI.

II.
ALEXAN-
DRI REG.
SCOT.
OBITUS.
Veofmun.
in Floril.
Vualfingh.
in Edvard.
I.
Io. Maior.
lib. 4. cap.
11. Boet. lib.
11. ad fi. Bu-
chan. lib. 7.
in fi.

vulgò *Billetarum* vocant, ab aquâ five à Salvatore in eâ búlliente : ubi hactenùs vifitur cella in facellum mutata, unà cum prædictis vafe, cultro & trabe inftrumentis miraculi: quod narratur à Nangio[a], Villanio[b], & Antonino[c], alüfque, atque etiam infigniter ab authore Fortalitij[d] Fidei : præter antiqua prædicti conventùs monumenta, quæ edita fuére Parifiis Latinè & Gallicè anno millefimo fexcentefimo quarto.

Hoc item anno tempore Quadragefimæ ponunt hiftorici Angli[e] obitum *Alexandri* Scotiæ Regis eius nominis tertij, principis fingularis virtutis : cùm Scoti[f] iam anno millefimo ducentefi-

qui & fermone patrio vaticinales rythmos fcripfit, undè & nomen accepit *Rythmus vates*) pridie eius diei quo Rex periit interrogatü à Comite Merchiarum num aliquid in pofterum diem novi eventurum effet, refpondiffe imminere vehementiffimam procellam, quæ univerfæ Scotiæ maximam calamitatem illatura effet. Nec defuit fides oraculo, quamquam obfcurè prolato. Siquidem Rege fine liberis defunéto, cùm plurimi contenderent de regni fucceffione, duóque ceteris propinquitate longè anteirent, Ioannes Baliolus & Robertus Brufius ; turis utriufque iudicio ad Eduardum Angliæ Regem à primoribus regni delato, poft

DE REGNI
SUCCES-
SIONE DI-
SCEPTA-
TIO.

In the year of Christ one thousand two hundred ninety a singular miracle happened in Paris concerning the most blessed Eucharist. When a certain Jew loaned a Christian woman at interest and under pledge of her clothing a certain amount of money and she for the coming Easter requested to have the clothing back. The perfidious Jew offered to restore it at no cost if the woman would pass on to him the Body of Christ she was about to receive and having held the Eucharist in the mouth and enclosed in a napkin brought it to the Jew. Then the sacrilegious in a subterranean cell of his house placing it over a fire in boiling water and it remaining the same pierced it with many stabs of a knife, whereupon copious blood poured forth which made all the water red. The matter having been detected by Christians, the blessed Eucharist in yet more evident manifestation of the crime rising from the water vessel came to rest posed in a bowl. The Jew captured and burned by fire, the most blessed Host was solemnly borne to the parochial church of St. Jean where of itself and whole it is conserved to this day. The house of the Jew was converted into a temple with the monastery adjoined of the Brothers of the Charity Blessed Mary under the rule of St. Augustine, whom in the common language they call Billettes, from the water or from the Savior boiling in it. Where to this day is visited the cell made into a chapel together with the aforesaid vessel, knife and bowl instruments of the miracle. Which is narrated by de Nangis, Villani, Antonino and others, as well as by the author of Fortalitia Fidei and ancient monuments of the said convent published at Paris in Latin and French in the year one thousand six hundred and four.

4-7.   Ferry de Locre, *Maria Augusta Virgo Deipara in septem libros tributa'* R. Madhuy Typographia Iurati, 1608.

Monasterium Humilitatis Nostræ Dominæ..

CAPVT 60..

ID·Philippus Pulcher in vrbe Lutetia·, anno ferè· 1290. compofuit, nomine *Humilitatis Nostræ Domi-næ*,.vulgò *des Billettes* infignitum..Occafionem Aegidius Corrozetius.& Petrus Bonfonius afferunt.eiufmodi.: Perfidus quidam Iudæus emptam.& acceptam à quadam muliercula Sacro-Sanctam Dominici Corporis Hoftiam,.cultello nefariè quum.perfodiffet, emanans.ex ea plurimus fanguis, aliaq; varia prodigia in.lucem abeuntia, populum primò, inde Regem.mirificè perculerunt.. Vnde fumpto, de fcelerato.ifto, fupplicio ; ædes eius diruere ; afceterium ibi.collocare ;. Anachoretas ex Diœcefi Cabilonenfi aduocare, ac.locum incolendum.dare ; vbi in hanc. vfque diem perfeuerarunt..

Aegid. Corro-
zetius.l. de an-
tiquite, Pari-
fienf.
Boaonius l. 2.
eiufdem argu-
menti, f. 14.

Philippe le Bel in the city of Paris, in the year 1290 founded a monument in the name of the Humility of Our Lord, commonly, of the Billettes. The occasion was related by Gilles Corrozet and Pierre Bonfons in this manner: A certain perfidious Jew purchased and received from a poor woman the Sacred Host of the Lord's Body, with a knife vilely stabbed it, much blood emanating from it, and further various prodigies having manifested, overwhelmed first the people then the king with wonder. Hence the cost of this crime being punishment, his house being seized to locate a hermitage there, calling anchorites from the diocese of Chalons to establish a dwelling where to this day they remain.

4-8.   Jacques Marchant, *Hortus pastorum sacrae doctrinae polymitus*, Candelabri Mystici, Tract. IV
Lyon: Sumptibus Societatis, 1752 (1638)

In Gallia, in urbe Parisiensi, quoddam templum est
quod vocatur *Salvatoris Bullientis*, ratione miraculi
quod contigit anno 1290. Quidam Judæus pactus est
cum inope muliercula, se ei vestem (quam oppigno-
ratam habebat) gratis redditurum, si modo ei traderet
Hostiam quam in Paschate erat sumptura. Tradidit
illam infœlix, urgente paupertate, Judæus verò cum
accenso igne Hostiam in sartagine vellet assare, vidit
non mutare formam nec colorem: ut ergo odium sa-
tiaret gladio eam transfixit, sed statim sanguis ema-
navit. Res detecta fuit supervenientibus Christianis,
& punito Judæo, ejus domus in templum conversa
est, quæ etiam nunc Salvatoris Bullientis nomine com-
pellatur, ubi Hostia Gladiusque ostenduntur. Testis est
Baptista Fulgosius, l. 1. Factorum memorab. cap. 6.

In Gaul in the city of Paris a certain temple is which is called of the Boiling Savior, by reason of a miracle which occurred in the year 1290. A certain Jew made an agreement with a poor little woman, that he would return her clothing (which he had in pledge) only if she would bring to him the host which was consumed at Easter. The unhappy woman brought it to him due to the distress of her poverty. The Jew in truth over a raised fire wished to fry the Host in a pan, saw that it did not change form or color, thereupon overcome with hate transfixed it with a sword, but immediately blood came out. The matter detected by arriving Christians, the Jew being punished, his house was converted into a temple, which now is called by the name of the Boiling Savior, where the Host and the Sword are displayed. The text is Baptista Fregoso, book 1, Factorum memorab. Chapter 6.

4-9.   Thoma Le Blanc, *Psalmorum Davidicorum Analysis*, Tomus Secundus Cologne: Ioannes Wilhelm Friess 1698: 601 Psalm XXI Verse XXVIII

In France has grown veneration for the miracle that happened in Paris in the year 1290, where a Jew having purchased a host from a poor old woman that he might try to cut it into pieces. But the matter did not go as planned, and blood poured out from it. The house of that Jew was converted into a temple, and there they exhibit the host and knife, as the blessed Antoninus relates in the third part of his history title 20, sixth chapter. And afterward it was translated to the parish church, St. Jean. See Spondanus in the year 1290.

Notes

[29] Walker (1933)
[30] Tomita, comp. (2009: 146)
[31] Münster (1544: lxxxvii)
[32] Corrozet (1550: 95-96)
[33] Dufour IN Belleforest (1882: xv-xvii).
[34] Jacob IN Corrozet (1874: xv-xvi)
[35] Dufour IN Belleforest (1882: i)
[36] "more or less lying pieces" Bonnardot (1851: 69)
[37] Flacius, et al (1574: 1271-78)

[38] Capocelatro (1894: 398-99)

5.

The Transformation of the Jew's House

The location of the Jew's house was only known from the location of the chapel that was made from it. The chapel was a way of remembering and dismissing the Jew's house. That the chapel and its successors were made from or built upon the Jew's house was embedded in the memory of the place, repeated in written sources and elaborated over the centuries. In a history of Paris written after the Franco-Prussian war and the Paris Commune, Henri Gourdon de Genouillac envisioned the mob of enraged Parisians breaking into the Jew's house and destroying it after the host abuse became known.[39] With no support from any record, he showed the Jew being burned in front of the Jew's own house.

"The Jew was burned in 1290, before his house, to the great satisfaction of the people".
Gourdon de Genouillac (1881: 137)

"At the first news of this miracle all Paris dashed to the house of the Jew and to the church of Saint Jean-en-Grève,"[40] the authors of a historical geography of Paris recalled nearly half a millennium after the date of the miracle. The crowd headed to the church because the host had been brought there, and they headed to the Jew's house to apprehend the Jew.

Qualifying the dash to the house, the authors continue: "The house and the other goods of this abominable Jew were confiscated to the profit of King Philippe le Bel, and the prince gave a part of this property to Reignier Flaminge [another alternative spelling], bourgeois of Paris, who had a chapel built there called the Chapel of Miracles."

The behavior of the Paris crowd was motivated partially by rage at the Jew's sacrilege and partially by eagerness to obtain what they could of his goods before they were snapped up by the king. An important piece of property was the ledger book of the Jew that recorded the names of his debtors and the amount owed by each. Having secured this book, the king could collect on the loans, a considerable amount. Soon after the expulsion of the Jews from France in 1306 townspeople raced the king's agents to secure the credit records of the dispossessed Jews, which constituted as much as two-thirds of the Jews' total assets.[41]

A "Renier le flemane," "Renier the Fleming," listed as dwelling in the Grève at the time of the 1292 tally was the man to whom the king ceded part of the Jew's house.[42] At 30 livres-30 sous of taxes Renier was one of the most propertied bourgeois of the city. Philippe le Bel was extending his influence over Flanders at the time and saw the advantage in having supporters of Flemish origin in charge of a potentially lucrative property in the city.

The Jew's house was in the *"Fiefs aux Flamans"* a feudal landholding within the gift of the king. It was the *"censive et seigneurie de la Bretonnerie,"* a property of considerable extent on which tenants holding the censive owed an annual fee to the seigneur.[43] The property earlier had been agricultural land devoted to vineyards. The building of residential and religious structures, including the house of the Jew, had eliminated the vineyards but not the property rights.

At the time of the miracle the seigneur was Jean Arrode, also a high-taxpaying bourgeois of Paris who became the sixth "mayor" of the city in 1291.[44] The king had pre-empted Arrode in seizing the Jew's house and granting a portion of it to another bourgeois. Arrode was a trusted councilor who had been on diplomatic missions for the king, including to Flanders, and likely was party to the king's plans.

The king may have granted the space, but he could not authorize the construction of a chapel. To this end Flaming petitioned the bishop of Paris and hence Pope Boniface VIII, who responded in the form of a papal bull on August 16, 1295.[45] This was during the first year of Boniface's papacy, before his travails with Philippe le Bel.

> Boniface bishop servant of the servants of God to his brother Paris bishop greeting and apostolic benediction. The petition of the beloved son Rayner Flaming a citizen of Paris shown to us contained here, that he in that place of the city of Paris in which a certain Jew having obtained a revered Eucharist punctured it with a knife and immersed it in the boiling water of a cauldron placed over a fire, where the very water by a divine miracle was recognized to be converted into blood; that he proposes to construct a chapel in honor of our Lord Jesus Christ, and to assign to it sufficient revenues of his own properties of adequate value by which a chaplain may be perpetually sustained to serve there, by law the patronage in the chapel for himself and his heirs reserved. As the same citizen has humbly beseeched us to command for himself the protection of apostolic favor, by which it is enough to fulfill his vow of this kind, so we direct. Therefore in this

part of the citizen's laudable proposal recommending, and through your oversight having full trust in the Lord, we command by apostolic writing to thy brotherhood, to construct a chapel in the stated location in accordance with the citizen's request, if the place itself belongs to that citizen or afterward is lawfully acquired, provided he offers that he lead the work, you may extend a license by our authority, without prejudice of foreign law, by law to reserve patronage in that chapel to him and his heirs in perpetuity. Given at Anagni, 16 of August, year 1 of our pontificate.

King Philippe le Bel granted Raynier Flaming part of the Jew's house, and the Pope granted him, through the bishop who made the petition, the right to construct a chapel there, provided he and his heirs dedicate property to the support of a chaplain and take responsibility for the construction. If the house was fairly acquired, and in accordance with French law, Raynier Flaming was entitled to patronage of the chapel forever.

Patronage (*patronatus*) meant the right to gain the spiritual benefits of donating a structure or ceremony of worship. It also was a form of ownership extending from church to state to layman.[46] Benedict's gliding footwork between civil legality, royal writ and strongly asserted papal authority was the dominant dance of his papacy, and a set of moves that embroiled him fatally with Philippe. In this early granting Raynier Flaming patronage he endorsed Philippe's wishes with a tremor of self-assertion.

The Pope's conception of the miracle "where the very water by divine miracle was recognized to be converted into blood" centered on its unique feature. Bleeding hosts and hosts escaping molesters by flight appeared in local miracles throughout Europe, including one at the nearby church of St. Gervais, but a host turning the boiling water of a cauldron into blood (not just bleeding into it) was unprecedented. Philippe le Bel and Pope Boniface VIII recognized its potential to attract the faithful. The image of the "boiled god" was deeply implanted in the mystery and name of this miracle.

There are two different versions of the next step after the Paris bishop and Raynier Flaming received the papal license in 1295. In the 16th century, Gilles Corrozet, the historian-guide who identified himself only as "a Parisian," cut through the complications by having the king and queen purchase the Jew's house, found a church there and install a religious brotherhood. In the 17th century historians of France and Paris maintained that the Jew's house was "razed from floor to roof" for the chapel to be built.[47] They projected into their forebears a wish to obliterate all material connection between the Jew and the chapel of the miracle, leaving only the miracle.

Another version was assembled by writers in the 18th century who wanted to demonstrate continuity between the house of the Jew and the chapel. They defended the credibility of the miracle against critics by proof of heritage and succession. Theodoric de S. René, a Carmelite monk, drew upon the archives of the chapel to provide the text of a sales contract which he assured his readers was evidence that King Philippe le Bel had confiscated the Jew's house after the host abuse and miracle.[48]

The contract itself was dated 1308. It confirmed by authority of the provost of Paris the transfer of the house from the heirs of Guillaume Morel Prêtre to the *Frères de la Charité de Notre Dame*. S.

René explains that the sale of the house completed one year after the miracle in 1291 was not registered until 1308 with the resale of that year.

Maciot l'Archier de Morlignon and his wife Anne held the censive of the property being exchanged, for which they paid 42 sous annually. They sold the house, which was "in the hand of the king," in trust after being confiscated, to Guillaume Morel Prêtre for 57 *livres de Paris*. The heirs of Guillaume then sold it to the Frères de la Charité de Notre Dame in 1308. At the very least the house was extant and was being passed with payments along the feudal channels guiding urban real estate transactions.

After being granted part of the house by the king and patronage of the chapel to be made from it in perpetuity by the pope, Raynier Flaming was shunted aside by the well-connected Guy de Joinville in 1299. There is no documentation of what Flaming did to fulfill his charge between 1295 and 1299. That the king wanted to contribute to the enlargement of the chapel and to having services performed there "with greater regularity and solemnity" implies royal disapproval of the way they were conducted under Flaming's regime. Events in the house that became the chapel signaled divine displeasure, which the king took responsibility to address in a suitable manner. The "reparation" of the wrong done to Christ's body by the Jew had to be sincere and perpetual.

The historian Dubreul did find in one of the lessons of the Easter liturgy of the chapel a reference to the transfer from Flaming, "who with his wealth cared for the chapel (by the name) of miracles in 1299, then by the manager Guy de Joinville gave it over to the brothers of the charity of Mary of Châlons."[49]

Guy III de Joinville, lord of Dongeux, founded an order of hospitaliers to attend a hospital for the poor of both sexes at Boucheremont in his native region of Champagne in 1284, which, coincidentally or not, was the year that Jeanne, Countess of Champagne and Queen of Navarre married Philippe le Bel (Philippe IV) of France, making him the sovereign of both principalities. Philippe confirmed this foundation with letters patent issued in 1286.[50] The connection between Champagne and the miracle blossomed in the 16th century and outlasted even its Paris sites.

Champagne, in the northeast of France, and Navarre, in the northeast of Spain, had been united under the same sovereign by the marriage of Jeanne's mother Blanche to the King of Navarre. The early death of the king left Blanche vulnerable to depredations internal and external, and she sought the protection of Philippe III of France. Her daughter Jeanne was raised with the heir to the French throne, Philippe le Bel, and married to him at age eleven.

The descendant of an old line of Champagne nobles, Guy III de Joinville, sought a foothold in Paris for his region, and found it in the management of the chapel of the miracles. With the king's written approval in the form of letters patent he brought the brothers hospitaliers to Paris and to the chapel of miracles. The king placed the rest of the house of the Jew at the disposal of the brothers through letters patent issued in 1299. He expected the brothers to reside in the building and conduct regular services in the chapel.

Joinville dedicated a considerable amount of property to the upkeep of this establishment. He obtained an amortization from Jean Arrode, the feudal lord of the Bretonnerie, the fief where the Jew's house become chapel was located. This legal instrument authorized the transfer of the property to the religious establishment of the brothers hospitaliers, relinquishing the dues and services due to the lord from the property owner.

If God and the Jew are not counted there were four levels of rights, benefits and obligations in this property: the king's rights, the Church's rights, the feudal lord's rights and the tenant-owner's rights. They all were fluid rights subject to assertion. The king, Church and feudal lord were acting on God's behalf, or at least they wanted it to be thought that they were. The spiritual benefits of owning and transferring the property were made concrete in the form of indulgences granted by the Church which in turn led to even more revenues from pilgrim visits, subsidies given for regular services and occasional donations.

The mesh of family, regional and urban kinship and trade relations, in which the Jew was a participant because of his wealth and access to Jewish networks, was in a constant play of revision through trade, marriages, births, deaths and unexpected innovations. The unexpected (not entirely unknown) innovation attributed to the Jew, trade of cash and goods for the host, was a disturbance in the network that profited everyone except the Jew, who lost property, family and life to the other players. Guy de Joinville completed the restructuring by introducing a religious brotherhood from his native region, formed to serve in a charity hospital, to take charge of the reparation services that had to performed on the site of the Jew's house.

The feudal lord, Jean Arrode, an officer of the king's household, would normally have demanded a fee to grant amortization, but the king's interest in the transaction and the hospital service formation of the brothers[51] extinguished the demand. The transformation of the Jew's house into a chapel and then into a reparation institution was a step in the centralization of the French state: the Breton lord of a fief in the city approved its transfer from a Fleming to a lord from Champagne, recently incorporated into the holdings of the monarchy, all under the aegis of the Church. The memory of the residence and rejection of the unconverted Jew was preserved in an institution that formed the miracle in a local, national and universal context.

Synagogues or, less frequently, dwellings of Jews in many parts of Europe were remade in reparation for sacrilege and other crimes attributed to Jews. Or at least the structure had the reputation of a Jewish place of worship rededicated while retaining the Jewish association. That association was retained and celebrated because it confirmed for Christians progress in the spread of the Gospel and conversion of infidels in advance of Christ's Second Coming.

The house of the Jew was absorbed into the fabric of the small temple attended by the brothers hospitaliers of the charity of Our Lady. As the brothers hospitaliers were replaced by the Billettes the house of the Jew descended into the earth, and it became a subterranean grotto housing the relics of the miracle where it was claimed to have taken place. The house continued with a mysterious physicality both ceremonially sought and built away from. It was guaranteed continuity as the stage set of the miracle reenacted in services. The house of the Jew became a temple of the Passion of Christ enacted upon the host. The host itself was elsewhere.

Notes

[39] Gourdan de Genouillac (1881: 135-38)

[40] Hurtaut and Magny (1779: 62)

[41] Taitz (1994: 220-22)

[42] Géraud (1837: 117)

[43] Sellier (1910: 193n94)

[44] Lombard-Jourdan (1976: 325-26)

[45] Félibien (1725: 295-96)

[46] Corrozet (1581: 155-56)

[47] "la maison rasée de fond en comble" Bonfons and Dubreul (1608: 308); "la maison rasée" DuPleix (1624: 453)

[48] S. René (1725: 270-73)

[49] Dubreul (1612: 979)

[50] Raunié (1893: 219n1)

[51] Davis (2013: 127)

6.
The Billettes

The men who came to Paris from Boucheremont in Champagne to conduct the chapel of miracles were not part of a regular church organization. They were seculars who in their service at the hospital had placed themselves under the protection and patronage of the Virgin Mary, hence the full name of their community: Brothers Hospitaliers of the Charity of Our Lady (*Frères Hospitaliers de la Charité de Notre Dame*). Guy de Joinville had petitioned Pope Boniface VIII and obtained a release from the authority of the bishops of Châlons-sur-Marne in the form of a bull given on May 12, 1299, which did not refer to the men by any title. The hospital was independent of the Holy See, and in recognition of that was to present the Apostolic Chamber with two pounds of candle wax annually. The Pope called for a cemetery to be established for the community.

Joinville, a layman, set the rules of everyday life for the "brothers" and "sisters" and the inmates of the hospital.[52] Brothers and sisters dwelt apart from each other. The brothers elected a superior; the sisters' superior was appointed by the ordained priest who ministered to them. Dress was prescribed for all, including an identifying scapular (one possible source of the later Billette emblem). Joinville made it clear that no one was admitted to the hospital in any role without his approval. He would manage the punishment of any member who refused to submit him/herself to communal discipline and required restraints. Each evening all were to pray for the king and queen, Joinville's family, and others he would name.

Only the men of this organization came to Paris in 1299. A body of members remained in Boucheremont performing their tasks at the hospital but there were no such tasks on the Rue des Jardins. Their sole purpose being there was "to honor Jesus Christ in the Eucharist," and of course to represent Joinville's interests and the house of Champagne in the seat of the realm and the site of the miracle. Queen Jeanne left a bequest to the chapel in 1305, as did a later Champagnaise queen consort, Blanche of Navarre, the wife of King Philippe VI, at her death in 1398.[53] Other queens without a direct connection to Champagne also made donations to the hospitaliers after they were established in Paris.

After occupying the half of the house of the Jew bestowed on them by the king, and expanding the chapel "as much as the smallness of the place would allow", the brothers initiated an annual festival on Quasimodo, the Sunday after Easter, in memory of the miracle. This was in 1323, at the beginning of the reign of King Charles IV, a son of King Philippe le Bel. At that time a Latin text of the miracle story was composed and deposited in the church archives.[54] Thirty-three years after the date of its occurrence the story of the miracle was consolidated ritually and narratively. Through word of mouth, ritual performance and visual representations the miracle became widely known. The ritual performance was in part the responsibility of the brothers hospitaliers of the charity of Our Lady.

They retained that name and a connection with their house of origin in Champagne. They were secular brothers who of their own volition took the Third Order of Saint Francis, which had been created to allow laypeople to follow the rule of St. Francis without making the monastic vows of the First and Second Orders. The Third Order in the early 14th century became associated with the Beguine and Beghard movements, in which lay women and men attended to the poor and ill without adopting the formal standards and discipline of a religious order. A line of popes declared them to be heretics. The Paris secular authority took charge of the burning at the stake of the mystic and prominent Beguine, Marguerite Porete, on the Place de Grève in 1310 (together with an unnamed Jewish convert who had relapsed).

The Avignon Papacy began in 1305 with the election of a French pope, Clement V, who refused to move to Rome upon his election but remained in the southern French city of Avignon. A total of seven popes, all French, kept the papal court in Avignon until the controversy (and a brief schism) was resolved by the Council of Constance in 1417. Under these conditions the brothers hospitaliers were especially susceptible to the accusation that they were schismatics who had followed an independent rule for decades.

One of the Avignon popes, Clement VI on July 27, 1346 answered the petition of the brothers to be released from the Third Order of St. Francis and instead be placed under the Augustinian Rule, making them members of a religious order who adapted monastic life to urban settings.[55] The Beghards and others who had assumed the habit of the Third Order without papal approval had been condemned by the Council of Vienna in 1311. The pope absolved the Billettes of blame for not having sought papal permission earlier. The brothers elected a General and a Visitor, both resident in their house of origin in Champagne, and adopted a "less primitive" garb dictated by the pope.[56]

Religieux Hospitalier de la Charité de N. Dame.

Helyot (1715: 3, 389)

With this modification the brothers were no longer in danger of being considered strictly a parochial organization devoted to an indigenous miracle. They had been legitimized by a French pope, and maintained their dedication to and the protection of the French monarchy. Their unruly character was a persistent theme in their history no matter what rule they fell under.

The brothers in 1381 exchanged houses and land their order owned in Mesnil to acquire signeurage rights to the *fief aux flamands* where their house was located in Paris, thus allowing them to sell and buy land within the fief without the approval of the lord.[57] Only the agreement of the monarch was required. Their holdings of land and buildings both in Paris and outside the city were a source of revenue and livelihood.

The patronage of the monarchy and contributions of the populace, due to the proprietary miracle they maintained, enabled the brothers to purchase an adjoining house and plan to construct a passageway between them. They petitioned King Charles V to make this modification, and after years went by without it being done, to tunnel an underground passage between the two buildings. The continued expansion of the campus backed by the nobility seeking merit and the people in thrall to the miracle led to a complete rebuilding of the church and the addition of a cloister, both consecrated on May 13, 1408.

The rise of the street bed during construction caused the original structure, still identified as the house of the Jew, to fall below street level. Acquiring a lower level caused the church of the brothers of the charity of Our Lady to resemble other ancient churches with a grotto or crypt located in the floor, often beneath the altar. The Jew now had performed his outrages upon the host on an anti-altar below, in opposition to the three altars on the upper level of the church.

By the 17th century this lower part of the church was designated the *cave* or basement and was marked by an inscription in the stone of the lintel: *Cy-dessous le Juif fit bouillir la Sainte Hostie,* Here below the Jew boiled the Blessed Host.[58] The culmination of the miracle story in some texts, and in some versions its chief wonder, was the water become blood and the apparition of Christ crucified when the Jew threw the indestructible host into a cauldron of boiling water.

One of the brothers' property acquisitions was a house deeded in November, 1337 by an heir of the bishop of Laon, to "the brothers of the hospital of the charity of Our Lady dwelling in Paris where was boiled by the Jews the Holy Sacrament of the altar."[59] The boiled host designated precisely who was the recipient of the legacy and where they lived.

The boiled host or the boiled god wording was strongly associated with that place perhaps because it was a memorable not often part of Christian or Jewish sacred imagery. There was no other occurrence of the boiled god. How it came to be associated with the miracle and place would be a matter of speculation. For a piece of wafer as fragile as a host to survive boiling was a miracle in which a sacred body endured familiar dangers of the domestic sphere (knives and fires). The apparently fragile host, which seemed likely to disintegrate in water, had hidden reserves to endure searing abuse. This was a powerful translation of Christ's Passion into terms of everyday life, including the potential violence of everyday life.

The archives of the church of the miracle were compiled and summarized by writers before they were removed to the state archives at the end of the 18th century. Among the documents kept in those archives were notarized contracts for the performance of a Mass in memory of a named individual or for an anniversary Mass. "On May 20, 1401, Pierre des Essars, Gentleman Squire to the Lord of Charnay founded an anniversary Mass before Vincent Chaon and Jean Lyure, Notaries of Paris in the church of the Billettes, where God was boiled"[60] reads the earliest of these in S. René's collection.

A poem found in a 15th century manuscript about the churches and monasteries of Paris also marks the place in terms of the boiling:[61]

> Thereafter a chapel
> Dedicated to a miracle fine
> Of a Jew who in his house
> Boiled the sacrament of the altar
> And made the water all vermillion

Many of the documents recorded during the 15th century identify the church by the same formulaic phrase "*dans l'Eglise des Billettes, où Dieu fut boüilli,*" "in the Church of the Billettes, where God was boiled." The "boiled God" phrase by itself was used to locate the church in some of the letters patent issued by kings during the previous century, and in such documents as the October 2, 1528 testament of Clemence of Hungary, wife of King Louis X. She left a sum of money to the "*couvent où dieu fut bouliz,*" 'the convent where god was boiled."[62] There could be no mistake where she intended the coins to go.

The Huguenot (French Protestant) minister and prolific critic of Catholic beliefs and practices Pierre Du Moulin (1568-1658) in a 1609 work quoted a Latin inscription on the Billettes chapel *frontispice* (pediment) different from the usual French wording.[63]

> With a spear the Jew pierces Christ's diaphragm (*cuspide iudaeus Christi praecordia sigit*)
> A wave boils with the rosy spreading bloodflow of God (*unda dei bullit roseo perfusa cruore*)

"If one believes them," Du Moulin wrote, the thick droplets of blood that poured from the host were seen painted on the inscription. *Christi praecordia* pictures the host as actual anatomy of Christ and was not used by any other writer and *roseo perfusa cruore* was a stock phrase in Latin poetry for waves of blood. The blood spattered on the sign was showmanship by Catholic clergy bound to excite the masses. That Du Moulin could present this satire as belief implied a distance already separated the inscription from whatever precipitated the miracle narrative.

In the early 16th century the "boiled God" was much less frequently used and "Billettes" took precedence as the label for the building, street, and especially the people still formally known as the brothers hospitaliers of the charity of Our Lady. Gilles Corrozet used it in his 1581 guidebook to Paris, applying it to the church, a college on the premises and the street, as did Bonfons in his 1608 history of the city. Arcangelo Giani tacked an Italianization of the name onto the brothers' formal title, "Nostra Dama de Bigliet" in his 1618 history of the Servite order.[64]

The earlier guidebook authors and historians did not attempt to explain the Billettes name. They assumed it was self-explanatory since it was attached to "boiled God" in most usages:

"*billette*" can mean "kindling" used to start the fire that boiled the water and the host/God. At a greater distance from the word's original usage it was taken to be a form of the verb "*bouillir*," "to boil" and the hypothetical form "Bouillettes" was constructed.[65] Or it conveyed the radiant source of the heat to boil the water, the humoral "anger" of the Jew, from the Greek "*atras bilia*"[66]

Antiquarian interest shifted from the boiled God to the house of the Jew, which was marked by an ensign (billette) or the local pay station for a tariff similarly marked.[67] Interpretation of the name's meaning finally settled on the scapular worn by the brothers, formed of small rectangular pieces of colored cloth in a row sewn into the garment front and back. They resembled the rectangular bars arranged on some heraldic shields.[68]

The church was never decorated with billettes in their architectural form of rectangular stone bars with rounded faces protruding on cornices. Following a general trend, the street and the church building both took the Billettes name and were marked as such on maps, supplanting the boiled god references. Guides to the "mysteries of Paris" to this day take up the boiled god banner but it is not present on maps, whereas the temple of the Billettes remains. Eventually the chapel's inscription was changed to read: This Chapel is the Place Where a Jew Outraged the Host. The scope of the Jew's abuse broadened from the vivid boiling to a series of violent abuses. He became *a* Jew, any Jew rather than *the* Jew, but the boiling was clouded by time.

In the lower chapel, where the Jew allegedly outraged the host, were kept three relics of the miracle: the knife (*canivet*) used to pierce the host; the cauldron (*chaudière*) in which it was boiled; and the bowl (*ecuyère* or *vaisseau*) with which the good Christian woman rescued it.[69] The knife was spotted with the blood of the host and, as the starkest relic, was exhibited regularly, on the occasion of the annual festival, on the Sunday after Easter. Later sources say that two of the relics (knife and bowl) were enclosed in reliquary statues,[70] or held by figures of saints or angels, which added to their grandeur. The relic cult centered on contrasting male and female objects corresponding to the Jew and the good Christian woman.

The archives of the Billettes retained a contract dated November 10, 1469 between a Paris notary and his counterpart from the town of Troyes (in Champagne).[71] The Billettes ceded the knife and bowl relics to the church of that town for a period of three years for an annual payment of 50 *livres tournois* in addition to a fund of 30 *livres* set aside for the fashioning of silver reliquaries. Theodoric de S. René put this agreement forward as further evidence of the sanctity of the relics, in demand in the provinces for their healing powers. The document was prepared by the notaries and filed in the church archives to dispel suspicions of "illicit traffic in holy objects." In case someone noticed that the artifacts were elsewhere.

John Calvin's 1543 *Traité des reliques* cited the *canivet* of the Paris miracle as an example of an object so revered by the "poor Parisian fools" that it rivaled the paramount sacramental, the host.[72] The curé of St. Jean-en-Grève, a Sorbonne doctor named Guillaume Duchesne, declared that those revering the knife (and just as much the lance, nails and thorns) that violated the precious body of Jesus Christ were worse than the Jews who crucified him. Calvin detected a rivalry between the clergy at St. Jean-en-Grève who sheltered the host of the miracle, and the Billettes, who enshrined the knife and other relics, to their profit.

The Paris printer and commentator on human foibles Henri Estienne in 1566 asked why such devotion extended to an instrument used to harm the Blessed Sacrament.[73] Estienne grouped the knife with a horse that ate a host and was the object of reverence. His comments were deeply embedded in his 1566 two-volume treatise aligning ancient events with modern parallels. It was the 19th century before Estienne's observation became known, by which time the relics had long vanished.

Trading off the relics for cash rent, and attracting the ire of reformers, was only one of the Billettes' transactions with the community. The church since the middle of the 14th century was the site of chapels to patron saints of guilds and religious societies not directly related to the miracle. The *menuisiers*, fine woodworkers, formed a confrerie (religious society consisting of four master artisans) dedicated to a chapel to Saint Anne in one of the bays of the nave. The Billettes held religious services on the saint's day including an exposition of the Blessed Sacrament with a sermon by a famous preacher.[74]

The Billettes extended themselves into the city in a number of ways, most solemnly by holding religious processions annually on the day of the miracle (displaced to the Sunday after Easter) which included exposition of the reliquaries containing the instruments of the miracle (perhaps accompanied by the host itself, which was at St. Jean-en-Grève).

In turn the population of the city extended itself into the church by arranging for services for special occasions and in memory of individuals. Most churches were the burial site of prominent persons placed beneath a plaque in the wall or the floor. The church of the Billettes contained entombments and accompanying epitaphs, of Billettes and other religious, a carpenter, an apothecary, viscounts, advocats before parlement and administrators from the 14th to the 18th centuries.[75] A personal devotion to the miracle, the Holy Sacrament, as well as having been a resident of the parish were important factors. Two historians, Jean-Papire Masson (d.1611) and François-Eudes de Mézeray (d.1683), whose heart was in the Chapel of Ste. Anne in the nave, were the most often recognized among those entombed there.[76]

The presence of these two humanists, Masson a former Jesuit who became a jurist, Mézeray a Secretary of the French Academy, both authors of histories well-regarded in their time but obscure afterward, suggests the attitude toward the miracle among 17th century French historians who looked beyond the absolute authority of traditional chronicles. The divine dispensation was not questioned as an article of faith and not examined as a fact of history. A heart-burial denoted a special gesture of devotion to the place of final rest: the historian's heart was with the miracle, the rest of his body was in another tomb. Neither historian felt called upon to consider critically the miracle or its custodians. Their presence in the church until Judgment Day was an assurance of that.

The Billettes became lax in the performance of their religious duties, their numbers fell, and those remaining dissipated the revenues they received from their properties and donations. They quarreled among themselves and with other church institutions. Indocility, the unwillingness of religious to be meek in their daily life, and unruliness (*dérèglement*) brought them to the attention of the king and parlement, who in 1628 ruled that they had to be reformed.[77]

Reform could best be achieved by placing them under the discipline of a stricter religious order. They balked at conforming to rules composed for them by the Friars Minor, and after more negotiations agreed to accept an arrangement with the Reformed Carmelites of the Observance of Rennes, a town in the ecclesiastical province of Toulouse. The Carmelites would assume control of the priory of the Billettes, all their properties and revenues, discharge the duties of their foundation including the performance of all religious services, and pay all their debts. The remaining Billettes could continue living in the convent where they would be fed and cared for, and receive a pension if they chose to retire.[78]

The Carmes Billettes formed by this merger were more financially stable than the Billettes alone. The few original Billettes remaining quietly merged themselves with the new regime, though one of them protested. Alexis Langau in 1652 declared himself ready to turn to another order, the Congregation of the Sacred Heart (Picpus).

An incident in 1659 implies that the Carmelites did not render the Billettes any more docile. The physician and man of letters Gui Patin began a letter dated December 12 to his fellow physician André Falconet remarking on the execution of a 21-year old woman on the Place de Grève.[79] She was a great thief and a great receiver of stolen goods, quite dedicated to her dishonest profession. "Over the past year she had the whip and the fleur-de-lis on her back."

She also was a member of the *Confrerie de Notre Dame aux Billettes*, an association of laypeople attached to the church. The condemned woman asked that one of the Carmes Billettes, who had heard her confessions before, be the one to absolve her. The chosen confessor found on arrival that a Sorbonne Doctor of Theology already was present asserting the university's priority in hearing the sins of prisoners. The two came to blows before the officers present intervened and removed the Carme-Billette.

The Billettes' original body of hospitaliers in Rouen also came through the centuries with a reputation for "morals hardly edifying."[80]

This not entirely reformed order continued the restoration and expansion of the church and adjoining properties, though any growth in size and congregation embroiled them with the clergy of Saint Jean-en-Grève, the proprietors of the host, the chief relic of the miracle. Their predecessors had agreed not to challenge the other church's dominance by attempting to increase their congregation, add more chapels and accommodate larger crowds for miracle-related events. The Carmes Billettes purchased a garden adjoining the church, the remainder of what once made up La Rue des Jardins, and pressed to expand their crowded dwelling space (the convent).

With the advent of the 18th century the church sat with an entrance on the Rue des Billettes between the cloisters, with a separate entrance on the street on the left, and the chapel of the miracles, with a separate entrance and stairway leading down on the right. The convent was reached through a street entrance opening on a vestibule and another door. The garden, not reachable directly from the street, spread behind the rear wall of the convent, with its own entrance. The church had a wide apse extending into the garden; and the cloister also had an entrance into the garden.

Expanding and increasingly enclosed, at this time the history of the Billettes was written. It was in response to a challenge from a Protestant historian who reviewed the miracle in the context of other comparable miracles. Jacques Basnage de Beauval (1653-1723) was the descendant of a family of Protestant nobles in Rouen who was in the midst of a career of state service when the revocation of the Edict of Nantes in 1685 forced him to flee to the Netherlands, where he eventually established himself as a Protestant minister and author. He composed some polemical works, a history of the Christian church, and a history of the Jews.

In the ninth volume of the history of the Jews Basnage examined charges leveled against the Jews, blood libels and accusations of mistreating sacred objects, including the host. He asked why abuse of the host did not arise until the 13th century, after the doctrine of transubstantiation became dogma. "But what use was this crime to the Jews, who certainly exposed themselves to the cruelest reprisals? It seems that the Jews fell into such excesses only to give the Transubstantiators an occasion to persecute them."[81]

Before reaching the miracle of the Billettes he cites a description of a miracle in a Spanish chronicle toward the end of the 14th century where the host was thrown into a pot of boiling water in place of the heart of a pig. All the pigs in the town died and the Jews were killed.

Basnage held up the absurdity and viciousness of these beliefs. Some rumors of Jewish host abuse and other crimes led to an outbreak of civil disorder that the authorities curtailed by punishing the Christian rioters. The Jews did not benefit from their presumed beliefs; neither did the Christians.

A Carmelite of the Billettes, Theodoric de S. René (1665-1728), named Basnage's *Histoire des juifs* in both the dedicatory Epistle and at the beginning of the Preface to his *Remarques historiques…*(1725) as one of the reasons he wrote the book. S. René believed that Catholics might have forgotten the miracle, and its proof of faith. He begins his long book with a survey of miracles and their incontestability. Miracles are the direct evidence of God's intervention in human affairs not reliant on reason.

S. René presents many pages of support for the miracle, from a French translation of the Latin miracle narrative to a chronology of publications by eminent figures after each of which comes the pronouncement "*On l'a prouvé,*" 'It has been proven." When he arrives at Basnage's specific points he maintains that the mass of responses to the miracle from 1290 onward constitutes proof that it occurred. The Jews have given such evidence of hostility to Christianity and Christians that their attacks on the host occurring since the late 13th century are just part of an entrenched pattern. S. René does not address the apparent recurrence of the Paris miracle several times and in different places.

Both books contain a much more than this exchange. The point of contact is where S. René as a Carme Billette mounts a defense of his personally constitutive belief against a Protestant who denies transubstantiation, exculpates the Jews and even makes them the victims. The guilt of the Jews and of this one Jew is crucial to his identity. Basnage died before S. René's book appeared. His evidence and arguments anticipate observations on the miracle by other Protestants and some Catholics in the years to come, as S. René's reaction was repeated and grounded in politics.

The Bishop of Boulogne, for instance, wrote in his pastoral instruction of 1767 that S. René had confounded the Protestants and especially Basnage, giving them little further to say, and he had instructed lax Catholics "in the faith a sensible person owes to miracles worked in favor of the Real Presence [of Christ in the host]."[82] Disputation of the pastoral instruction did not even mention the miracle.

S. René's dispute of Basnage epitomizes the frame of mind of the Carmes Billettes in the midst of the Enlightenment. Summoning the miracle to faith for those in danger of lapsing. For the church hierarchy, S. René had defended the miracle as a proof of transubstantiation, which the Protestants dismissed as a fiction. *On l'a prouvé.*

The Carmes Billettes defended the miracle but its location underwent changes. The inscription on the chapel of the miracle's stonework identifying it as the place where the Jew boiled the host disappeared in the course of renovation, to be replaced by a different inscription: "This chapel is the place where a Jew outraged the blessed host." The new less specific inscription and the chapel survived the next reconstruction.

The number of Billettes had grown from 14 in the 17th century to 50 in the middle of the 18th. The reconstruction of their church and convent was an ongoing effort resisted by the marguilliers (lay officers) of St. Jean-en-Grève who were certain that a larger building would draw more pilgrims and cut into their revenues. Defying the non-expansion agreement reached in 1632, the Billettes asked the architect Jacques Hardouin-Mansart de Sagonne, who had just been given a major commission by King Louis XV, to make a plan.[83] Mansart's 1744 proposal reoriented the entrance of the church to a larger street and increased its capacity from 960 to 1200 people.

The consequent opposition by the architect of St. Jean-en-Grève and intervention by the procurer general of parlement led to another plan for a larger church, also kept at a standstill. Mansart was paid by the Billettes and though records do not state whose plan was being followed when construction finally began in 1754 (completed in 1758), the general design and decorative features of the church tie it stylistically to Mansart.

Guidebooks have since the late 18th century attributed the design and supervision of construction to a Dominican monk named Claude.[84] Complaints of the "bizarre" ill-proportioned façade, the "mean and disagreeable" portal, the lack of structural support for the galleries and the organ reflected the continuing battle over the church. The Billettes continued to attract pilgrims and donations.

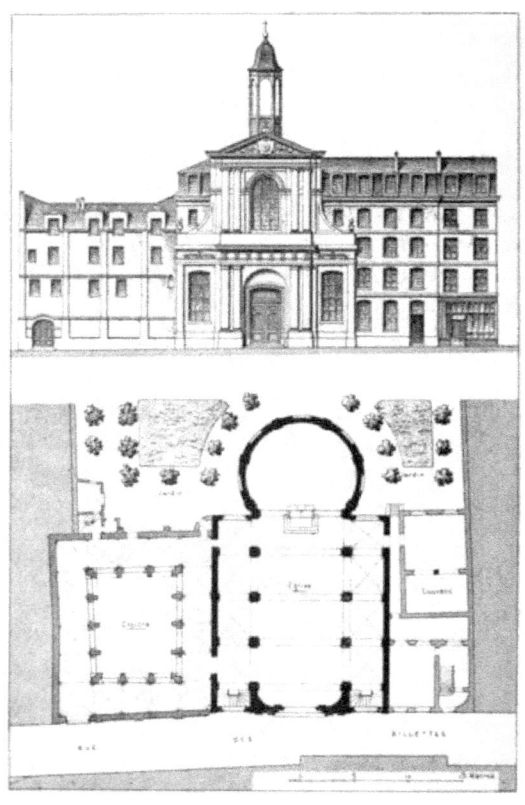

Lenoir (1893: 216) 1754-58 Reconstruction of the Église des Billettes

Joanne (1863: 418) Subsequent changes to the church of the Billettes.

Not all the *procès verbaux* concerning the Billettes, statements of legal actions, that flew about Paris in the 18th century were occasioned by the church reconstruction. On November 6, 1759 at half past midnight a police inspector named Louis Marais came before Pierre Thiéron, an attorney of parlement, to ask that he accompany him "to witness the debauchery and the capture" as he executed an order to arrest Father Elizée (Maximilien-Joseph Bulletot), a 28-year old Carme Billette, at the eau-de-vie bar of Chassé in the marketplace.[85] Having found Father Elizée "in this scandalous place in the state he was at this outlandish hour" drinking together with a coachman and an unemployed man, the officers conveyed him as ordered to his superior at the convent. A letter from Marais to the lieutenant of police adds that Father Elizée had spent three quarters of an hour in the company of a *femme de debauche,* surnamed Leroy.

These documents were found in the trove of police records that fell into the hands of the people who stormed the Bastille in 1790, and were published for the first time in *La chasteté du clergé devoilée (The chastity of the clergy unveiled)* published in Rome that same year. The book uncovered the ease with which monks and priests escaped official sanctions for violations of the law and their own rules that enjoined chastity. Father Elizée was one among many whose debauchery was detected, recorded and left to the discipline of his order without further comment.

Prior to that 1790 breakthrough for critics of the clergy and the *ancien regime* that supported them there were other less specific publications that caught up Father Elizée's activities in the interim. Eighteen years after his 1759 arrest, the *Gazetier cuirassé*, an assemblage of gossip about regime figures "printed a hundred leagues from the Bastille at the sign of Liberty" contains a paragraph referring to the Carme-Billette.[86] "Mademoiselle Contat, accused by Mr. Barois of having "implacable uterine ardors" ("*des ardeurs utérines implacables"),* was fundamentally cured by the begging brother of the Carmelites who took advantage of his community's secret for this marvelous cure."

"Implacable uterine ardors" was one phrase for hysteria in the sense of an unquenchable desire for sexual intercourse. The begging brother of the Carmelites was a member of the order who went about seeking alms. In this case he was known to be Father Elizée. Many of the orders fielded begging brothers but those of the Carmelites were reputed to be particularly craven.[87] The Carmelites as a community had a remedy for this complaint that came to be known as "the heat of Mademoiselle Contat" (*"le chaleur de Mademoiselle Contat"*). Such pharmaceutical readiness also was a component of the reputation borne by Father Elizée.

Further exploits of Father Elizée came to light with the early 20th century discovery of the records of "the house of Madame Gourdan," the elite Paris brothel of the late 18th century. In 1782 Father Elizée sent a note to Madame Gourdan asking that the back door be kept open and ordering up a *"collation"* for the time of his arrival.[88] *"Coquet,"* not food, will be his primary need. Sophie, a resident of the house, complains in another letter that this *"diable de Carme"* made her so sick with his attentions that her surgeon told her she would be out of service for two months.

Father Elizée's first reported arrest in 1759 doesn't seem to have inhibited his patronage of Madame Gourdan's establishment 23 years later. The well-funded licentious behavior was supported by revenues brought through the miracle they attended. Small wonder that the Carmes Billettes, numbering 25 at the time, resisted the stirrings of the revolution in their quarter.

A crowd broke into the sacristy in 1791 and carried off a collection of pikes and guns.[89] The religious demanded that they be allowed to keep the sacred vessels and other pieces of silver for the celebration of Mass. These objects, and a collection of records and books, were transferred to the state archives, located not far away on the Place des Billettes, now called the Place des Archives.

The Carmes Billettes order, created by the state and only licensed by the pope, was suppressed at the time of the Revolution and their buildings were sold. In 1808 Napoleon authorized the City of Paris to reacquire the buildings of the Billettes by purchase from the private owner and to hand them over to the Consistory of the Lutheran Church (Augsburg Confession), which occupied the church as a temple was still known as the Temple des Billettes.

Napoleon's imperial government had made concordats with major religious bodies represented in France as part of their effort to integrate a conquered Europe.[90] The Lutherans were especially appealing because they had a hierarchy and a tradition of compliance with government (unlike the more democratic Calvinists). Census-takers discovered that the Lutheran population of Paris was closer to 10,000 than the 1600-2500 originally counted. The availability of the buildings, the needs of the population and the broader plan of religious integration were the reasons for giving the former Billette properties over to the Protestants, but the gesture held an unintended irony.

The historian Amédée Gabourd surveyed the chapel of the miracle's transitions in his general history of Paris and commented ruefully on its final disposition.[91]

> The Catholics might well have wished that a place where happened, before a whole population, one of the most astonishing miracles that attested to the sanctity of the Sacrament of the Eucharist, would not have fallen to the enemies of their

dogmas, to those who recount, with a smile on their lips, the abominable profanation to which Paris was witness in the 13th century.

Gabourd's comment reflects the persistence of the miracle in the absence of its dedicated attendants and Dionysian practitioners. Nothing of the chapel of the miracle survived, and the church itself was transformed on the inside into a Lutheran place of worship. The medieval cloister remained, the only cloister from that period extant in Paris. The large Lutheran population for whom the temple was provided did not live in the same area. It was out of the way for the workers who inhabited the Faubourg Saint-Antoine.[92]

The revival of the miracle and the associated anti-Semitism during the late 19th century stopped at the boundaries of the Lutheran temple, but nostalgia become antiquarianism endorsed investigation into the remains of old Paris specific to the church of the Billettes. When this inquiry turned to them, the relics of the miracle and the records of the Billettes were scattered. In the catalogue of the Musée de Cluny, the national museum of medieval art and artifacts, which had been created in 1843, was listed from the church of the Billettes a "processional ensign in metalwork of beaten copper, cast, set and adorned with imitation stonework, depicting the mystery of Jonathas and so on."[93] This ensign was carried atop a staff in processions apparently no longer held.

The further careers of the Billettes' relics of the miracle can be traced only to a point. The knife (*canivet*) was removed from its reliquary and placed in a new one on November 10, 1469.[94] "The authenticity of the relic was recognized after the verifications of usage in a similar case." The Billettes making the relic transfer compared the Jew's knife to one known to have been miraculously bloodied, which reassured their followers and patrons. The last time anyone recorded seeing the "deicidal knife" was in its reliquary in the Church of the Carmes Billettes when the revolutionaries entered in 1790: 500 years after the miracle.[95] The knife then lost its identity and became either trash or an unnamed artifact.

Lucien Michaux's 1888 inventory of the contents of the Temple des Billettes for the French national art survey unsurprisingly did not turn up anything related to the miracle.[96] The minutes of the meetings of the Commission Municipale du Vieux Paris from its founding in 1897 do contain a number of references to the Temple des Billettes. The Commission is an official body formed of architects, historians and archaeologists charged with examining the material remains of Paris history in their contact with current development, the patrimony of Paris.

Several times it was announced at the meeting of the Commission's subdivision for the district that included the Temple that a fugitive piece had been unearthed. For example a marble plaque inscribed with an epitaph also recorded in the written record and dated 1732 was found in 1898 and transported to the Musée Carnavalet, the museum of the history of Paris.[97]

The Commission and the Musée Carnavalet were mandated to check the destruction of architectual features and artifacts in the course of development, which often meant reviewing construction activity. Laying a drainage pipe across the cloister for a set of toilets in residences on the Place des Archives brought inspectors from the Musée Carnavalet who secured an inscribed board from the rubble and demanded that they be notified of any future work.[98] The Temple des

Billettes had become Paris history under threat from the Paris present. The Lutheran church and the surrounding neighborhood had their own history superimposed on the layers of formation and revision that preceded them.

Excavators only go so far into the past underground before encountering resistance in the present. They never penetrated far enough to reach the Jew's house in any of its transformations. At a 1902 meeting following up on excavations in the underground of the Temple des Billettes the Commissioners considered the sparse material of varying ages found in a narrow chamber beneath the nave of the church.[99] Fifteenth century architectural fragments, gilded molding that once held a painting and human bones led them to the conclusion that they had found the rubble of the monastery of the Billettes and its cemetery, the original church described by S. René in his 1725 *Remarques historiques.*

The limitations of the findings led one Commissioner to question the value of further fossicking. Another reminded him that the results of tunneling can't be known in advance. An analysis of the debris brought to the Musée Carnavalet supported the hypothesis that the 15th century church was destroyed at the time of the transfer to the Lutheran consistory. The mixture of 15th and 18th century material would have been created by churning the foundation without sifting out the artifacts.

The house of the Jew and its successor chapel of the miracle had slipped away into the rubble at the turn of the 19th century, no longer discernible at the turn of the 20th. Perhaps Napoleon's imperial government, inventing an empire on the ruins of a kingdom, had looked the other way after transfering the property to the Lutherans, knowing they would erase any remains of the old rallying point beneath the Billettes.

After that everything of the miracle at 26 Place des Archives was either rubble, art or artifact. The Commission's opinion after the 1902 diggings tended toward the rubble. The Temple des Billettes was stamped with an *"avis desfavorable"* ("unfavorable opinion") in 1907, one of the few buildings in a survey of Paris religious architecture that drew such a judgment. On the brink of the First World War the sculptures in the cloister were "deteriorating."

The Temple's 20th century history was tied to the miracle only as a reference point. Other parallel, interlinking histories had kept the miracle supplied with place and personnel within its original cosmology and then in a broader cosmos of ideology and politics, with no possibility of material eradication.

Pagniol de la Force (1742: 172excerpt)

Notes

---

52 S. René (1725: 10-12)
53 Delisle,ed. (1885: 14n62)
54 De miraculo hostiae, *Recueil des historiens des Gaules et de la France* 22(1865): 32-33.
55 Helyot (1715:3,394-95). Helyot discusses other effects of the Avignon Papacy on religious orders in France.
56 Lenoir (1893: 219n1)
57 Lenoir (1893: 223)
58 Le Maire (1685: 409)
59 Lebeuf (1863: 379)
60 S. René (1725: 417)

> 1401.
>
> Meffire Pierre des Effars, Ecuyer
> Sieur de Charny, fonda un Anniverfai-
> re pardevant Vincent Chaon & Jean Lyu-
> re Notaires à Paris le 20. Mai, dans
> l'Eglife des Billettes, où Dieu fut boüilli.
> On conferve l'original de cet Acte dans
> les Archives des Billettes.

61 Bordier,ed. (1856: 38)

> *Puis siet apres une chapel*
> *Dediée par miracle bele*
> *D'un Juif qui en son ostel*
> *Bouilli le sacrament d'autel*
> *Dont trouvez fu vermaus entiers.*

62 Helyot (1715: 3,394)
63 Du Moulin (1609: 25)
64 Giani (1618: 106). Giani attempted to claim the Billettes as Servites.
65 Jacquemart (1792: 190)
66 Dubreul (1612: 982)
67 Sauval (1742: 117)
68 Helyot (1714: 1,376-77)
69 Le Maire (1685: 408), Le Rouge (1742: 273-74).Later sources mention two or even just one. The knife is always the one remaining.
70 De Gaulle (1839: 320n1)

[71] S. René (1725: 388-90). Troyes is the site of two churches with stained glass representations of the miracle story.

[72] Calvin (1921: 137-38).Calvin (1817: 430n1)

[73] Estienne (1735: 279)

...I recall the blessed Knife, that is, the knife with which a host was pierced in Paris by a Jew, which knife was has since then been included among the most precious relics, in one of the temples of said city (in Saint Jean-en-Grève, if memory serves) as if it was sanctified by such an act. That is how instead of holding these gods in contempt who let themselves be murdered, who let themselves be eaten by beasts, they have allowed themselves to adore them as before, and outside of that to adore those who eat and murder them: because I call murderer this knife with which the blow was made.

[74] The rules and by-laws of the *menuisiers* were published periodically. There are votary prints (1667,1743) of the Virgin Mary standing before her mother Saint Anne in the collection of the Bibliotheque Nationale. Below is a cartouche surrounded by tools of the profession and an inscription that indicates the confrerie was founded in the church of the Billettes, there are plenary indulgences and an exposition of the Blessed Sacrament on Saint Anne's day as well as preaching by famous preachers and two masses for the dead each year.

[75] Lenoir (1893: 229-38)

[76] Belin and Pujol (1843: 117), for instance, list them immediately after the two relics of the miracle in the church. Pagniol de la Force (1742: 313) attributes Masson's presence there to his devotion to the miracle.

[77] Lenoir (1893: 224)

[78] By contract ratified by parlement on July 24, 1631. Lenoir (1893: 224)

[79] Patin (1846: 168)

[80] Farin (1738: 19-20)

[81] Basnage (1716: 9,1, 381)

[82] de Pratz de Pressy (1767: 140)

[83] Cachau (2004: 2,1253)

[84] DeGaulle (1839: 322)

[85] Rémi, et al. (1782: 683-84)

[86] de Morande (1777: 140)

[87] The narrator of Denis Diderot's *Jacques le fataliste et son maître* (1765-80) describes the rapacious gleanings of a Carmelite *frère quêteur* who visited his village and debauched his brother Jean.

[88] Defrance (1908: 152)

[89] Lebeuf (1863: 379)

[90] de Lanzac de Laborie (1907: 367-68)

[91] Gabourd (1864: 2, 80-85)

[92] Les deux nouveau temples de Paris, *Le lien: journal des églises reformés de France*, 49 (1841): 365-66.

[93] Sommerard (1881: 413n5070)

[94] Lecanu (1866: 644n1) citing a memorial in the archives.

[95] Delarc (1895: 217)

[96] Michaux (1901: 94-99)

[97] Commission (1899: 10)

[98] Commission (1901: 26-27)

[99] Commission (1903: 91-94)

7.
St. Jean-en-Grève

The three relics of the miracle, once revered at the Church of the Billettes, form a bridge between that church and the other pole of the miracle's cosmos: the church of St. Jean-en-Grève. Taken by themselves they seem like the instruments of a ritual processing of the host from object of violence, to object discarded, to object gently received and transported to safety. From male butchery to female sheltering: their order could be a paradigm of domestic abuse. From the Dionysian Billettes to the Apollonian clergy, it could be the diagram of a myth.

St. Jean-en-Grève was not the nearest church to the house of the Jew, nor the most prominent, but the house of the Jew was in its parish. The church was at first the baptistery of St. Gervais, one of the oldest churches of Paris, and in 1212 it became the parish church for part of the area formerly served by St. Gervais. St. Jean-en-Grève was eclipsed in front by the Hôtel de Ville, which forms a side of the Place de Grève, and to the rear it met an alley leading to the Place de St. Gervais. The church was enlarged toward the Hôtel de Ville after the miracle increased its congregation, but its presence never became overwhelming. Projective maps only show its steeple rising behind the hulk of the Hôtel de Ville.

A Eucharistic miracle centered on the church of St. Gervais had occurred in 1274.[100] A thief stole the pyx, the silver box where the hosts were kept, and carried it to the field of Lendit, where an annual fair was held near the town of St. Denis. Wanting only the precious metal, he discarded the host, which flew up and fluttered around him. The peasants alerted the abbot of the monastery of St. Denis, who with the bishop organized a procession to the fairgrounds. The fugitive host glided into the hands of the priest who originally consecrated it. It was enshrined in a reliquary on the altar of St. Gervais, where weekly chanting of a canticle was decreed in addition to an annual feast on September 1.

The miracle of the Lendit host was incorporated into the sacred calendar of St. Gervais 16 years before the Jew outraged the host on the Rue des Jardins. The two miracles parallel each other in the host being abducted from the ritual precincts of the church, carried to another location, escaping destruction by innocent flight and finally returning of its own accord to consecrated hands and enshrinement. Expected monetary gain was the motive for the host's removal, the vain Christian woman to resolve her debt with the Jew, the thief to gain the precious metal of the pyx (not the host itself).

The man may have carried the pyx with host to the field of Lendit expecting to sell it without the host on the fairgrounds. The date of his crime is not given; it did not have to be during the period of the fair, June 11-24 each year, for trade to be his objective. Lendit was the site of religious and trade gatherings since pre-Roman times, and the accession of the Abbey of St. Denis to control of the fair in the 12th century sealed the fair's Christianization.[101] It was one of the abbey's three annual fairs, the largest, and truly international drawing buyers and sellers from as far away as Byzantium. The abbot of St. Denis was interested in rescuing the host and its container from a transaction of the grounds of his abbey's fair.

That fugitive host was returned to St. Gervais of its origins. The host that was brought to St. Jean-en-Grève after it escaped the Jew had originated in another church, St. Merry, where the woman who stole the host was a parishioner. Passing the host along to St. Jean-en-Grève supplied it with a connection to a miracle that other churches in the area already possessed, and this miracle affirmed transubstantiation in a unique way. It was the making of the church. The volume of worshipers following the miracle drove expansion accommodated by the demolition of adjoining houses without payment to their owners.[102]

During the period of growth after the miracle, and on the church's parochial centennial in 1312, St. Jean-en-Grève received a collection of saints' relics from the Archbishop of Lyon. The relics were from Lyonnais saints: St. Irenaeus, the second bishop of Lyon; St. Polycarp and St. Nizier, both of whom were patron saints of Lyon churches; and the largest collection, body parts, vestments and a manuscript sermon from St. Francis de Sales, absentee Bishop of Geneva, mystic and writer of devotional works, who had died in Lyon.[103]

The Archbishop of Lyon was by a 1079 papal bull "primatiale of all the Gauls," chief of the archbishops of all the major French cities. His cathedral was dedicated to St. John the Baptist, as was St. Jean-en-Grève. By the donation of relics St. Jean-en-Grève became the Lyonnais repository in Paris, a Lyonnais Notre Dame in Paris. The prestige conferred by possessing the miracle host, and the proximity to the seat of power, helped to affirm the link between the Paris and Lyon churches.

St. Jean-en-Grève was not attached to a monastery or convent of religious dedicated to the miracle. Feudal property rights determined who had the right to select the tenant of the church's main benefice, the chief presiding priest, the *curé*. The count of Meulan in Normandy held La Grève in fee of the Bishop of Paris, and made a gift of the fief of Monceau St. Gervais, encompassing both churches, to the Abbey de Bec and the Priory de St. Nicaise, both in

Normandy. The abbey owned property in France and in England and its abbots were protective of these possessions. The abbey and the priory were to alternate in selecting the curé of St. Gervais and of St. Jean-en-Grève which became fraught with conflict especially after the 13th century miracles enriched both churches.

The Avignon pope Benedict XIII asserted papal primacy in clerical appointments and conferred the office of curé on the theologian and chancellor of the University of Paris Jean Gerson in 1403, in an attempt to shore up his support at the university during the turmoil of schism.[104] It was several years before Gerson could reach an agreement with the Abbey de Bec, but finally he was able to join the St. Jean-en-Grève cure to his chancellorship, which provided little revenue. The additional funds allowed him to cease taking on student borders to make ends meet.[105] Gerson's writings and sermons do not include any words on the miracle of the Billettes. It contributed to his livelihood and that of his successors however indirectly.

Like the chapel of the miracle and the church of the Billettes, St. Jean-en-Grève was the site of regular devotions centered on the host. The host was enshrined in the church, where it was an object of pilgrimage. It was carried in procession on the miracle's feast day and when divine intercession was sought in a crisis, for instance in the appeal for the health of King Charles VI on June 3, 1412.[106] S. René accounts this and other processions in 1415, 1534 and 1538 to be among the proofs of the miracle.[107]

The processions were occasional, and the church offices were perpetual. St. Jean-en-Grève celebrated Mass and other rituals according to the calendar of the Roman Catholic Church. It also had a scheduled set of Offices of the Holy Sacrement peculiar to its history and mission printed in a collection of the church's offices in 1742, at a time when the miraculous host and the story of its origins were the target of vocal doubts. The Preface to that section placed the host miracle and the resulting unique liturgy in the greater history of the struggle of the transubstantiation doctrine to prevail over those who would cast the Eucharist merely as a ritual, and use it as a means of undoing the faith.[108]

The Jew was only an agent of demonic forces intent on disproving that the host is the body of Christ. The Feasts of Reparation held annually during Advent and Lent constituted a liturgical recounting of the story of the miracle in the nine episodes that had become established. The Office of the Feast of Susception was recited on the Thursday after the Octave of Easter. On August 13 each year a special Feast of Reparation for the Theft of the Host on that day in 1648. A "pretend reformer" Jacques Le Comte had stealthily removed the ostensorium with host, but was detected through traces he left behind. He was captured and the host was recovered. This resembled the St. Gervais theft of 1274, except that in 1648 the host did not fly to the hands of the curé and there was no miraculous translation to a safe haven. Its recovery by police action was ceremonially memorialized.

The host was kept in a sanctuary behind the church's main altar until the end of the 17th century, when a new reliquary was fashioned to enclose it.[109] Its three pieces were kept in a small box enclosed in a *soleil*, a sun-shape with rays of gilded silver (*vermeil*) of a reddish cast with contained an enamel of the priest in suplice and stole receiving the host from the good Christian woman who rescued it. A piece of the True Cross was also in the reliquary. Between the sun containing the host and a larger one above was an enamel plaque of the Jew holding a knife about to drive it down into the host on a table. Below it was a small model of a cauldron over which the host was suspended. This imagery was repeated in other visual representations of the miracle.

From the refashioning of the reliquary to the 1740's the church underwent a remodeling, the design and construction of two new altars in keeping with the neo-classicism of the period. The collection of paintings and sculptures spread about the interior depicted St. John the Baptist. The source of the funding for these improvements, the miraculous host, was not forgotten so much as framed by these augmentations. The marguilliers maintained their opposition to expansion of the Billettes properties that might cut into their part of the revenues. From documents associated with the church those revenues were estimated (in 1863) to be around 45,000 *livres* a year in 1764.[110]

The church of St. Jean-en-Grève was demolished as the result of a decision of the national assembly formed during the Revolution in 1791. The church was chosen because its neighboring church St. Gervais was older, and because it was engulfed by the Hôtel de Ville.[111] Before giving these reasons, Nicolas Jacquemart commented on the status of the church.

> One always will miss the order and the majesty of the ceremonies observed in this church, the precision of the canonical office, the propriety, the decency, the richness and taste of the ornaments, the beauty of the Main Altar, and the piety of the virtuous ecclesiastics who directed this parish. St. Jean-en-Grève was consecrated, so to speak, to the grandest of our mysteries. The Feast of the Reparation in Advent and in Lent, in September and in the time of Carnival, were a time of continual hommage rendered to the Eucharist by this edifying clergy.

In destroying St. Jean-en-Grève, an act documented in several contemporary paintings, the assembly made a rational decision based on size and relative importance of the church. They also demolished the sober pole of the miracle's Paris cosmology, the place where the *ancien regime* translated the imagined bloody rampage of the Jew into a repeated and sustained adoration of the Eucharist well regarded for its solemnity. That was not allowed to end with the dismantling of the church. The bones of its many sephulchres were in 1804 sent to the catacombs where they were stacked in orderly heaps without epitaphs or name tags. The relics of the Lyonnais saints disappeared.

At a meeting of the municipal bureau of the Commune of Paris on May 10, 1791 the church of St. Gervais and the new church of St. François d'Assise claimed the ostensorium and host of the miracle.[1,2] They could no longer profit St. Jean-en-Grève. Both churches based their claims on territorial sovereignty. In addition, St. François was without an ostensorium of its own. The bureau made the Solomonic decision to sunder two and give host to St. Gervais and the ostensorium to St. François.

The miracle-related remains of St. Jean-en-Grève, including the host itself, reliquary, tapestries and processional equipage along with the parish priest were nonetheless transferred to the church of St. François, which had formerly been the church of the Franciscan monastery. It gained the compound name St.-Jean-St.-François, attaching the patron of the former parish to the new one.

The presence of the relics was not noted in 19th century guidebooks and they did not reappear. St.-Jean-St.-François was best known for its organ and the organists who played it (as St. Jean-en-Grève had been)-until the revival of the miracle-inspired ceremonies after the middle of the century. At that time the host of the miracle was said to have vanished.

Obliterated with the church fabric of St. Jean-en-Grève were several representations of the miracle. They may have disappeared when the church was destroyed, but their *imago* transcended their material and spread far beyond sight of pictures. The St. Jean-en-Grève assemblage of miracle representations was the consolidation and broadcast of the *imago*.

Notes

[100] Lombard-Jourdan (1973)

[101] Lombard-Jourdan (1987: 273-74)

[102] Lebeuf and Cocheris (1863: 324-26)

[103] They were verified by the Bishop of Megara in 1550, whose listing was found when their casket was opened for the relics to be placed in a new one in 1724 under the direction of Cardinal de Noailles. Jacquemart (1792: 60-62)

[104] Valois (1901)

[105] McGuire (2005: 164)

[106] Sauval (1724: 179). See also Camille Salatko Petryszcze, *Le mistère de la saincte hostie, introduction, edition du texte et notes.* http://www.sites.univrennes2.fr/celam/cetm/Edition%20Hostie/ostie.html *Les reliques du miracle en procession*

[107] S. René (1725: 316-23)

[108] *Offices propres à l'église paroissiale de St. Jean-en-Grève, seconde partie contenant les offices du saint sacrement.* Paris: Mercier et Boudet, 1742.

[109] S. René (1725: 394-95)

[110] Lebeuf and Cocheris (1863: 360-61n31) Not considered a high revenue for a church at the time.

[111] Jacquemart (1792: 63)

[112] Lacroix, ed. (1905: 205)

M. Champion reported to the municipal Bureau on the claim of the curés and officers of St. Gervais Parish, who want to have a miraculous host that was at St. Jean-en-Grève as well as the ostensorium in which it is enclosed. They base their request on the fact that the territory St. Jean occupied belonged to the parish of St. Gervais, when that chapel was elevated to parish in 1212, at which time the chapel shared ornaments and revenues with St. Gervais. M. Champion also said that this same ostensorium was requested by the curé and parishioners of the new parish St. François d'Assise, that they are based the fact that they don't have any such thing, and because this new parish encloses in its allotment a great part of the territory of St. Jean parish.

The municipal Bureau, after having deliberated on the matter decided that the miraculous host will be sent to St. Gervais parish, and as for the ostensorium, it will be delivered to the curé of St. François d'Assise, for the service of this new parish.

8.
Services

Besides its ever mutating narrative and architectural forms, the Paris miracle went through time in the form of processions and services. Proceeding from stories, they were the basis of dramas. They took shape in a historical moment, yet by attachment to traditions of religious processions and services they expressed an aspiration to timelessness. They perpetuated temporal and spatial cosmologies.

The services and processions animated the transformed house of the Jew, the enshrined host and everyday implements and vessels become relics with a solemn enunciation of the events of the miracle. The story of the miracle was its liturgy, read at St. Jean-en-Grève on select days of the year according to a regular calendar. The readings were repeated year after year for hundreds of years. The original Latin text, preserved in the treasury of Notre Dame de Chartres,[113] was translated into French by a marguillier of St. Jean-en-Grève and printed in 1603.[114]

For so much time to pass before it was translated into the vernacular implies that the regular readings of the full text, routinely incomprehensible to an audience not versed in Latin, were supported by common knowledge of the miracle. The oral tradition carrying that knowledge dimmed. Increasing literacy in the population may have made the written translation seem an effective way to bridge the gap and preserve knowledge of the miracle.

Like the narrative of Christ's Passion and Resurrection that formed the annual and daily cycle of the Christian liturgy, especially the Mass, the Latin words of the miracle story sustained a rhythm expected by the congregants and equivalent to the normal passage of time. The text of the miracle readings, divided into nine lessons, announced the links between fallible human behavior and the redemptive power of the sacraments in their local workings. Dramatic events in domestic and commercial spaces were sacralized through reliable repetition.

The introductory paragraph summons up the faith of the listeners for its improvement to attend to the miracle which Christ has made, recognizing that some Christians are "stripped of faith, empty of hope, lukewarm in charity" and given to doubt. "In order to root out from the soul of Christians such a damnable error, and confirm in them the constancy of this belief" in this city of Paris, in the house of a certain Jew, Christ "wished to render a certain and doubtless argument, with an evidentiary demonstration of the real truth of his body in the sacrament of the very blessed Eucharist."

Having sharpened the focus of miracle to a point in Paris, the narrator speaks out the happenings of the miracle in a language figured with sin and judgment. The Jew engages his debtor, the Christian woman, to bring the body of her God in exchange for her pawned dresses and forgiveness of her debt.

> Just afterward at the hour of the first Mass she enters into the parish church of St. Mederic, and approaching with the other faithful near the holy altar, according to the ancient custom, and inflamed with the venom of her malice and greed, receives the venerable mysteries of Jesus Christ and by a projected artifice holds the blessed

host some little time in her accursed mouth and under the tongue of her infidelity. From there this great traitoress, guilty of the excess of such a great parricide, leaving the church goes toward the Jew's house and, discharging her impious promise, delivers to him this precious sacrament as she had agreed, and returns home, making little of having so casually and maliciously sold the body of her Creator.

The reader characterizes each person and object according the prevailing scheme of values and apart from the sequence of events. The woman's tongue and mouth themselves are accursed and unfaithful. The "projected artifice" she uses to conceal the host is nothing more than that, a mechanical device she had contrived for the purpose. Her own lack of devotion no longer is sufficient. It may have been a known device used to harvest the host for unsavory purposes. The woman's casualness, the superficial reverence of her approach to the altar, is subject to condemnation. She is a traitoress who killed her own father, and sold the body of her creator. The theft and resultant reward from the Jew excite no admiration for their deftness, as a well-planned and well-executed robbery might. The woman, not heard of again in this recital, cedes the stage to the Jew, who executes his program of abuse.

The reader apostrophizes the increasingly enraged Jew at length, asks him why the marvels of the host remaining whole in the midst of his knifings have not moved him, and invites him to join Christians in the adoration of the Blessed Sacrament. The Jew does not think to refuse; he is set in his course and will have none of it.

As much as this detestable Jew placed himself where he had to recognize his iniquity, so to the contrary; as much as he was miraculously instructed, so much he converted his thoughts to do worse, and hardened himself like Pharaoh.

God caused Pharaoh to harden his heart and so with the Jew. He resists all importunities whether of the reader or of his own family. Exhausted and confused, he retires to his room. The audience, hearing this read for one of many times in a language they do not try to understand as words, partakes of the Jew's intransigence as forward movement. They know what is going to happen but they listen expectantly just the same. Listening is virtue; understanding is artifice.

A series of inversions of the apparent damage to the host take place. The wounds become whole; the patch of blood becomes an admission of guilt; the ugliness becomes beauty and light. Those wishing to gain an "ocular faith" (*"foi oculaire"*) can see with their own eyes the new resurrection in the host on the altar of St. Jean-en-Grève. The church palpably surrounds the service of the narrative.

The Jew's son brags to the crowds arriving at the monastery of Sainte Croix (opposite the Jew's house) for Easter services that they won't find their god in the church because his father killed it. The good woman quickly enters the Jew's house, sees the bloody scene and receives the leaping host in her wooden bowl.

She makes her way to Saint Jean-en-Grève. The passage that describes her peregrinations about the church is longer than that of securing the host.

> Here one has it that after she entered the church she felt she had to leave. Not knowing exactly what to do, and since she could never find any of the doors, she went here and there wandering about the altars, as if invisibly bound by certain chains, until the curé noticed this strange case, approached her close with several assistants, learned what had happened and received from her this precious jewel.

Again the church encloses the events, and like others under the influence of the host in a church the woman is bound there. She is only released when the priest in charge of the church's services notices her odd behavior and takes the host into custody. In other versions of the story the host flies from the woman's container to the altar.

A crowd gathers at the church and on learning of the host's sufferings quickly brings the Jew who is just as quickly interrogated and, once the facts are established, urged to convert. St. Gregory is quoted, that a hearer listens in vain to outside advice if because of sin his heart is not full of grace. "Notable persons" pronounce the death penalty on the Jew. He is bound in a cart-the earliest report of a procession celebrating the miracle has an actor impersonating the Jew in cart on the procession route-and conducted to the square where wood is piled about him.

The Jew calls out that if he were not taken by surprise he could have availed himself of the arms he had. The Provost asks him what they might be. The Jew says a book. The Provost hopes to dispel his false faith by bringing it to him. It is bound together with him, and burned to ash with him, discrediting his protective magic and of course accomplishing the incineration of baptized. King Philippe le Bel and Queen Jeanne, the parents of the present King Charles (IV, 1322-28) had the Jew's house "improved" ("edifié") into a church. The poor brothers of Notre Dame Hospital on the river at Rogneron (diocese of Châlons) were brought to celebrate Mass daily at the church, and on the octave of Easter, Quasimodo Sunday, to carry out the "solemnity of the miracle," the present recital, with hymns. All to the glory of Christ.

St. Jean-en-Grève, where the liturgy of the miracle was recited according to a regular schedule among other liturgies and the regular celebration of Mass, was distinguished in the service from the church of the Billettes, where Mass was celebrated daily in reparation for the desecration of the host by a group of priests selected for that purpose. The liturgy of the miracle was read once a year, on the Sunday after Easter. The eternal present of the recital is the reign of Charles IV by which time the church of the Billettes had been formed from the Jew's house.

The Mass celebrated by the Billettes every day was not in content specific to the miracle but was as a whole dedicated to making amends for the torture suffered by the host at the hands of the Jew, just as the Mass itself is in part reparation for the torture and death of Christ. Reparation is only one of the reasons the Mass is regularly celebrated in Catholic Churches. The revival of the miracle in 19th century France centered on the restoration of the Mass of reparation and the liturgy of the miracle.

The 1637 publication of the *Officium Corporis Christi*,[115] the Latin *Office of the Body of Christ recited in the church of Saint Jean-en-Grève* made available in print the abbreviated text of the lessons and traité that was being recited because the full text was considered too long. The reformation from 1530 on of the Roman Breviary, the standard manual of prayer marking the hours of the day for Catholic clergy, included a shortening of the lessons for saints and festivals.[116] The services of the miracle were shortened accordingly and the *Officium corporis Christi* was the product.

As the title suggests the new St. Jean-en-Grève offices were not translated into the vernacular. Long exhortations and apostrophes were cut from the recital. The first lesson went directly to the Jew's offer to the woman without the drawn out courtship, hesitation and acceptance of the Jew's bargain as in the full lessons. The woman does as the Jew requests, brings him the host and leaves with her recovered dress. The Jew's knifing, boiling, scourging of the host are line by line acts. The woman who rescues the host does not wander about the church but quickly brings it to the priest. Of the string of notifications, of crowds and officials, only the bishop remains. The Jew is burned in a phrase without resort to his book. Matter-of-fact passages in the original became the standard for the entire sequence, about a fifth the length of the original. Less time was needed for the entire recital.

The Billettes by the late 16th century developed their own set of shorter lessons, a series of three in place of the nine read annually on the Sunday after Easter.[117] The three lessons of the second nocturne of the revised Roman Breviary were the model. The story of the miracle was reshaped into an even more curtailed version suitable to the Billettes' claims. They had been left with the instruments of the host's passion. The Billettes lesson places the host at St. Jean-en-Grève, then refers to the "knife, the blood spoken of, which flowed from the wound in plain sight, and the wooden bowl in which it was sheltered" that are at the church of the Brothers of Blessed Mary where they can be seen "with your own eyes" (*"corporalibus oculis"*). The old name of the group was deliberately archaized to make the lesson appear older than it was.

The cauldron relic of the boiled host was replaced with the blood that had flowed from the host (*pradictum sanguinem*) and stained it and which S. René says remained on the knife (*cultellum pennarium*). Possessing that bodily trace of the miracle would give the Billettes' collection of relics greater status than if it were confined to tools and vessels. Their revision of the lessons placed them in closer competition with St. Jean-en-Grève, where the lessons, now a different set, also were recited on the Sunday after Easter.

These lessons did include the passage of the woman's inability to leave St. Jean-en-Grève once she arrived there with the host and her surrendering it to the priest, and the Jew's request for his supposedly fireproof book. Those components were not part of the lessons revised for St. Jean-en-Grève. They were included to retain the resemblance to the old lessons otherwise abandoned. The construction of the chapel of the miracle by Reignier Flaming and the formation of the Brothers by Guy de Joinville and the bestowal of the house by Philippe le Bel, not in the old lessons, ended the short version read at the chapel. This service had become a recitation of the foundation story of the Billettes so old it did not include their name.

The Billettes' services also differed from those at St. Jean-en-Grève by the substitution of a *prosa* composed for the occasion for the hymn *Lauda Sion Salvatorem* in the Mass of the Holy

Sacrament. This rhymed, metre-less song, chanted to the rhythm of *Lauda Sion* had the traces of the early 14th century when Latin compositions with brief, cryptic lines were popular, around the same time the Office of the Miracle, the nine lessons with their references to King Philippe le Bel, entered the liturgy of the Paris churches. S. René included the text in his collection while noting that it had been redone in "better" Latin a dozen years earlier. Yet in keeping with his quest for signs of legitimacy he presented the older text.

From the beginning the *prosa* is atune with rhymed wordplay to the taste of clergy and Latin-speaking laity, a clever variation on a familiar lyric in the making of an indigenous Paris cult.

> *Mirabilis et insignis*
> *Res virtutis plena signis*
> *Et stupore.*
> *Sic perfecit Parisius*
> *Jucundius et latius*
> *Nove more.*
> *Anno Christi millesimo*
> *Bis centum octogesimo*
> *Juncto deno.*

Marvelous and renowned
Thing of virtue full of signs
And with awe.
So Paris finished
More joyful and more
In new style.
In the year of Christ one thousand
Twice one hundred eighty
With an added ten.

In two of its first words-*insignis* and *signis*-the hymn evokes signs, which are pointers set by God to high truths. The simple marvel of magical events has to give way to an understanding that the miracle occurs and repeats itself in words and images to enlighten its witnesses. The city is named on the brink of improvement. The date is as an additive cypher in the French counting style (1000+2x100+80+10=1290). This faithless Jew, his heart full of vile bitterness, an imitator of the wavering of his fathers [who did not see the truth].

This one, just before Easter,
Arid in the health of spirit
Became a merchant
Of the Lord's Body.

He acquires the host from a poor Christian woman and in ordered strokes, first, second, third…, knifes, nails and tosses the host into the fire, from which it leaps.

Deus invisibilis,
Qui pro eo mirabilis,
  Nam cum sit impalpabilis
  Comprehendi voluit
In corpore habuit
  Ex intacta virgine,
 Sine virile semine,
Maxime ab homine
  Scelerato.

Invisible God,
Who for this marvelous,
How when is impalpable
Flees the grasp
In a body he has
From an intact virgin
Without male seed
Farthest from the wicked
Man.

The host slips from the grasp of the wicked man as Christ born of a virgin without male contribution slipped from the womb. Yet when he is struck with the point of a knife on his body as hard as stone blood flows out. The "divine ram," which God substituted for Isaac about to be sacrificed by his father Abraham, is lanced and freely bleeds. Thrown into boiling water the host flies up, the crucifix appears and the water is wasted.

Seeing this, the Jew's wife and children ask to be among the faithful and leave Jewish errors. The Jew is consigned to the flames and the Eucharist is carried into the church. "As in the present they know sorrow so in the future they will glory. Amen."

The brisk, and reverent, completion of the miracle with Biblical allusions and doctrinal riffs in the 78 lines of this *prosa* counterbalanced the severity of the recited lessons. The *prosa* was chanted to the rhythm of one of the hymns that Thomas Aquinas wrote for the Mass of the Blessed Sacrament, and was so cherished that its language was corrected to meet current standards after it had been sung for hundreds of years. Yet S. René printed the archaic form after the revised one had been in use for years. The wish both to improve and to retain the *prosa* expressed the position of the miracle.

The revision of religious services associated with the reform of the breviary advanced to include the offices of the saints and festivals of Saint Jean-en-Grève in 1747. That year the *Offices propres de l'église paroissiale de Saint Jean-en-Grève (Offices proper to the parish church of Saint Jean-en-Grève* was issued by a Paris printer. The unsigned introduction compared the Christian services of the saints to the worship accorded heroes of pagan times, and credited participation in religion on the parish level with bolstering the faith in general. These remarks situated the compilation of offices in 18th century Enlightenment ideas of comparative religion, both universal and parochial.

A history of the church and of the acquisition of its relics placed its name saint, John the Baptist, and others imported with the relics from Lyon on its calendar, which was then summarized. The services of the miraculous host were only one section of the compilation. With this Saint Jean-en-Grève signaled that it had attained the degree of reformed sophistication that the publications of S. René displayed for the Billettes. A further advance toward popular presentation was printing all of the offices of the saints in the first section and of the Blessed Sacrament in the second in parallel Latin and French columns.

The table or calendar of celebrations set the first Thursday of each month for a procession of the Blessed Sacrament before high Mass, and each Sunday of the month for a presentation of the blessed hosts at first Mass. Services of the miraculous host are mentioned for Lent, Advent, Quasimodo Sunday, when the congregation was set to go "in station" to the Billettes, and on the Thursday after, when the Office of the Susception of the Blessed Host was performed.

The largest part of the second section of the book is taken up with the Office of the Reparation of the Blessed Host Outraged by the Jew performed annually on the second Sunday of Lent. Before the words of the service are given, a prefatory note charges the Jew with renewing in his abuse of the host the crimes of his whole nation against Christ in instigating the Passion. The author of this note, like S. René decades earlier, tries to dismiss the defense of the Jews by the Protestant historian Basnage. For there truly to be reparation for the crime, the Jews must be the guilty party.

The Office of the Reparation is composed of a sequence of hymns, psalms, lessons and short prayers that like all the religious offices are read and sung over a twenty-four hour period. Some of the office prayers figuratively identify Christians with the Jews in their plight, a not uncommon strategy. Other prayers indict one particular Jew for murdering Christ in the host.

The first Hymn of the Office of the Reparation begins:

True children of Abraham, you to whom the faith,
blessed mother, gave a spiritual birth! Sing, the
victories of Jesus Christ over a rebel son of Isaac.

The holy victim who was the prize of this world, alas!
An impious woman gives him in exchange for a lowly
garment, and retraces by this crime the sacrilegious pact
of the perfidious Judas.

Why does the earth redden, this divine blood of the land;
the blood that poured on the cross, washes away our iniquities?

Why does a blinded Jew again buying the Redeemer of This World
renew today the deicidal furor of his fathers?

The hymn sings to the "true" children of Abraham, that is, the Christians, whose Savior defeats a rebellious Jew. The children of Abraham as Christians are exalted over the contemporary Jews to the detriment of the latter. There follows the allusive condemnation of poor Christian woman, equated with Judas, and the Jew, equated with his people's heritage of deicide. This hymn and others draw lines from images of the miracle, the woman's sale of the host, the knifing and bleeding of the host, to other imagery with a strong valence in Christian history. The hymns are sung to show the events of the miracle suspended in the whole of the faith.

The story of the miracle is told as a linear narrative in the lessons, three of them linked together in the offices. The content is keyed to the miracle narrative but varies from one to the other. The lessons of the Lenten Office of the Reparation tell the miracle story as abbreviated from the full nine lessons formerly read and given in the 1637 *Officium*. The Advent Office of the Reparation contains three lessons that cut details to concentrate on the establishment of the churches of the miracle and their regular celebrations.

The Office of the Susception's first lesson quickly reaches and then elaborates upon the bringing of the rescued host to St. Jean-en-Grève, where it is enshrined. The lesson explains that the feast of the Susception, when the lesson is being read, is on the Sunday following Easter, though the miracle took place on Easter Sunday. The susception of the host does not trump Christ's resurrection.

The next lesson begins:

> Although God may have made various miracles over the centuries, to confirm
> the faith of the church in the Sacrament of the Body of the Lord, nevertheless
> there are few miracles as striking as the one that came in Paris in 1290.

The Paris miracle outranks other Eucharistic miracles, and is a source of pride for this Paris church. The lesson quickly reviews the story and elaborates upon the bringing of the rescued host to St. Jean-en-Grève, where it is enshrined. The lesson explains that the Feast of the Susception, when the lesson is read, is on the Sunday following Easter. It was transferred to that date because of the greater solemnity of Easter. The susception of the host, however reverential, does not trump Christ's resurrection.

The second of the two lessons in this office refers to the miracle only indirectly. The text warns those who would dare touch holy objects with an impure conscience, and who approach the altar of the Lord without fear, crimes of the Jew and the Christian woman, that they set themselves against the Lord's word. When the Hebrews brought the ark of Aminadab to Jerusalem those who touched it without purifying the conscience were punished with death. To eat and drink at the table of the Lord while impure, which for the congregants would be to take Communion in that state, is to invite condemnation. The miraculous host is a reminder that the faithful must not

82

approach the altar without having made confession. The miracle conveys this message to the congregant.

The offices are designed to keep the miracle from becoming merely an edifying story. They are an opportunity for the listener, hearing it in the vernacular, to identify with the subjects of the Lord from the time of the Hebrews onward, and know how to avoid the fire that consumed the Jew forever.

The Office of the Susception celebrated the return of the host to the church from which it had been visibly absent. Communion was restored by inversion of Communion, susception of the host back to the church, after the impure Christian woman passed it on to the impure Jew. The normally fragile wafer that melts upon being taken by the communicant endured the attack and remained a permanent exhibit of its resistant vulnerability. The Offices of the Reparation were meant to accomplish a restoration as well, of relations between humans and God damaged by an individual. This would forestall the divine retribution for touching the holy object, which does not distinguish between Jews and Christians. The ceremonies of reparation mingled expiatory religion and apotropaic magic.

The theft of hosts and a ciborium from St. Jean-en-Grève on August 13, 1648 by Jacques Le Comte also occasioned a Service of Reparation performed annually on that date. The first lessons of the service recounted the theft, giving the historical event liturgical form.

> In the year 1648, the night between 12 & 13 of August, Jacques Le Comte, Calvinist, one of the coachmen of the Duchess Henriette Catherine de Joyeuse, wife by the first marriage of Henri de Bourbon, Duke of Monpensier, and a second of Charles de Lorraine, Duke of Guise, having entered by a window into the church of St. Jean-en-Grève, and having mounted the altar, took the vessel where the Holy Eucharist was kept, carried it off and hid it in his attic. Before leaving the church, having taken the consecrated hosts from the ciborium he ate them, believing, he said, to show more respect to Jesus Christ, whom he was beginning to believe really was present in the Holy Eucharist, than by depositing them on the altar, or putting them on the floor.

This first part of the lesson is followed by a brief Biblical parallel situating Le Comte's crime in the history of sacrilege and retribution. Le Comte himself is located in the ranked society of Paris. The apprehension of Le Comte, recovery of the ciborium, his imprisonment and interrogation by a roster of named church authorities follows. The previous theft of hosts from St. Jean-en-Grève and the Jew's perfidious deal are recalled. Le Comte abjures his Calvinism and, condemned to death, makes a signed profession of faith which the co-adjutor of the bishop, who led the proceedings, deems all the more sincere for being made under imminent threat of execution. Nothing more is said of Le Comte's end.

"The guilty party having been punished, one thought to make reparation for the outrage done to Jesus Christ." A procession is assembled on September 16, stopping at other churches in the vicinity where the host was outraged and finally reaching Notre Dame. All the religious groupings taking part in the procession are listed, including the Carmes Billettes. At St. Jean-en-Grève the consecrated hosts are placed in a new ciborium. The Duchess of Guise, since the condemned man was in the employ of her house, contributed two wax candles to burn on the altar until they were spent, and instituted a Mass. The annual office was decreed in perpetual reparation for the sacrilege.

Further lessons allude to the restoration of Communion. The sharp discourse if it offends the faithful is like bitter medicine given to those with ailing stomachs to restore the balance of their humors. Whoever drinks and eats indignantly at the table of the Lord (as Le Comte did) "renders himself guilty of the body and blood of Christ." It is as if he caused Christ's torture. Le Comte reappears as the subject of a hymn.

> Le Comte had finally appeased the anger of the Lord, by his tremblings, by his tears, and by voluntary acceptance of his mother: a pure and sincere faith has just entered him: the Church his mother from which he had been separated by heresy.

Le Comte has become the expiatory sacrifice that repairs the breach caused by his sacrilege. Through the solicitations of those who share his pain his soul will be spared being consumed by the flames that consume his body. The hymn doesn't recur to the Jew's demise but it is obvious that the Jew was obliterated while Le Comte may still be purged of his sin by repentance and contribute to the task of reparation, deferring God's wrath.

Jacques Le Comte is embedded in the names of nobles, two of the most prominent families in France, primarily to pressure them to take responsibility for urgently needed ceremonies. The acknowledged role of the Duchess de Guise providing candles and a Mass is the visible expression of the success of that notice. Le Comte's history is made into a ritually reiterated exposition of violation and repentance. The whole of the service hovers on the edge of expected divine retribution for another seizure of the body of Christ in the custody of the church. It does not come into focus on the body of Le Comte as it did on the Jew incinerated with his book, but rather invests in the hypostatized body of the ideal sufferer which Jesus is begged to become again.

Le Comte's motives other than heretical are unclear. At the very moment of profaning the altar and taking the ciborium he seems to be projected forward to the confessory condition after his capture, and avows the real presence of Christ in the hosts. A Calvinist would not accept the real presence but Le Comte has changed. He was trying to protect the hosts by eating them.

Memories of the Lendit miracle where the thief took the ciborium to sell it and threw the hosts into the mud. And a similar profanation in the church of St. Sulpice the previous month. Le Comte's treatment of the hosts ranks him over that thief and the Jew, providing a resolution of host mistreatment by conversion that neither of the earlier violators could manage. Le Comte left evidence that led the church authorities to his dwelling and the missing ciborium: a part-burned piece of paper with the signature of a priest found in the church's confessional. It was considered a miracle that the signature remained to allow Le Comte to be traced.

The introduction to the reparation service (not the lessons of the service) contains this bit of information.[118] It also says that Le Comte's hands were cut off as he was brought to the place of execution. The conversion and purification that began as soon as he touched the hosts continued alongside the ceremonial recitation, which was kept free of these jarring details.

The reparation service of the theft of the host adapts a historic event and the motives of its actor to the cosmos of the miracle. The eternally repeated time of the host and the Jew added a lesser, symbolically complementary cycle to the whole. The miracle remained, with revisions.

Historic punctuation did occur. Single ceremonial events were staged under the weight of a royal occasion. The Adoration of the Blessed Sacrament was an exposure of the host openly and freely for a set period of time, or perpetually. An Adoration might be dedicated to a purpose. In 1604 and again in 1714 there was a Miraculous and Royal Adoration of the Very Blessed Sacrament of the Altar, not at St. Jean-en-Grève, where the fugitive host was located, but at the church of the Billettes.

According to a memorial brochure printed in Paris, the Adoration was held "to make honorable amends for the outrage to Jesus Christ done by a Jew in the underground of this place."[119]This adoration comprised a viewing of a host at the Billettes, and the relegation of the Jew's house to the caves below, a buried memory.

Notes

---

[113] The *thresor* was a repository of documents in manuscript, printed books and relics that formed the archives of the church. This text is titled *Tractatus Miraculi Biletani Super Sacratissimo Corpore Christi a Judeo confixo an 1290*. It was printed in Paris by Frederick More in 1601. Paget (1912: 282)

[114] Séguier (1603)

[115] *Officium Corporis Christi, recitandum in ecclesic Sancti Joannis in Gravia; ex concessione Joan. Francisi de Gondy, Archiepisccpi Parisiensis.* Paris: Ant. Vitray. 1637

[116] S. René (1725: 213); Collette (1880: 5-6)

[117] S. René (1725: 116-23). This text is identical to the manuscript text cited in Chapter 3, footnote 14. In different places S. René dates it to the early 14th century (the Brothers of the Charity of Notre Dame, not named Billettes here) and to the late 16th century.

[118] *La Gazette de France* 144(1648): 1038-48 describes the chain of traces from the signature on the paper to Le Comte.

[119] *L'Adoration Miraculeuse et Royale du Très-Saint-Sacrement de l'Autel, pour faire amende honorable à Jèsus-Christ de l'outrage commis par un Juif dans les caves de ce lieu.* Paris, 1604 and 1714. Corblet (1885: 2,569)

9.
Processions

Processions and services are interconnected in performance and purpose. They may emerge from each other. They unite and divide churches, neighborhoods, parishes, secular and religious associations. They are recurrent and historic. A procession typically held on a specific day every month or year might be dedicated to achieving a specific end on that one day, to meet the wishes of a patron.

Processions are the carrying of relics and figures from where they are kept through the surrounding area to a destination according to a prescribed route or one made to order for the occasion. Ranks of persons precede, carry and follow the relic, their dress and demeanor adopted to energize the spirit of the procession. There may be an office of the procession, prayers and hymns before, during and after. There are processions of the Blessed Sacrament which bear a Eucharistic relic in an ostensorium.

Processions of the miraculous host originating in St. Jean-en-Grève or the Billettes were held from the late 13th century onward. They were part of a city-wide processional system which linked parish churches and abbeys to each other often through one of the ancient churches of great national importance such as Notre Dame or Sainte Genevieve.[120] Locally originated processions were a facility to be called upon when needed for the city as a whole.

The early 15th century was ripe with occasions to call upon them, and it yielded the earliest descriptions of processions of the miraculous host longer than cursory entries in chronicles. The ruling monarch, Charles VI (reigned 1380-1422), was sometimes carried away by bouts of madness and beset by challenges to his rule from powerful lords. The king drew upon the resources of his Paris subjects to fund his armed quarrels. One of his biographers quoted the votaries who carried candles in a 1412 procession asking God "to make peace between the king and the lords, or at least bring victory to the king."[121]

From late May 31 to July 13, 1412 rounds of processions were scheduled to help the king overcome his uncle the Duke of Berry who was under siege in the city of Bourges. The processions were organized and coordinated by clergy at the central churches of the city, Notre Dame and the Sainte Chapelle, the chapel of the royal palace. They were, in the word of Jacques Chiffoleau, "polysemic": they simultaneously partook of religious, political and urban structural meaning.[122] The carrying of the miraculous host on June 3, 1412 began as the king commenced his campaign with an assault on Dun-le-Roy, and the day after the annual feast and procession of Corpus Christi (*Fête-Dieu*). [123]

> The following Thursday, 3rd day of June in the said year, was made the most beautiful procession that ever was seen. All the parishes and orders, whatever their condition, went barefoot, carrying as said before, relics or candle in devotional dress, together more than 40 thousand persons, all barefoot and fasting, with no other hidden abstinences, more than 4 thousand burning torches. In this way they came carrying the holy relics to St. Jean-en-Grève, then they took the precious

body Our Lord that the false Jews boiled, with great sorrow, in great tears, in great devotion, and it was delivered to 4 bishops who carried it in the said monstrance to St. Genevieve, in such a company of common people, it was affirmed, that they were more than 52 thousand. There they sang the great Mass, then carried the holy relics to their destination fasting.

This account is from a contemporary journal (1405-1449) of a Paris bourgeois who witnessed many other processions. The full route of the procession can be reconstructed by adding this to the briefer notation by the registry clerk Nicolas de Baye,[124] who wrote that the procession proceeded from St. Jean-en-Grève to the gate of the palace (Louvre, Sainte Chapelle), where the court was in attendance, thence to Notre Dame, Ste. Genevieve, and back to St. Jean-en-Grève and the Billettes to return the relics.

The procession formed by aggregation from parishes on the right bank of the Seine, and it linked religious and political sites fundamental to the history of Paris to build a unified motion from disparate parts of the city. The route mimicked the ancient reflex in response to danger, of carrying the relics kept at and brought to Notre Dame uphill to the mount where the abbey of Ste Genevieve was located, and the unifier of the Franks and first Merovingian monarch Clovis was buried. Nearby was St. Etienne-du-Mont, site of a stained glass representation of the boiled god version of the miracle.

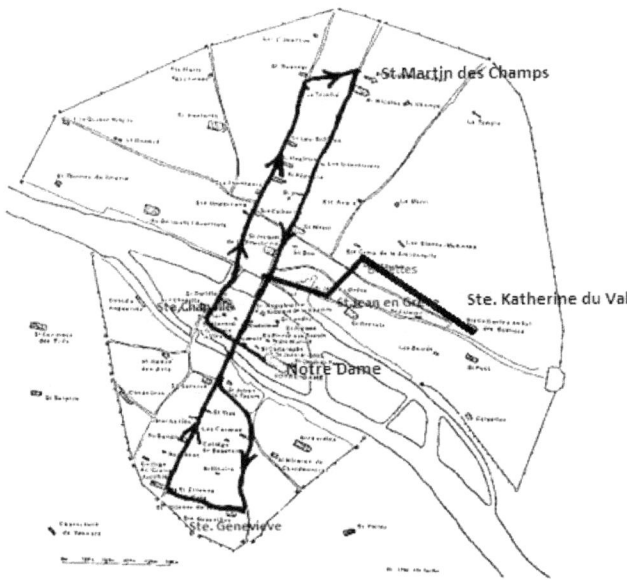

Paris 1412-1444 processions. Modified from Chiffoleau (1990)

The procession arrived at St. Jean-en-Grève already bearing the knife, cauldron and bowl from the Billettes and other relics carried by people who joined along the way. There they received the abused host in its monstrance carried by four bishops. The register of parlement for this date reads *"vacant curia"*.[125] The members of the deliberative body joined the procession as a mass. The penitential character of all the marchers, calling upon God's mercy by performing austerities, going barefoot and fasting, formed a brilliant line on the dark streets of the city. Their egalitarianism of dress "whatever their condition" was offset by the appearance of distinguished church officials who kept control of the host in its monstrance.

The large gathering crossed the Seine from right bank to Ile de la Cité, stood before Notre Dame and the residents of the palace at the Sainte Chapelle, then to left bank as far as Ste. Genevieve at the old city walls, and back again making the absent, deranged king seem to be present and in command. The lines of people who followed the course of the march so impressed the journal writer that he attempted to count them. If his unverifiable number of 52 thousand is correct at least a third of the population of Paris at the time had taken to the streets to form the glowing contingent.

The host and other relics were adopted into a mass expression that joined other enhanced local processions to exceed the parochial and become a display of urban and national solidarity in its glory. The larger and more brightly shining the greater the unity felt, and the more the parochial contributions were made parts of the whole. The miracle relics were incorporated into the symbolic rescue of fundamentals in a time of danger.

The success of the 1412 processions (Bourges was taken and a treaty signed) and the prominence of the Paris miracle procession among the dozens made it a resort as the civil disorder continued. The continued display of the miracle was penitential, grandly cowering before a divinity displeased by the treatment of the host who manifested that displeasure through national misfortunes.

"To appease the anger of God" the Chapter of Notre Dame, the ruling body of Paris churches, decreed three days of processions September 19-22, 1415.[126] On the third day, a Sunday, a procession carried the miraculous host from St. Jean-en-Grève to the Priory of St. Martin des Champs, an ancient monastery and church located at the pole of the processional circuit across the city opposite Ste. Genevieve. A high Mass was sung at the terminus. St. Martin contained a painted panel-by-panel representation of the miracle story which was considered to correspond to the oldest written account.[127] Ste. Genevieve and St. Martin enclosed the terrain of the miracle within the precincts of Paris.

The clergy dressed in capes (*en chappes*). This widely enfolding garment gathered at the front, contributed a waving motion in the march to the spectacle of the procession. Accounts of processions detailed distinctive material, colors and ornaments of the capes worn by the clergy.

This effort at appeasement did not have the tangible effect of the 1412 processions. On October 25 the French forces, the debilitated king again absent, suffered a celebrated and consequential defeat by the English at Agincourt. Processions traveled the Paris routes during the following years but without the appreciable fervor previously recognized by chroniclers.

When the king made an entrance into Paris (itself a ritual) on December 1, 1420 he was accompanied by his heir by treaty, Henry V of England, the war having gone that badly. They were greeted by ornamented streets, a *"piteuse"* ("feeling") and magnificent mystery play of the sufferings of Jesus on a huge scaffold, and processions of cape-wearing and relic-bearing clergy chanting benedictions.[128] All the while starving due to the astronomical increase in the price of bread.

This joy amid famine would not be uncommon during the ensuing years, which included the death of Charles VI (1422), the efforts of Charles VII, his son, to be crowned despite the English insistence that Henry VI's sovereignty take precedence and the English occupation of Paris (1422-36) to ensure that, and the ultimately successful efforts of Joan of Arc (1412-29) to ensure otherwise. St. Jean-en-Grève, the miraculous host, the Billettes and their relics were little noted amid the processional news of these years.

In early 1441 King Charles VII undertook a siege of the strategic town of Pontoise, close to Paris and held by English forces since 1437. Besides acceding to the king's demands for supplies and funding, the people of Paris sought to bolster the force of arms by holding daily processions. Scarcely a day went by that the university, the religious or the parishes did not hold a procession.[129] The clergy of Notre Dame coordinated them as they had in the past. St. Jean-en-Grève made their contribution on March 27. After a long siege and many more processions in Paris, Pontoise surrendered.

The Paris bourgeois recorded another procession of the miraculous host on June 15, 1444, just two weeks before a major truce was concluded at Tours. The familiar wording, praise of theatrical proportions, made this "one of the most feeling and devout ever seen in Paris."[130] The bishops of Paris and of Beauvais, and two abbots, shouldered the host ("the body our Lord") in its ostensorium at St. Jean-en-Grève and carried it as far as the Billettes where they added the *canivet* the Jew used to stab the host, a piece of the True Cross, and other relics without number. From there they proceeded to the church of Ste. Catherine du Val des Escolliers.

> Five thousand illuminated torches led the way, with nine or ten thousand persons besides those of the church. After these holy relics the entire mystery of the Jew who was tied up on a cart, where there were dried thorns as if he were being led to a burning, and afterward came the judge, and the Jew's wife and children. And amid the streets were two scaffolds for very sorrowful mystery plays and the streets were decked out as for the Feast of the Blessed Savior. This procession was made because there was good hope of having peace between the kings of France and England.

For the first time a description of a miraculous host procession included a dramatization of the Jew rather than just a reference to his deeds and punishment through relics. The central figure of the miracle story joined the other enactments of sacred mysteries along the route of the procession. The Jew emerged from the narrative of the lessons and the implicit action of the relics into the celebratory environment of the streets. King Henry VI of England had not joined King Charles

VII of France to enter into Paris this time, but there was a villain being carried in a cart to his final destination.

Ste. Catherine du Val des Escolliers was a 13th century church, in this case a priory established by a movement of university scholars who took vows of chastity and abstinence. Unlike Ste. Genevieve and St. Martin it did not have a relationship to the story of the miraculous host. The church was located at a directional point from the Billettes-St. Jean-en-Grève axis that completed the circle north-south-east-west about Paris within the wall. During the 32 years between 1412 and 1444 major processions bearing the host and artifacts had gone in each of the cardinal directions at least once. This defined Billettes-St. Jean-en-Grève as the axis of a sacred body-miraculous host-evil Jew cosmos.

From the viewpoint of the end of the procession the miraculous host was "the precious body of our Lord Jesus Christ and boiled sacrament of the altar."[131] Jean Maupoint, the prior of Ste. Catherine at the time of the 1444 procession and the author of a Paris journal, was at the church with the other clerics of his convent, to receive the relics one at a time. Besides the host and a piece of the True Cross from Notre Dame, Maupoint listed body relics of a miscellany of saints, an arm of St. Thomas Aquinas and a portion of "St. Innocent," a boy who allegedly had been murdered by Jews for his blood.

Maupoint began his entry focusing on the conclave of dignitaries gathered at Tours for the peace talks, and then naming the abbots who accompanied the bishop of Paris in the procession, followed by those who gave the sermon and celebrated the Mass. His was an ecclesiastical view of the procession as an official transfer of relics including the boiled god to build support for peace in the burdensome quarrel of kings. The lay Paris bourgeois saw it as a street spectacle that had grown more theatrical over the years he monitored.

The 15th century miraculous host processions, enmeshed in war, peace and the health of kings, were the largest and grandest manifestations. A few objects that date from that time lasted long enough to have their images recorded including the previously mentioned processional ensign (*insigne*) once part of the Billettes ensemble catalogued in the collection of the Musée de Cluny (now Musée National du Moyen Age).[132]

It is a cast and trimmed bronze assemblage, covered with pressed copper, gilded and finished with pearl that was carried atop a post by the leader of the Billettes section of the procession.[133] A housing in the form of a Gothic chimney cap (a practical touch) supported by two posts surrounds three figures: to the left the Jew Jonathas who tends the fire beneath a cauldron, the Christian woman to the right receiving the host in a bowl and the crucified Christ rising in glory over the cauldron. The configuration resembles the stained glass window representation of the host miracle in St. Etienne-du-Mont in Paris, the only church-held miracle representation in Paris that remains in its original place.

The piece came from the diverse collection assembled by the Russian diplomat Pierre Soltikoff. After its stay in the medieval museum it was placed in the Musée d'Ecouen outside Paris (Musée National de la Renaissance), where it presently resides.

At the opposite social class extreme is the pressed lead medallion recovered from the Seine River near the Hôtel de Dieu in 1848,[134] unlabelled except for the INRI acronym on one face, a knife, specifically a *canif*, a small very sharp-pointed pocket knife. On the other side a haloed figure with three marks on his chest displaying three pieces of the host raises both hands in benediction as he rises from a cauldron. This was a token distributed to those accompanying the procession, the knife and boiled god imagery a signature of the Billettes' side of the miracle.

These two objects probably figured in 15th century processions when the Billettes were present with or without the St. Jean-en-Grève contingent. After June 3, 1456, when a meeting of the court was cancelled for the assembly to join a procession of the miraculous host, there are no records of processions devoted exclusively to the miracle for the rest of the century, but a number in which the Billettes are listed among the religious orders in the line of march. For instance, on February 7, 1483 the Billettes were part of the procession from Notre Dame to Saint Denis with the stated purpose of relaxing the "wind" ("*vent de bize*") of the reigning king, Louis XI, who died soon afterward.[135]

The Reformation was the next challenge to be met by religious processions in Paris. At first it took the urban form of placards questioning Catholic dogma such as transubstantiation and the validity of indulgences. King François I, the first French monarch of the Renaissance, presided over the burning of the heretical placard-posters and others identified as Lutherans or Calvinists. One grandee who did not abide by Lenten fasting rules because of his Protestant convictions was obliged to stand penitent in his shirt on the stone pavement before Notre Dame cathedral, had his property confiscated and was banished from France for five years.[136]

The king wished to avoid repercussions for the insults heretics in his domain directed against the Blessed Sacrament, and decreed a general procession to be held on January 21, 1535. Barriers were erected and archers posted to prevent the common people from interfering with the march. The king himself, gravely dressed and carrying a burning taper, followed the Blessed Sacrament borne by the Bishop of Paris, under a canopy supported by the Dauphin and other nobles, part of a line that included many religious orders carrying relics, the provost of Paris and other officials and dignitaries as well as more archers. The most detailed contemporary source, *Cronique du Roy Françoys*, makes no mention of St. Jean-en-Grève, the Billettes, the miraculous host or the knife-cauldron-bowl relics.[137]

The streets reserved for the procession extended from St. Germain to Notre Dame and St. Denis. The *Cronique* remarks that the Notre Dame bridge was decked with tapestries and an elevated altar that "among other histories" displayed edifying poems denouncing heretics.

The Registers of the Deliberations of the Paris City Bureau for this same procession adds that at the end of the bridge was a *repoussoir*, a visual "draw."[138]

> On said bridge were very pleasing histories, even the history of the Blessed Sacrament that was pierced with a knife (*canivet*) by a Jew, which Blessed Sacrament is at St. Jean-en-Grève. Well played at length and there was a beautiful illumination, and it brought the people great devotion to see it, and was inscribed around the base [in Latin]: "They shall perish, but thou shalt endure."

The "histories" ("*histoires*") were dramas repeatedly enacted for the passing crowds, likely performing the text of *Le mistere de la saincte hostie* issued in a third edition by a Paris press around this time (see Chapter 12). The illumination may have been similar to the paneled painting of the Paris miracle at St. Martin-des-Champs. The inscription around the base of the illumination was a quote from the 102nd Psalm, line 26, and from St. Paul's Epistle to the Hebrews 1:11. In the latter citation the words were taken to refer to the Catholic Church and the Pope.

A representation of the crucifixion was among the other mysteries recorded. Beneath a ceiling of woven ivy hung burning chandeliers, wreaths of triumph and knotted scarves among which were pronouncements and inscriptions "in praise of the faith and the Very Christian King." The rage of the Jew was a lure to attract the attention of passersby to the message of triumph over the heretics and security for the Body of Christ.

The Blessed Sacrament was the central subject of the procession. The host of the miracle kept at St. Jean-en-Grève once stood for the Blessed Sacrament in general. Its story was too specific to Paris to evoke the general principle that had to be defended against the heretics. The drama of that host was a lure to bring the wayward notice of literate urbanites to the melding of faith and royal power manifest in the procession, in the exhibits on the bridge and the burning of heretics by the dozen, whose names were listed in the *Cronique*. The miraculous host was only one manifestation of the Blessed Sacrament and the Jew was only one of those heretics.

The Billettes were part of the funeral train of Alberto III Pio, the Prince of Capri in January, 1531.[135] The banner of St. Jean-en-Grève, but not the host, was carried in a procession ordered to celebrate another treaty in the endless royal wars, on June 21, 1538. Among the others in the line of march were the Billettes in capes, carrying the reliquary containing the knife.[140] The annals of Notre Dame cathedral record general processions after that date which included some representation from St. Jean-en-Grève but again not the host, and the Billettes bearing their own relics to add to the sacred force.[141]

The pressures exerted by the continued posting of Protestant placards were reflected in reduplications within processional system repeatedly bringing out relics to counter impieties. The January 21, 1534 procession was repeated in its ceremonies on August 24, 1536; and the procession of October 19, 1534, followed by another three days later, was repeated on January 21, 1535. A January 10, 1536 procession was directed at the "impieties committed at the church of Saints-Innocents."

The processions that called for the participation of the two churches and their personnel in the following years followed the same format of evincing a presence without the accompaniment of the host of the miracle. Individual clergy, church officers and organizations associated with the church took part and the church banner headed their contingents.

The February 17, 1556 procession to celebrate an entente between Henri II of France and Charles V, Holy Roman Emperor, traveled from St. Jean-en-Grève to Notre Dame, where a Mass was celebrated.[142] The march included the Provost and principal merchants, the curé of St. Jean-en-Grève in a magnificent gold-threaded cape with his clergy, a group of children from that church's orphanage, the mendicant orders, the Billettes also in capes, and ranks of peddlers of salt, vegetables and other fare.

A splendid dinner was provided on the return to St. Jean-en-Grève. No host or other evidences of the miracle were recorded. The Provost and merchants made a separate procession to the church before they all proceeded to Notre Dame. The procession expressed the wealth and prosperity of the parish where both the church and the Hôtel de Ville were located.

Parlement decreed that the St. Bartholomew's Day Massacre of Protestants (primarily Huguenots) beginning August 23, 1572 in Paris and spreading to other cities was to be commemorated by an annual procession on that day, which never was celebrated.[143] This tested the limits of what deeds might conscionably be institutionalized in Paris processions. (Other cities such as Rome did celebrate the massacre.) In addition to the regularly scheduled processions held by the churches, certain occasions of politico-religious polysemy still precipitated general processions mandated by the king, legislative assembly and church authorities. The death of King Charles IX and the accession of Henri III moved the city to a general procession on October 9, 1574.

Resistance to and then a declaration of loyalty to the heir to the throne after the death of Henri III took the form of a series of general processions in 1593-1594. King Henri of Navarre was a Protestant who agreed to convert to Catholicism to become King Henri IV of France. The January 13, 1593 procession culminated in a sermon in Notre Dame conveying the papal message that Henri's conversion was faked and that accepting it constituted apostasy. The May 22, 1594 procession at his entrance into Paris as king receiving the submission of officialdom was made into an annual procession on that date except when it fell on a day in the week of Easter, at which time it would be moved to after the Sunday following Easter, to exclude interference with Easter and the miracle's annual celebration.

Processions of the relics of Ste. Genevieve were scheduled to halt heavy rain, bring on rains and assure a good harvest. They also celebrated the birth of the children of Henri IV, and, on August 13, 1638 the news that the queen, wife of Henri IV's son, Louis XIII, had become pregnant after 23 years without the birth of an heir. Processions were decreed to promote and rejoice in fertility and prosperity.

The next new procession and the last one specifically to concern St. Jean-en-Grève was in reparation for the sacrilege committed by Jacques Le Comte, who as recounted before, broke into the church, opened the ciborium, consumed the hosts and carried away the vessel. The annual performance of the office and procession was on September 6.

Le Comte's theft and punishment took place during the first phase of the Fronde, a revolt first of the Paris bourgeoisie against the demand that they pay to field the French army in the Thirty Years War (1618-1648), the nobles (who revolted later) having also refused. Officers of the Paris Parlement pushed for the adoption of reforms they had proposed and resisted the imposition of taxes. Cardinal Mazarin, who had succeeded Richelieu as first minister of state, was emboldened by the return of the victorious French army following the signing of a peace treaty in August, 1648 to have many officers of the Parlement arrested. Paris broke out into open revolt, forcing Mazarin and the royal party to flee.

As this environment developed, on the night of July 27-28 men broke into church of St. Sulpice in the Paris faubourg of St. Germain. They forced open the door of the ciborium, tossed the hosts onto the floor of a confessional in the church's Ste. Barbara chapel, where they trampled them.[144] This action and stealing the ciborium seem to have been the object of their visit.

The church was undergoing a long reconstruction that would make it the second largest church in Paris after Notre Dame. The curé, Jean-Jacques Olier, removed the ornaments from the altar until the hosts could be replaced in a new ciborium. The report of the desecration in *La Gazette de France* is mostly taken up with the prayers offered in pity for the sinners who exposed the hosts, the outfitting of the church for the reparation, the visit of the queen, and the order of the procession which was scheduled to be repeated annually.[145] The procession culminated in the translation of the hosts from a Notre Dame ciborium to a new one on the St. Sulpice altar. The author of the *Gazette* article took care to describe the sequestration of the place where the spilled hosts were found behind a balustrade, the silver lantern positioned to illuminate that spot, and a copper tablet inscribed with the history of the incident.

Procession in reparation for the St. Sulpice sacrilege. Hamel (1900: 77)

Le Comte's behavior during his St. Jean-en-Grève break-in and the response in August-September, 1648 mirrors this earlier sacrilege: Le Comte ate the hosts rather than throwing them on the floor, claiming that he was suddenly converted and wanted to protect them from desecration. Le Comte was a Calvinist, living in St. Germain where St. Sulpice was the main church. One of the St. Sulpice desecrators was later captured and executed.

During this period of social and political upheaval at least two Paris churches suffered removal of hosts from the ciborium, which were sullied by unconsecrated touches and worse. The thieves were caught and punished and the invasion of sacred space was countered by a regular procession. These acts of impiety directed at the host brought an enduring response. Aside from promoting fertility, both human and natural, processions were instituted anew to address God's wrath at the violation of the body of Christ.

When St. Sulpice suffered another invasion on October 25, 1665, four ciboria removed from the altars, the report began with a recollection of the 1648 robbery.[146]

This time, however, the robbers "confused the hosts with booty," took them along with the vessels, and did not throw them on the floor, acting like "Turks or Jews" in their disrespect for sacred instruments. The consequent procession, which like the 1648 one included royal participation and a translation of hosts into new ciboria, did not become a yearly procession, but a commemoration on the day of St. Simon-St. Jude when the robbery occurred. The robbers may have recalled the punishment of those who made a point of profaning the hosts for all to see and stayed within the lesser impiety of robbery alone.

The symbolic series that began with the Jew's desecration and the miraculous response of 1290 and continued with the two desecrations of 1648, one of them in the church where the host the Jew stabbed was enshrined, did not go without comment by contemporary writers.[147]

This series reached closure on August 3, 1670. During the elevation of the host in Mass at Notre Dame a man stepped forward and slashed at the host with a sword.[148] The priest, lightly wounded, dropped the host on the altar and fled as the man made an attempt to slice it. In the melee that followed the ciborium suspended over the altar was opened spreading hosts across the altar stone and floor, and a woman who cried out was wounded. The attacker ran off, to be brought to ground by a lackey who avoided the thief's sword by yanking his coat from between his legs and causing him to pitch forward.

The man was twenty-two year old François Sarrazin, who had been a Huguenot, then a Catholic, and presented himself as a Jew wearing white taffeta and a green ribbon, as he claimed Jews dressed. He was in all these modes "an enemy of the real presence" of Christ in the host. He had studied with the Jesuits but then fashioned his own religion. Escaping from his mother's house, where he was confined as a madman, he made his way from Caen in Normandy to Paris and to Notre Dame.

He asked a priest if the archbishop was to officiate at Mass and, receiving an inconclusive reply, made his way to the chapel of the Virgin where he comported himself with seriousness and gravity until he launched his attack. He told the interrogating officer that he intended to prevent idolatry and attract notice with his gesture.

The bishop who attempted to convert him after he was condemned to death found him composed and self-assured. Sarrazin contended he was not opposed to the king or the courts, only to the Church. He maintained a mannerly demeanor as his hands were cut off and, paraded to the place de Grève wearing signs front and back that read "Impious Sacrilege", he was burned alive and in the open without being strangled to death beforehand. He did not cry out as others did. The diarist d'Ormesson was astonished to find such firmness in a spirit that had committed these execrable acts. One would expect such a person to be actuated only by passion.

The altars of Notre Dame were stripped of ornaments and no Mass was celebrated until after the church was purified on the following Monday. A three day fast and forty hours of prayer were accompanied by processions of the parishes and religious communities. A general procession of reparation to Notre Dame on August 12 included the king, courts and civic officials. All shops in Paris and the faubourgs were closed by order of the police.

Sarrazin was punished with such severity because like Le Comte he had set out to desecrate the host. The sword blow was aimed at the host after consecration, to prove that it would not take flight or bleed, that it was just a wafer cut by the sword. The Jew had attempted the same experiment with bloody result, but the aftermath of Sarrazin's cutting at the host was not given out in any account, nor was it elaborated according to the Passion as the Jew's had been. Sarrazin was not a Jew though his name did suggest a Saracen, a Muslim antagonist of Christians. The Jew's reenactment of the Passion on the host could not be imposed upon Sarrazin's actions, and the blood libel mythics were not emphatic for Saracens.

There was a precedent for the insane. A young scholar named Edmond de la Fosse on the day of Saint Louis, 1503 insinuated himself into the chapel of the Sainte Chapelle where Mass was being performed and snatched the host from the priest's hands as he elevated it, shouting "And this act of madness will last forever."[149] He was chased down by attendants who seized him by the hair since he was still holding the host, and dragged him to the vicinity of the palace, where he dropped it. A priest placed it in a chalice, and the area of the pavement where it fell was covered with a gold damask cloth lest anyone set foot there.

Under interrogation de la Fosse claimed to be Hercules or Zeus, and did not allow any heaven other than the Elysian Fields. He did not change his views and make reparation with the passage of time, so the hand that had taken the host was cut off and he was executed by burning. An alternate version has him breaking the stolen host into pieces with no further outcome. The crime had been taking the host with unconsecrated fingers, punishable by losing them, and without repentance, to be burned as a heretic whether demonstrably insane or not.

Parlement would not act so violently toward any offender other than another François Sarrazin, wrote Louis-Sébastien Mercier. And no doubt there would not be another. Mercier did not mean that no one would ever try to slash or seize a host again, but that the circumstances of Sarrazin's endeavor would not be repeated, and not only because of the deterrence of punishment. The Thirty Years War and the wars of religion had produced instances and accusations of host profanation, but the few that occurred in the sacred space of Paris churches were severely punished. The host's miraculous response to being cut by the Jew was replaced by a blur for de la Fosse and Sarrazin that did not justify the cost of trying again in the same place with witnesses present.

The procession of reparation for Sarrazin's desecration took place only once and did not become a fixture as reparations for previous desecrations had become.

A manuscript researcher discovered in 1864 a sonnet datable to the day of Sarrazin's attack, entitled "On the crime of divine lèse-majesté, committed at Notre Dame Sunday August 3, 1670 at nine o'clock in the morning by one named François Sarrazin, a native of Caen."[150]

Detested by mortals, abominable spawn,
Dare you stir the point of your iron,
Against a God whose name makes all hell tremble,

And whose power awes the demons?

What? Furious monster! The terrible presence
Of Him whose arm confounds Lucifer,
Who made known by his death how dear you are to Him,
Couldn't you restrain your brutal insolence.

Lord, the crime against your majesty is great!
But it is an uncontested truth
That the author of the deed long was taken mad...

It seems his madness was there from the cradle,
And when we wander to altars, we forget
The heart has no part in the defects of the mind.

    The transcriber attributed this sonnet to the dramatist Pierre Corneille, because of other works present in the manuscript and because Corneille had portrayed a deliberate desecration of a pagan altar by a Christian convert in his 1642 tragedy *Polyeucte*. The turns in the sonnet, from an apostrophe to the sword-wielding desecrator, to God and finally a solo ending in an epigram defend Sarrazin without approving his actions. A transcendent heart remains in spite of the distortions of mind wrought by madness. This resembles the course of one of Corneille's protagonists, who torn between love or loyalty and belief chooses to sacrifice himself for belief. Outward madness cannot conceal the truth of the heart.

    Rather than desecration or even heresy Sarrazin is guilty of the crime of divine lèse-majesté. The host is not mentioned in the sonnet. The early lines of the sonnet focus on the power and majesty of God whom the offender has slighted, and acknowledge the offense is great, but end in an appeal for mercy due to insanity. Divine lèse-majesté, parallel to human lèse-majesté, was any challenge to the sovereign person of God, or king, both punishable by a scale of exactions, torture and execution. The desecrator's crime having disrupted the state under God, and the church under the protection of the state, the archaic punishment was an affirmation of the king's absolute authority. The judicial procedure and consequent punishment of the guilty took the place of reparation processions newly scheduled.

    The Jew's crime was resolved historically by the encompassing machinery of the church and state, but the Jew's image was not.

Notes

---

[120] Descimon (1998: 94-95)

[121] Juvenal des Ursins (1653: 240)

[122] Chiffoleau (1990)

[123] Tuety, ed. (1881: 20-21). S.René (1725:1, 316-17) cites "these very angry deeds" (*"ces faites très facheuses"*) of the king as a motive for the procession.

[124] Tuety, the editor of the Journal, extracted de Baye's contribution from a manuscript in the *Archives Nationales* (1881: 20n2)

[125] S.René (1725:1, 316-17)

[126] *Offices propres* (1747: seconde partie, 4)

[127] S.René (1725: 2,169n1)

[128] Tuety, ed. (1881: 144-45)

[129] Tuety, ed. (1881: 441)

[130] Tuety, ed. (1881: 372-73)

[131] Maupoint (1878: 30)

[132] du Sommerard (1881: 413-14)

[133] Vloberg (1946: 1,214)

[134] Forgeais (1858: 31)

[135] Félibien (1725: 2,877)

[136] Lalanne, ed. (1854: 438)

[137] Guiffrey, ed. (1860: 113-29)

[138] Bonnardot et al., eds. (1886: 2,196)

[139] The dispossessed prince, a humanist and diplomat, had sided with François I against the Holy Roman Emperor, and fled to France, where he became embroiled in a controversy with Erasmus.

[140] S. René (1725: 1, 321-23). From the *Registres de l'Hôtel de Ville* for that date which were subsequently destroyed in the revolution. Also printed in a pamphlet *Ordre de la procession du 21 janvier 1538 à Paris* (1539).

[141] Dubu (1854: 200-)

[142] Bonnardot, et al., eds. (1886: 4,409-10)

[143] Voltaire (1769: 148) wrote "These times were so morbid, fanaticism or terror so dominated spirits, that Parlement ordained that each year a procession would be made on the day of St. Bartholomew, to render thanks to God. The chancellor of the Hospital thought otherwise, writing [in Latin]: "let that day be excised." The procession was not made, and in the end one was horrified to consecrate what should be forgotten forever."

[144] Hamel (1900: 76-78); d'Ormesson (1,550) wrote that the hosts were tossed into "ordure."

[145] *La Gazette de France* 1648: 1038-48.

[146] *La Gazette de France* 1665: 1091-1102.

[147] *La Gazette de France* 1648: 1108 contrasted the impiety of the act with the outburst of piety and the justice of Their Majesties that followed.

[148] *La Gazette de France* 1670: 771-96; d'Oremesson (1861: 2, 596-98); Mercier (1782: 3,44)

[149] d'Auton (1834: 3, 33-34); Lonergan (1896: 33)

[150] Jacob (1864: 559)

10.

Imago

An *imago* is a devotional scene implanted by verbal, visual and atmospheric representations which then serve as cues for its recollection and reenactment. It is an event that assertedly occurred in the past and is supported and sustained in the present by material figures. Any figuration of an *imago* is proof that its event has occurred and is recurring in ritual and ceremony. The means of its expression change from time to time, assisted by the evolution of technologies.

Evidence of the miracle's earliest *imago* was not presented in any form accessible to us today until the beginning of the 17th century. The story of the miracle as recorded and remade in its many versions from the late 13th century onward bear the *imago* in linking objects in the narrative- the host, the knife-to objects viewed in the same places as relics. The written texts of the miracle, unreadable to many of its adherents because of their inaccessibility, were a design for implementing its *imago* from pieces that might be viewed. Authors of the later accounts attempted to refer objects present in their own time back to the time of the miracle literally and by heritage in order to obtain historical continuity. They attempted to restore the miracle from the texts and the remains.

Gilles Corrozet in his 1550 Paris *Antiquitez* simply recounted the miracle story and mentioned that the knife used by the Jew is on exhibit in the city, a reference to the *imago* generated in those well-known sites. The Latin text of the chronicle's miracle narrative was printed in 1604, firmly designating it as "the miracle of the Billettes."[151] In that same year came a text that advanced the claim of the miracle's other pole.

In 1604 a book was printed that placed the *imago* of the miracle before the literate public who might or might not visit the chapel of the Billettes and St. Jean-en-Grève. The publication of this book marked a separation between the ground of the miracle, the chapel and church where its ritual base was performed, and the population of votaries.

No author is listed on the title page of *Histoire miraculeuse de la saincte hostie gardée en l'Eglise de S. Iean en Greue* (*History of the miracle of the blessed host kept in the Church of St. Jean-en-Grève*). The book focuses on the host as the enduring body of Christ. The name of Jérôme Séguier has long been associated with the brief publication, indicating the remains of communal reputation surrounding a printed work.

Séguier was the descendant of a family of landholders in the Auvergne, a councilor and eventually the president of the grand council of state, thus a member of the provincial gentry who spent most of their time in Paris conducting official business. Why he in particular would assemble an emblematic collection of writings on the miracle is unclear. He did compose religious and historical verse in French and Latin, including an epic on King Henri IV, the progenitor of the kings of the Bourbon dynasty, one of whose props was the Paris miracle.

The longest text in the book is a translation, from Latin into French, of an "extract from the treasury of Chartres" by a marguillier of that church. This is a recital of the story of the miracle, not strictly a narrative, rather a homiletic in an instructional voice.[152]

To conserve eternally the solemn memory of the holy and glorious body of our Lord Jesus Christ, in the sacrament of the Altar, and renew in the heart of the faithful faith in such a great mystery which can be secured there, I thought it would not be amiss to repose in sincere writing a miracle that our Lord, following the custom of parental bounty, deigned to make in this time and before our eyes, in the form of his own flesh.

Christ recognizes, the introduction continues, that many in his church "are barren of faith, empty of hope and lukewarm in charity, and would come to doubt" the sacrament of eating Christ's flesh and drinking his blood "under the species of bread and wine." To strip away "an error so damnable" Christ chose to make a demonstration of "the basic truth of his body" in the city of Paris in the house of a certain Jew.

The events took place as a divine dispensation to renew faith in the Eucharist. They were not arbitrary happenings but a set of fixed characters acting according to Christ's plan. They moved step by inevitable step leaving evidence with each.

1. The Christian woman wishes to redeem her garment given as collateral to the Jew and the Jew offers to return the garment and forgive the debt in exchange for a host
2. The woman's falsely receives the host at St. Merry
3. The woman gives it to the Jew and receives her clothing in return
4. The Jew stabs the host and it bleeds
5. The Jew hammers the host and it bleeds
6. The Jew throws the host into the fire, which it flies from, and into boiling water, followed by a manifestation of Christ crucified
7. The good Christian woman learns of the Jew's actions and enters his house, where the host flies into her bowl
8. The good Christian woman carries the host to St. Jean-en-Grève, where the curé receives it
9. The bishop (named) is alerted by the crowd
10. The Jew is arrested and examined by church officials
11. The Jew refuses to repent and convert
12. The Jew is executed by burning at the stake

It is not a step by step narration as in the chronicles. Each action is couched in the first-person narrator's exclamation of the parallels to scripture and the sacred template being fulfilled. The rhetorical rules of simile and yoking give the *imago* the dimension of sacred time. After the Jew has tortured the host, the narrator declaims:

We can also notice here that as much as this second crucifixion carried out in the precincts of the holy sacrament of the altar equals as a crime the first crime committed by the Jew, to the same degree was it accompanied by miracles. For no more or less than our Lord suffered the first passion, infirmity was exchanged for force, the bonds of death broken and shattered. As for these outrages of which we treat, the deadliness of the wounds has been converted into integrity, the stain of blood into plainness, ugliness into light and beauty, as by a new generation of resurrection that then today can be observed by all those who would be curious to draw an ocular faith of this truth. For always and so many faithful people come to adore this blessed Host honorably positioned in the church of St. Jean-en-Grève in Paris, they can see it with their bodily eyes in whole and with no change.

The miraculous history of the torture of the host seen in the spirit's eye coincident with the Passion and Resurrection of Christ, can be recollected by the fleshly eye's view of the host itself, unchanged on the altar of St. Jean-en-Grève, the location in Paris stated for those who might make the pilgrimage from elsewhere.

After the Jew has refused to acknowledge the miracle and accept conversion, the narrator quotes a passage from St. Gregory: "In vain the hearer is excited by exterior admonition (*avertissement*), if his heart because of sin is not full of inner grace." The Jew's inner state does not permit him to form the *imago* no matter how strongly the message has been conveyed by the miracle. The "hearer" is the hearer of the lesson, as in the present one. If you are not impressed, you must be sinful.

Details fill out each phase of the admonitory lessons: the initial acquiescence to the host abuse then horror of the Jew's wife; the Jew's request for his book, which fails to protect him from burning. The host and the Jew are apostrophized by the narrator.

This recital was translated into French from the Latin of the series of nine lessons given at the annual service in commemoration of the miracle on the Sunday after Easter.[153] Liturgy was made narrative in the vulgar language for this publication. Each scene can be visualized where it occurred and in the abstract of language and ceremony. The translation is at the point of intersection of story and ceremony, of church language and popular language.

After the translation is further affirmation of the miracle in the form of comparable Eucharistic miracles adapted into church ceremonies. The hosts that a Jew attempted to abuse in Brussels, Belgium were transported by a miracle to the church of St. Gudule, where they can be seen. The translator gives a bibliography of the present and other miracles, using their inclusion in books as further support for the Paris miracle. The Latin original and then a French translation are given from a passage of a royal biography that tells of a crucifix that bled when lanced by a soldier. Variants of the same story have not spread elsewhere. They are all challenges to recover the belief Christ has decreed in many miracles.

The *imagines* of all these miracles converge on the transcendent truth of transubstantiation, beyond all doubt because real flesh and blood.

This collective *imago* referring to a greater doctrine is reinforced by the final section of the book: a translation by "H.S.P." (Hieronyme Séguier, Prêtre?) of the four lessons composed by Thomas Aquinas for the feast of Corpus Christi decreed after the Eucharistic miracle of Bolsena, Italy (1264).[154] This first French translation of these hymns generalizes the *imago* of the miracle. There is one reference to a cruel Egyptian (Pharaoh of the Old Testament) but none to Jews or vain women. The first verses are addressed to Christ in the Eucharist.

> I love you devoutly
> Sacred hidden divinity
> Who self-contained and not there to see
> Is truly beneath these figures

Sight is denied in favor of belief throughout the hymns. The substances of Christ's body, like the bread of the host, conceal the divine essence and convey it. Blood, the flesh of Christ, and the host are recurrent themes.

> As for the blood: what the eye does not perceive
> Nor the human spirit conceive
> Is set by belief

Séguier's book was a composite contribution to making the *imago* of the miracle separate from its things and places, an assertion of its internationality and independence from the material evidences while drawing crowds to them. It was a apparatus for making the seen unseen but imagined according to the strictures of faith.

Neither the chapel of the Billettes nor the Billettes themselves figured into the *imago* of the 1604 book. St. Jean-en-Grève was present from the title of the book; the curé and the bishop were prominent in the sequence of host rescue and interrogation of the Jew. In the wake of the 1631 reform of the Billettes by absorption into (or of) the Carmelites de Rennes another book was published that made the *imago* of the miracle portably figural.

The name of the author of *Le sacrifice de la croix representé en l'Eucharistie par l'hostie miraculeuse de Paris (The sacrifice of the cross represented by the miraculous host of Paris)* only appears after the dedication that immediately follows the title page: *P. Milon, docteur en theologie.* The P. may stand for the author's first name, or for his status as priest. He prostrates himself in small type before the object of his dedication, the most eminent Cardinal Duke de Richelieu.[155]

> Since I do not see anything in the eminence of all your dignities and grandeurs greater and more elevated than that of priest, by which you have Jesus Christ, the very Son of God subject to your powers, submitted to your will, and obeying your words. Also I do not find anything in the grandeur and sanctity of our mysteries more worthy to present to you than the thoughts and discourses that it pleases God to inspire us with than that of the Eucharist you offer him on your altars.

This introduction performs the rhetorical act of litotes setting before the Cardinal the seeming impossible fact that a man can command Christ, which Richelieu can do as a priest at the altar. This introduces the transition to the Eucharist in which form Christ is held in the hands of the priest. Not far into the introduction Milon brings up the reformed religious order and later the House of the Miracle and the Convent of the Billettes. The approbation of two doctors of theology and a privilege of the king to print and distribute the book complete the package of front material.

Milon is then prepared to recount a history of the miracle slightly different from that of Séguier. Both the artifacts enshrined at the Billettes and the host and processions of St. Jean-en-Grève are included in his review. His section on the proofs of the miracle, citations in published books and printed testimony of witnesses of the artifacts, is much longer than Séguier's. A long poem "on the history contained in the figures of the book" anticipates the chief exhibit of these pages. After an elegy and a sonnet, both dedicated to Milon, comes a set on nine discourses, "on the sacrifice of Jesus Christ in the Eucharist," all but one of them preceded by a copperplate engraving.

The engravings each depicts a scene from the miracle; the following discourse by Milon discusses the scriptural analogue of that scene. A quatrain printed on the bottom border of each print is a transition from the specifics of the scene to the spiritual commentary, the history in the figure, as the poem anticipated.

How accursed is this commerce
Woman to redeem the dress
It is your heart that you undress
To sell at last Jesus Christ

On the downhanging cloth of the table is written in cursive script, "*juif,*" "*Jew,*" and the woman's casaque is inscribed with "*vite,*" "quickly." She is making haste to sell Jesus. The discourse that follows is titled "Jesus Christ sold." It decries with exclamations that Jesus gave himself to us only to be sold for petty gain. The engravings complete the link between a past event and the framework of human sin and the possibility of redemption inherent in the *imago* of the Eucharist.

The engraver signed each of the prints, "F. Ragot fe," "F. Ragot ma(de)(it)." He was most likely François Ragot (the elder) whose son by the same name was a master engraver of the mid-17th century. The family name Ragot is a French idiom for trickery, and there are a few tricks in this series of engravings, which are related to the grave discourses that follow them only in subject.

The fifth engraving captures the Jew standing with flail and scourge in his hand beating the blood-spurting host nailed to an upright as his wife remostrates with him. On the wall behind them is a framed print of him driving a javelin down into the host on a table. The artist fit all the Jew's tortures in an inset without adding a separate picture to the set, the same as in the fourth engraving. On the floor a small dog is dashing about and barking, as well it might. The dog was a fixed emblem of the Jew in Christian visual discourse.

The blood cannot stanch
The faithless rage of the Jew
For with a cruel wand
He continues to drain it out

"Jesus Christ flagellated" is the title of Milon's accompanying discourse, which frames the Jew's reference to Christ's Passion and not a domestic scene. In the sixth engraving, the Jew takes a lance to the host, while the dog is curled up on the floor asleep, the Jew's soul unawakened.

During the 19th century bibliophiles collected copies of Milon's book for what one called "the curious and well-enough engraved vignettes."[156] They were free to exercise connoisseurship in place of the *imago* and thus to grade the skill of the engraver rather than using the prints to visualize the history of the miracle figurally. The engraver domesticated the miracle for his contemporaries.

In the 1633 publication the engraver made the now enumerated (1-9) phases of the miracle into genre prints, which made them "curious" to later viewers. The figures, dressed according to class and station, were updated from the 13th century timing of the miracle to the 17th century. The Jew covers his hair with a chaperon, wears a doublet and goes bare-legged in boots, the dress of a frugal tradesman of the time. His facial features seem to be caricatured only in the first print; he looks like other men after that. The other men are the priest, bishop, church doctors and soldiers of the second and the last three prints, all of them dressed and carrying the objects (crozier, pikestaffs) of their station.

The Jew's wife appears in a hennin, a conical aristocratic headdress with trailing veil that was making its way into the ranks of the middle class in the cities in the 1630's. Her chemise and skirt are in keeping with this status. The Jew's household is not without pretense. The corrupt Christian woman wears a coif, a hood covering her head and reaching down over her shoulders, and a casaque over her loose dress (sack) in all three of her appearances. Her wish to replace this clothing with the one gown she owns but which is held by the Jew causes her to misappropriate the host and exchange it for the gown. The good Christian woman is dressed the same but without the coif. She has nothing to hide.

In the one print where the good Christian woman is present she is in church, delivering the rescued host to the priest. For a woman to be in church without a head covering (even the corrupt Christian woman wears one) she must be in an unusual state of grace and hurrying on a sanctified mission. The prints in their depiction of the commonplace branch off into specific allegories that serve the general analogy between the history of the miracle and Christ's Passion.

The corrupt woman kneels at an altar in the second print, a priest facing her brings the consecrated host to her extended lips. At variance with the group receiving of Communion, she is alone facing the priest, the archwork of a church framing the figure of the crucified Christ in the distance. The quatrain below begins, "So it had to be that a kiss/alas betrayed again." The discourse that follows brings up Judas' kiss of betrayal paralleled by the woman's lips meeting the host. The conceit superimposes a moment from the Passion of Christ upon a seemingly unrelated episode of the miracle.

The Jew without repenting
Dies amid the torture
Let us pray that such a sacrifice
May make us all convert

This last print, which combines the interrogation of the Jew with his execution, leads with an abrupt visual: the bare buttocks of a halberd-bearing helmeted soldier face the viewer. His braies have slipped down exposing what looks like a tail between the two cheeks. The learned doctor whose finger indicates the Jew burning in the distance might just as well be pointing to the soldier's behind as he expounds the meaning of events to the bishop beside him. With his left hand he holds to his chest a paten cloth placed over the chalice on the altar. Another doctor beside him looks toward the soldier, his hand raised in amazement at the manifestation of doctrine.

Rather than a suggestion of sodomy (the satanic tail) it is another jarring pun they are calling to attention: *selle* (excrement) runs down both sides of the cleft, a homonym for the *sel* (salt) which according to the Gospel we will be salted with fire (Mark 9: 49 "For every one shall be salted with fire, and every sacrifice shall be salted with salt."). Milon alludes to this passage in his discourse. The fire of God's love and of God's justice salts us all, and the Jew, intransigent unbeliever, burns with hellfire of God's justice. The quatrain draws the analogy between Christ's sacrifice on the cross and the Jew's condemnation to fire, which should convert us by emulation of one and rejection of the other.

The visual component of the *imago* associates sights seen with scripture through the names of things and actions. The engravings were designed to be a repository of these allegorical associations. They were said to be based on a sequence of 13th century tapestries that hung in the chapel of the miracle or in the church of St. Merri. François Ragot *père* was known as a reproducer of paintings and tapestries in engravings; his son had greater renown in this craft. It is possible that Milon's book engravings were copied from tapestries meant to capture the mystery of the miracle in a visually arresting form, as the tapestries were meant to settle the *imago* for the public.

If that is how the prints were made then there was another cycle of copying the tapestries and making them into paintings and then into prints (postcards) yet to happen in the 19th-20th centuries.

Whichever initiated the cycle, the engravings established the seen form of the miracle copied many times over. Because they manifested sacred history as commonplace events grown wondrous they spatialized the *imago*. It could be staged in processions, in different churches and other books that partook of its universal time. There was no anachronism in the dress of the figures. The miracle always was going on as the Passion of Christ went on in the mass. And the role of the Jews in bringing about Christ's Passion was also perpetuated as a cause for punishment which then returned to the Passion.

The obscurity of the allegory was a depth of time that might be penetrated, and catch the viewer whether layman or bishop in its mesh of references. A Carmelite du Saint Sacrement (Billette) who had taken the name Léon de St. Jean in 1664 issued a revised edition of Milon's book. The first title page was designed by Ragot (*fils* this time, given the date). Between two scrolls mingled with putti at the head of the page is a figure of the miracle's boiled god apparition not appearing in the 1633 publication.[157]

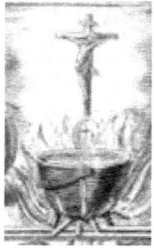

The title on this page is the same as 1633, but a plain print title page that follows adds wording that places the miracle in the convent of the Billettes. The dedication is not to Richelieu, long since deceased, but to "Monsieur (no further name)," the title long accorded the eldest brother of the reigning king, in this time Philippe I, Duke of Orleans, brother of Louis XIV. In the course of the dedication "Monsieur" becomes "Monseigneur," the title accorded a church official and a signature of secular power coexisting with religious authority. Léon does not make the same obeisances to Monsieur that Milon did to Richelieu; he does place before him the Maison du Miracle but not the church of St. Jean-en-Grève.

The section on proofs and the nine discourses are reproduced from the 1633 book, as are the copperplate engravings, using the same plates as before only with a significantly improved impression. This is a stronger assertion of Billette control of the miracle than Milon's book. It consolidates a tradition of representation, fixing the boiled god, the emblem of the Billettes' interest in the miracle, in the forefront of the *imago*. Ragot's seventh engraving, absent from Milon's book, was present in sequence here.

Who was not in downcast
To see Jesus in these flames
Once more to say to our souls
That all is consummated

The Jew, wearing a turban, raises his hands in astonishment as the crucifixion and the host also bearing a crucifixion appear over the cauldron perched on a fireplace tripod as the maid raises the flames with a bellows (*soufflet*, suggesting *souffri*, suffered). The little dog is stirred by the dark shadow of those arriving to bring the Jew to justice. The quatrain concludes with another dark pun, a reference to Christ's word as he dies on the cross given in John 19:30 as *tetelestai*, it is consummated, but also referring to a boiled concentrate of meat or vegetables, a consommé, which might be in the pot.

This Billette *imago* centered on the crucifix and host over the cauldron became the most disseminated figure of the miracle with or without the word-image play. It already formed the frontispiece of the *inventaire* (inventory) of the Billettes property placed in their archive in the 16th century.[158] Here the crucifixion over the boiling cauldron accompanied by the host appears between the Pope (Boniface VIII) and the Virgin Mary holding the Christ child, each of whom holds up a cloth sheet like a parted curtain. The good Christian woman kneels on the left side of the flame stoked by the Jew on one knee applying the bellows. Behind them on either side is a row of black clad, tonsured monks, the Billettes.

This scene either is the singular representation of the miracle des Billettes or forms a component in a sequence.

The personnel vary but the crucifixion accompanied by the host over a cauldron of boiling water always is the core of the picture. It appears as a central component of a stained glass window sequence that still exists at the church of St. Etienne-du-Mont in Paris and another stained glass sequence (1540-50) in the church of Saint Eloi in Rouen, now in that city's Musée des Antiquités.[159] The church of St. Etienne de Bar sur Seine in the Champagne region also contains a 16th century stained glass rendition of the crucifixion emerging from the cauldron where the host was thrown by the Jew.

These and other picture sequences in various media prominently featuring the cauldron-host-crucifixion are the keynotes of an *imago* that absorbed the host of St. Jean-en-Grève into the Billettes' relic narrative of the miracle. Léon de St. James' book is the model: the details of bringing the host to the church are dropped in favor of the unique sacrilege, trial and punishment of the Jew. They are abbreviated, the boiled host picture always remains, and serves as their center.

The memorial pamphlet of the 1714 rite of adoration of the host in the church of the Billettes in Paris conducted in the presence of members of the royal family "to make honorable amends to

Jesus Christ." was accompanied by the nine engravings of Léon's book. The entire miracle in its *imago* of religious and secular power was sited in the church of the Billettes in the presence of the monarchy.

The Billette S. René on March 13, 1715 saw late 13th century embroideries of the miracle at the church of the Billettes.[160] He connected their subject to a painted tableau in the church of St. Martin-des-Champs in Paris and Séguier's 1604 book to form a network of proof across place and medium. The miracle of the Billettes reached out to embrace disparate forms to make an *imago* of content and staging, a transpatial miracle at its origins under the aegis of the Billettes.

A devotional copperplate print for sale at the printers on the Place de Grève in the 1750's is an artifact of this unification in the miracle's *imago*.[161] Surrounding the text in the center are the nine phases of the miracle as in Ragot's engravings (but not reproducing them). In the top center of the print much larger than the other illustrations is the cauldron-host-crucifixion. The Jew recoils on the left as the good Christian woman receives the host on the right. "The Jew tosses the host into a cauldron of boiling water. The host is transformed into Christ crucified" reads the plain inscription.

This was the *imago* ready to survive the conversion and destruction of the church fabric, indifferent to the struggles between the Billettes and the marguilliers of St. Jean-en-Grève.

Source gallica.bnf.fr / Bibliothèque nationale de France

Notes

[151] *Tractatus miraculi Biletani super corpore Christi a Iudaeo confixo, anno 1290.* Lutetiae [in Paris], 1604.

[152] Séguier (1604: 5)

[153] The Latin original was printed in 1637 as *Officium corporis Christi recitandum in ecclesia a Sancti Joannis in Gravia e concessione illustrissimi et reverendissimi archiepiscopi Parisiensis.*

[154] Séguier (1604). The hymns begin on page 37 of this brief work. They are French translations of the four hymns composed by Thomas Aquinas for the Office of Corpus Christi: *pangis lingua; sacris solemnis; verbum supernum; lauda Sion.* These hymns were composed at the request of the pope after the Eucharistic miracle at Bolsena (1263).

[155] Milon (1633: 1)

[156] Leber (1839: 56/3320)

[157] Léon de St. Jean (1664: first title page)

[158] *Relevé des documents interressants du Departement de Seine et Maine.* Fontainebleau: Ernest Bourges (1893): 170

[159] Listed in the 19th century catalogue of the Musée des Antiquités. Des traces de l'antisémitisme médiéval à Rouen, https://pierrickauger.wordpress.com/2014/01/30/des-traces-de-lanti-Semitisme-medieval-a-rouen

[160] S. René (1725: 231-33)

[161] *Histoire miraculeuse de l'hostie outrage par un juif l'an de grace 1290. Se vend à Paris chez Vautié, Place de Grève sous les piliers de fort Samson.* BnF Hennin 8740.

11.
Configurations

The miracle was a belief about an attack on the host in one place, at one time, by a Jew, told and performed as a historic event. Relics, services, processions and institutions were taken as proof that it actually had occurred. Underlying the historic miracle was an exemplary account of the behavior of Jews toward Christian material culture and related beliefs. The miracle story spread, and was reported as recurring, within and outside of France in forms adapted to local beliefs and styles of expression. It took on shapes and narratives clearly related to each other because the Paris story was an adaptation of an exemplary story about Jews and the host being told before it was grounded in that city and time. This led to representations independent of but possibly converging with the Paris story and its variants.

A pre-1290 form of the story was found in an *exemplum* from a sermon delivered by the Franciscan Jacques de Provins to a group of poor parishioners in a Paris church during Lent, 1272.[162] Sermons to the people were delivered in the vernacular and set down in Latin sometimes with vernacular notes. *Exempla* were stories often with vivid details that preceded the moralizing of the sermon. They were gathered in collections for the use of preachers, sorted by saint's day and time of year in the liturgical calendar. The *exemplum* Jacques de Provins devised for his sermon was under the heading of the Eucharist.

The Jews here are a character type bent upon subjecting the host to a test to determine if it is Christ's living body. They obtain a host from an old Christian woman who assures them it is consecrated. They pay her in silver, toss the host into boiling water, then into the fire, and then stab it.

> They took that blessed host, and had prepared a large cauldron over a blazing fire, and threw it into the boiling cauldron, and looking saw the host in the aspect of a most beautiful boy playing with the waves of boiling water, and thought to capture him, and immediately he returned to his former aspect. Then some of them said, "Certainly we test it this way."

> Having taken the host, he threw it into the middle of the fire and covered it with burning coals, saying, "Thus we are freed of the god of the Christians." And taking the tongs strongly agitating the coals, he saw the host whiter among the burning coals and cleaner than snow. Then they said, "Thus we test it." One who came in said, "This is not enough..."

> "...give it to me and I will prove it once and for all." And he took a large fork, a large blade and stabbed, and blood came on the earth in great abundance. So that host was well tested, in fact, the true body of Christ in humanity and divinity, and "by water they boil it, and by fire they burn it and by arms pierced." Then all those Jews were stupefied at the marvel.

They were so stupefied, de Provins explains, that they sent the host to the Jewish community in a neighboring town with letters on the events that had occurred, prepared to accept their opinion and convert to the faith of the Christians if they think they should. The host is discovered before it reaches that town and the Jews are arrested and imprisoned. de Provins denies knowledge of what became of them.

The *exemplum* is structured by the Jews putting the host through three judicial ordeals used to test the veracity of an accused person: by water, by fire and by iron. Each time the host proves out. There is no talk of torture or deicide, nor of reparation by religious rites.

The Jews test the host and witness the Eucharist in the *exemplum*. The miracle stories originating in Paris years after this sermon was delivered lead to conversion after the same events, but a conversion that is forced, not inspired, and when resisted an excuse for capital punishment. Specific locations and persons, dispossession of the Jews by the crown and the formation of religious establishments by the church on those sites are added to the story of a Jew assaulting (not testing) the host. The ordeal-based formula of the Jews' testing the host was modified to dramatize their ability to corrupt Christians with money and violently threaten the pure and innocent embodiment of belief, thus justifying their dispossession and, if noncompliant, their execution.

The Paris miracle configured a story fabricated to proclaim the real presence of Christ in the Eucharist to suit the persecutional politics of the time and place. The key element of the miracle story missing from the *exemplum* was addressed in a *quodlibet* (academic question and answer) composed during Advent of the same year as the miracle, 1290. The theologian Henri de Gand asked[163]

> Should civil justice punish a Jew who pierced a consecrated host and who, seeing
> that it responded with blood flowing from its wounds, is converted and baptized
> after having seen the miracle?

Henri's answer to this question drew upon academic reasoning and popular traditions surfacing in his words. He treated it as a legal *casus* (instance of reasoning by principle): how should the Jews like those imprisoned in the *exemplum* be treated? The intent of the actor, a principle shared by jurists and spiritual directors, decides the issue. Was the host pierced out of malice, intent to harm the body of Christ, or was it pierced out of skepticism? If malicious, the act is culpable; if skeptical, it is a step toward a sincere conversion.

This answer fills the space left open at the end of the *exemplum* with a contingency requiring an evaluation of the Jew's intent as he goes about his work of destruction. The Paris miracle introduces a solution in the dramatization of the Jew's rages which are the result of a historic and culpable malice against Christ and his embodiment.

The Jew uses the rhetoric of inquiry and exposure of idolatry but his persistence and lack of mercy against all pleas, and his refusal to accept conversion lead to his classification as a heretic. This is the area of the miracle story most susceptible to basic variation. The Jew and his entire family may be converted and spared; the Jew alone may refuse to convert; he may be denied the right to convert; he and his entire family may be burned whether converted or not. The penalty phase responds to Christian-Jewish relations where the miracle story is being retold or reenacted. The retellings take place in a field that includes the *exemplum,* the *quodlibet* and the original miracle story.

The *exemplum* aspect predominated in the configurations of the miracle in Spain. A retablo painted between 1363 and 1375 by the Catalan painter Pere Serra for the Monastery of Sijena contains a frame clearly referring to the story of the Jew and the host.[164] It is one of many frames in this tall retablo devoted to the Virgin Mary (as was the monastery), and "centered in turn on the exaltation of the Eucharist with strong anti-Jewish implications."

Within one corner of an architectural enclosure the woman sells the host to the fork-bearded Jew. At the center the Christ child emerges from a black cauldron over a fire, the Jew plunges a knife into the broken and blood-spattered host on a table while his wife wearing a neck cowl with diadem looks on and a boy, likely their son, stands facing to the right as he holds up his arm toward the two miraculous manifestations.

All the elements of the *exemplum* are present in the order they are given, with the addition of the boy who is heralding the discovery by the authorities of the Jew's host abuse and the resultant miracles. The single Jew rather than a group might be a concession to the limited space to tell the story.

Accusations of host profanation against Jews arose during the mid-14th century in the Kingdom of Aragon (where Sijena is located). A Jew in Perpignan in 1367 was accused of receiving a stolen casket containing hosts which were then removed. The focus shifted from the thieves to the Jewish merchant, and the investigation, driven by the heir to the Aragonese throne, Infante Juan, involved

115

important Jewish scholars and led to the execution of three Jews in Barcelona that same year.[165] The representation of the profanation in the Sijena retablo was cast in the better known form of the de Provins *exemplum* translated into the Paris miracle, in response to heightened antagonism against Jews for their commercial activities and religion.

The retablo also contains a portrayal of Judas as an archetypal hook-nosed Jew seated at the table of the Last Supper in contrast to the others present, a partially scratched-out figure of a demon at his side.

Jews were not the only "foreigners" defamed in the retablo. The next section to the right of the host profanation encapsulates a known story of a woman who consults with a dark-skinned Muslim magician to regain the affections of her husband through a love spell. She brings him a host only to find that it has been transformed into a child. The Muslim does not have a chance to handle the host.

In the middle of the next century two more works containing scenes of host profanation by Jews were painted for a monastery and a church. The Monastery of the Virgin Mary in Vallbona de les Monges (Lerida) exhibited a retablo and altar frontal (both around 1450) by an unknown master. Two horizontal strips of scenes surround a central panel of the Holy Trinity in the retablo. The last two scenes on the lower right of the retablo continue into three scenes on the upper left of the frontal centered on the Virgin and Christ Child.

The sequence of images begins with two men with forked beards wearing tailed cowls standing at a wooden table in an open space with flat patterned backing. One of them knifes a large host recognizable from the IHS inscription. Streams of red radiate from the host's disc over the raised edge of the table as the other man gestures toward the knife. In the next panel one of the men thrusts a lance vertically into the host at the peak of the arched frame while two others watch. Panel three: one of the men stands over a flaming brazier where the host rides above the opening of a pot suspended by a chain over the flames. His hands are raised palm outward in the fourth panel as a woman crouched on the other side of the now empty pot supports the host in the palm of her right hand. The final panel of this sequence consists of the host mounted in a monstrance on an altar with the figures of two hovering, haloed figures, angels, above and to the back.

The other panels of the paintings depict a Corpus Christi procession, Eucharistic miracles, the Last Supper and scenes from the conversion of Jews. The Eucharistic miracles are not confined to thwarted Jews but all are instances of the real presence of Christ in the host being made plain to doubters and those of weak faith.

The five panels of the profanation of the host bridging the two paintings are clearly the central events in the order of the Paris miracle, only lacking the initial sale of the host and the manifestation of the cross over the boiling water where the host was thrown. The punishment of the Jew is absent from all the Spanish representations. This is the earliest pictorial evidence of the awareness of the story contents and sequence specific to the Paris miracle in a Spanish context. The final panels are an innovative two-frame progression of host retrieval followed by the enshrinement.

Alfonso de Espina, a Franciscan monk, in the Third Book of his *Fortalitium Fidei* (1464), relates his encounter with two monks of the Cluniac order in the market town of Medina del Campo. The monks acquainted him with the Paris miracle story, which he made part of his book.[166]

The *Fortification of Faith* is a handbook for preachers in a set of seven books with instructions and examples of how to confound the arguments of those who deny the divinity of Christ, and of the impossibilities and cruelties of heretics, of Jews, and of Muslims. The Paris miracle is one of several used to counter Jews who question the real presence in the host by illustrating what happens when a Jew attempts to test it out. de Espina's Paris miracle includes new elements that clearly were fabricated to add an almost comic zest to the Jew's pursuit of the host manifested as a beautiful child around the cauldron of boiling water, the scampering of the children to herald their father's child abuse and the expulsion of the Jews en masse after the abuser is burned.

Other examples in de Espina's book correspond to other panels in the Vallbona de les Monges paintings. They were part of a growing armory of assertions and anecdotes against outsiders to the faith, who were classed as less than human.

The Retablo of the Eucharist in the parish church of Villahermosa del Río in Castellón province was completed in the Italianizing style of the late 14th-early 15th century by a painter in the circle of the Serra family, most likely Llorenç Zaragoza. The central shaft of the altarpiece is formed of two large panels of the Crucifixion and the Last Supper. The figure of Judas dressed in an engulfing cowl is seated with his back to the viewer while the haloed Christ and the apostles stand facing outward on the other side of the table. Judas separates two three section panels that form the bottom course of the retablo.

The figures in three groups kneeling and standing on a tiled floor that stretches from one side to the other and enclosed in an architectural frame divided by pilasters. The Christian woman receives Communion from a priest and then is standing at a table facing the fork-bearded, cowled Jew as she hands over the host. Even the lower lappet of the Jew's cowl is forked. A pile of coins is beneath their outstretched hands on the table and the both hold the empty gown up to full length in the front plane of the panel. Two Jewish women, heads inclined at the same angle and wearing a tight-fitting headwrap (*sudar*) surmounted by a diadem, watch from the upper portion of the scene. The figures are repeated with different hand gestures in each of the remaining sections.

The Jew stabs the blood-spattering host on a wooden pillar. In the first section of the opposite side he hammers the host on an anvil on the post as the two women, and two men look on, their hands raised in alarm. The host is on a wooden table spurting blood over the edge as a young man holds a sword over the heads of the crowd ready to strike again. The Jew, another bearded man the same as the previous panel and the two women crowd in watching. Two beardless men, the Jew and the women stand over the host floating in the chain-hung pot over the flames which are raked by a small child standing to the side. The child resembles in position the Jew's son in the composite panel of the Sijena retablo.

The Villahermosa panels follow the story line of the Paris miracle without the ending, like the later Vallbona panels. There is a striking similarity between the Villahermosa bleeding host and the Vallbona bleeding host-lines arching out and over the edge of the table-despite the stylistic distance between the two. In this they both differ from the earlier Sijena panels, which configure de Provins' *exemplum*. Once the Paris miracle became known to the ecclesiastical patrons who set the plan of the paintings it dominated representation and recounting of the miracle and carried pictorial strategies across stylistic boundaries. The distinctive headgear for Jewish men and women, and the beard style for men remained the same in all three of these and in other paintings. Jews were marked as distinctive.

The painters of these religious works configured the miracle according to the *exemplum* and then the Paris relation, with some themes common to all of them. As history led up to the definitive expulsion of the Jews from the united kingdom of Castile and Aragon, and the defeat of the last Muslim kingdom on Spanish soil, Granada, both in 1492, devices like the miracle gave way to other configurations.

During the 14th to 15th centuries the Paris miracle provided a model for the representation of opinions and actions against the Jews in Brussels, Belgium. The story of the miracle was not reconfigured in separate local forms as it was in Spain, but served implicitly to organize the response to a theft of a ciborium with hosts from a church, and as a justification for burning several (or many) Jews at the stake.

The history of the miraculous hosts of Brussels was first set down as a published narrative in French by Steven Ydens, a priest and canon of the church of Sts. Michel et Gudule.[167] Ydens referred to earlier, unpublished source manuscripts some of which he quoted in Latin. His account was illustrated by a sequence of copperplate engravings that set the standard for the visual ordering of the miracle, including a print of the golden cross in which the hosts of the miracle were deposited. Ydens occupied a portion of his book with stories of healing of ills and debilities attributed to the hosts' influence, and with other Eucharistic miracles in the Brabant.

During the history of the miracle Brussels was located in the Duchy of Brabant, a state of the Holy Roman Empire. The cultural and linguistic bivalence of the Brabant was the basis for one of the tensions in the development and dissemination of the miracle story. The church of Sts. Michel et Gudule, with its paired international and local saints, later declared the Belgian "national church," embodied this dualism. Ydens' book as the bearer of the miracle story, was published in French, later translated into Flemish, and had further editions in both languages over a span of forty years.

This initiated alternating French and Flemish accounts of the miracle and of the church. In 1720 another priest and canon of Sts. Michel et Gudule, Petrus de Cafmeyer, issued through a Brussels press his Flemish history of the miracle, published concurrently by the same press in a French translation.[168] This publication included a new set of illustrations clearly based on those in Ydens, but in an updated style.

On the 400th anniversary of the miracle in 1770 a group of priests associated with the church of Sts. Michel et Gudule produced a history illustrated with the de Cafmeyer copperplates, in a French original with a Flemish translation.[169] The story of the miracle that had been handed down from Ydens to the 1770 book is as follows.

A Jewish merchant named Jonathas living in the town of Enghien commissioned a Jewish convert to Christianity, Jean de Louvain, to procure hosts he could use to disprove the divinity of Christ to Jews who were converting. Jean de Louvain was persuaded by the sixty *moutons* of gold Jonathas offered. Called "sheep" from the Lamb of God icon on the coin, these *agnels d'or* resembled the wafer-shaped host.[170]

Jean stole into the Chapel of Ste. Catherine in Brussels one evening in October, 1369 and removed a ciborium containing consecrated hosts. Jonathas accepted delivery of his prize, but was murdered by thieves while walking in his garden before he could make any use of the hosts. His wife hastily disposed of the vessel and its contents to the Jewish community of Brussels.

The Jews, an accursed nation, the authors write, were not always the tranquil people known today (1770), but were given to savage rages against Christianity. The Paris miracle is one instance of this. Unable to destroy the Christian religion, they held private conventicles in which they directed their wrath against the enemy faith, and especially against the Blessed Sacrament. The hosts that fell into the hands of the Jews of Brussels were stabbed and beaten in one of these tumultuous gatherings. The authors quote earlier writers and histories to substantiate their assertion.

The blood spurting from the victim hosts frightened the abusers, who commissioned Catherine, a Jewish woman converted to Christianity, to take them to the Jewish community in Cologne, where they readily could be eliminated. Catherine had second thoughts, and informed the church authorities, all named, who assembled the chapter and interrogated her, examined the hosts she carried to verify they were stained with blood, then called upon the magistrates who under the authority of the Duke and Duchess of Brabant arrested all the Jews of Brussels and Louvain. Some confessed to the crime under torture, others did not. All had their property confiscated, were torn with heated pincers, and were burned at the stake on public squares on the Feast of the Ascension, 1370.

The authors maintain that neither the original nor copies of the final order (*arrêt*) can be found in the public archives, which had been destroyed "by the injuries of time." There is, however, a record in the Register of Accounts "where it is made that nothing can be suspected of supposition and falseness" which reads as follows:

> Received from the Jews who lived this year in Brabant, so much of their annual tribute, as well as their confiscated property, after they were burned, around the Feast of the Ascension of Our Lord, and declared infamous, for having pierced the Blessed Hosts furtively taken from the Chapel, so much of said property as entered in my receipt.

The total amount taken came to 1413 *moutons*. The authenticity of this record was verified by comparing the copy to the original manuscript in 1605, and again in 1730, though it was difficult to read the 13th century script. This was the only contemporary record that authenticates the story. The authors were, at the 400th anniversary, especially eager to demonstrate the reliability of the documents.

The primary matter of the theft-abuse-miracle, the hosts themselves, was divided between two Brussels churches: the parish and collegial church of Sts. Michel et Gudule, and Notre Dame de la Chapelle. The three hosts allocated to Sts. Michel et Gudule were enclosed in a gold crucifix. Grand processions established the transfer of hosts as genuine, and annual services with processions were decreed in reparation of the crime.

The hosts remained in their respective churches for hundreds of years, through attacks by Calvinists and attempted robbery. Those in Notre Dame de la Chapelle were lost due to lack of vigilance on the part of their protectors. From November 24 to December 16, 1789 the Sts. Michel et Gudule hosts were hidden while they were threatened by spreading revolutionary violence.[171]

The main threat to the Brussels miracle was not destruction of the hosts, but that their viability as evidence that the events occurred depended upon documenting that they did occur. The authors of histories of the miracle relied on imagery that was so ensconced in the tradition of the miracle that it had become reality. The rage of the Jews upon the hosts looked like this to the illustrator of Ydens' 1605 book.

Ydens (1605)   de Cafmeyer (1720)

The right-hand engraving was signed by L.-J. Fruytiers, but it is identical to the engraving of the same scene by an unidentified printmaker in de Cafmeyer's original edition of 1670. The differences in figure drawing, composition and chiaroscuro place the two prints in different centuries. The dress of the Jews is variously Oriental and Classical in the 1605 print; it has become standard Jewish in the 1720 one.

The host bleeds in both, and the plunged knives and raised blades are at the same position and angle. The brawl has claimed two victims. The fork-bearded man to the left of the table has exchanged his turban for a cowl and his knife is in the hands of another. The 1720 printmaker has not so much reinterpreted the 1605 print, as he has restated an eternal scene. The brawl and miracle occurred and had been occurring for a long time. The fumbling violence of the Jews against the host is manifest.

The written evidence for the miracle in the form of documents dating from 1370 and later times is similarly stereotyped. They are listed, described, and sometimes quoted from one history of the miracle to another, which established them as an unassailable body of evidence supporting the perfidy of Jews, the bleeding of the hosts and the justice of the punishment meted out. As long as these were accepted beliefs the validity of the documents was not questioned. The receipt for the Jews' confiscated property, a reading of which was quoted above, and two other 1370 documents alluded to stabbed and bleeding hosts only with tendentious reading of the original script, which was reproduced in transcription or translation in the histories.

The depositions of six named ecclesiasts who had contact with the miracle, taken down at the orders of a bishop in 1402, thirty-two years after the events, were enshrined in the history of the miracle as testimony. No writer seeking to verify the miracle for another generation failed to cite, summarize or quote them. One historian used the status of Pierre de Heede as a witness to underwrite the validity of another blood miracle (not involving Jews) that was said to happen in 1371 in a Brussels church.[172]

The first difficulty that these evidences ran into was political. The government of the Brabant in 1786 suppressed the publication of a "dissertation" on the miracle by the Jesuit J.J. Navez, which relied heavily on the 1402 depositions.[173] Ducal officialdom was uneasy about the nationalist sentiments spurred by the reassertion of the miracle during a time of revolution. The book was published in 1790, when the Revolution did come to Brussels. Its effect was the opposite of casting doubt on the evidence.

It was reprinted in 1820, as was the 1770 history, for the 450th jubilee of the miracle. The jubilee was celebrated by gala processions and original publications on the miracle and of the history of the church of Sts. Michel et Gudule. The priest and archaeologist P.-J. Bruyn used his survey of the tapestry scenes of the miracle adorning the interior of the church to register his horror on seeing the punishment of the Jews. Bruyn found that one Jew who made a few injudicious remarks on the proceedings was arrested, convicted and burned, his confiscated property added to the Duke's benefits. The children of the Jews were forced to watch their parents devoured by flames before being forcibly baptized.[174] Bruyn did not question the verity of the miracle, but he recoiled from the brutality of its effects.

His book was reprinted with a new introduction for the 500th jubilee of the miracle in 1870. At that time there were more trenchant critiques of the evidence supporting the miracle and the beliefs it seemed to confirm. The phrase "*faux miracle*" in the title of both pointed to the fabrication that these authors concluded had made the miracle.[175] Further research over decades enabled historians to refine the criticism and isolate the events that could be supported by the documentary record.[176]

> If the condemnation of the Jews, under the crime of sacrilege, is attested by contemporary documents, the assurance of the miracle is not explicitly put out until later…In the month of October, 1383, an expiatory procession is organized at Sainte-Gudule to evoke the memory of "the theft of the most blessed." This ceremony envisaged a simple rite of reparation. Not the least allusion to the miracle. Did they not believe in it yet at this time?…In conclusion, we judge that the discovery, in 1370, of a theft of consecrated hosts bearing the traces of laceration, a crime in which the work of the Jews of the city was seen, gave birth to the theme of sacrilegious transfixion, with vengeful miraculous effusion of the victim, and perhaps to the theme of the punishment inflicted on the guilty the following day.

There had been a theft of hosts from a Brussels church in 1370. They were found abused. Jews were accused of the crime, their property was confiscated by the Brabantine ducal government, and they suffered the penalty of sacrilege on the Feast of the Ascension. This much can be established from a single extant 1370 document which if carefully read states that sacrament was "abused" (*"punito"*) and not that it was "punctured" (*"puncto"*), as writers since Ydens had claimed.

Two other crucial documents have not survived as originals. Confirmed from an entry in a 1474 catalogue was a letter sent by the Bishop of Cambrai (his see including Brussels) to the parishioners of Notre Dame de la Chapelle concerning the division of the hosts that had been profaned by the Jews between that church and Sts. Michel et Gudule, both of which claimed a share.

The 1402 depositions, known only through later copies, collectively refer to hosts profaned by Jews but not to the action of profanation or to a miracle that occurred when the hosts were mistreated. There is no reason to believe that the depositions were assembled around 1530 to justify the expansion of the cult of the hosts after an epidemic. The depositions were transmitted to the bishop with a request for permission to grant indulgences to pilgrims but there is no original text or contemporary copy of the bishop's reply.

A 1435 request by a layman to construct a chapel of the Blessed Sacrament in the Coperbeek district of Brussels where a synagogue had been makes no reference to a crime of host desecration or a miracle. The request was not approved by the church authorities with a provision for the granting of indulgences until 1441. The clergy of Sts. Michel et Gudule had opposed a rival for the pilgrim indulgences trade.

The essential features of the Brussels miracle do not appear until the middle of the 15th century in the form of a Flemish reading for the Eucharistic holy day, Fête-Dieu, written into a codex kept at the priory of Rouge-Cloître in the Forêt de Soignes to the south of Brussels.[177] This "legend" sets the course of the miracle as related in all later sources, from Ydens to the 1770 jubilee version.

The documented association of the Jews with the theft and mutilation of hosts in 1370 Brussels, and their consequent punishment stimulated the unknown author of the legend ("reading") to extend it with components of the Paris miracle story, which starts with the same basics. The Paris miracle was not needed to charge Jews with host crimes: that was a commonplace accusation. The record of thefts and reparations makes it clear that when Christians were apprehended stealing and casually abusing the host they also were punished by torture and burning. The Paris miracle model contributed three elements that allowed the author of the legend to make it more characteristic of Jews.

First the element of commerce in the hosts was added, in the Brussels case a false Jewish convert to Christianity instead of the vain Christian woman seeking the return of her pawned gown. Instead of a single host abstracted by taking Communion, the Brussels thief takes a ciborium with a number of hosts from a church otherwise not involved. The theft has been commissioned by a Jew with the same name, Jonathas, often given to the Paris receiver of the stolen sacrament and the sixty *moutons* he pays out is double the Judas number. This Jonathas is murdered walking in his garden (trace of the Rue des Jardins?) and his wife donates the hosts to the Brussels Jews.

The multiplicity of hosts is maintained by adapting the second new element, the Jew's frenzied attack on the host with knife points, to a group and making it into an orgy of stabbing. This leads to the third element, the bleeding of the hosts leaving stains that make them into relics. Ydens' reading of "*puncto*" in the manuscript of the 1370 receipt was driven by the introduction of stabbing and bleeding into the legend. The three stained hosts enclosed in the cross reliquary in Sts. Michel et Gudule supported the legend.

The introduction of a Jewish Christian convert woman who contracts to take the bloodied hosts to Cologne where a more sophisticated Jewish community can manage them, but who has qualms and brings them to the authorities instead, is a reflection of the good Christian woman in the Paris miracle. The attempt to redirect the hosts to a more learned community in another city is a recollection of the *exemplum*, in which the hosts never reach that other community. Likewise in the Brussels miracle: the hosts never reach Cologne, and serve as testimony against the Jews.

The contentious split of miracle relics between two churches, and the founding of a miracle chapel where the Jews once dwelt or worshiped are extra-legendary parallels between Brussels and Paris. The Paris miracle was a model for the legend of the Brussels miracle as well as for its institutional history. Both miracles reached centennials in the late 19th century that were an occasion for revivals and a renewed contest over their anti-Judaic bias and verifiability. Neither of the Brussels churches was destroyed as St. Jean-en-Grève was, or given over to Protestants as the Chapel des Billettes was. One of the churches was Sts. Michel et Gudule, the national church of Belgian Catholicism, whereas St. Jean-en-Grève was only an imitation of Notre Dame, and the Billettes were a product of the Paris miracle.

The influence of the Paris miracle on the Brussels miracle made them appear the same from a distance. A late 19th century list of representations of the Paris miracle outside of Paris included the pictures exhibited at Sts. Michel et Gudule.[178] The 1433 papal gift of a miraculous host to Philippe le Bon, Duke of Burgundy came with a written brief. Philippe had been of considerable assistance to Pope Eugenius IV in his struggles with the papal Curia at the Council of Basel. This host did not have the storied background of the Paris, Brussels and many other enshrined hosts. In the French translation of the pope's Latin brief the host had been "pierced in several places by the enraged brutality of a certain wicked man."[179]

The blood flowing from the stabbed host was said to have formed on the surface of the host the image of Christ resurrected bearing all of his wounds, which coincided with the marks left by the wicked man's stabs into the host. This constituted the most succinct print expression of the real presence: the image of the pierced Christ flowed from the wounds of the stabbed host. "The Eucharistic wafer has transformed itself into an enduring relic, flecked with blood but paradoxically incorruptible."[180] Even more incorruptible in what it represented, which nonetheless changed.

This host formed a distinctive picture reproduced in paintings and prints. The earliest pictures of the host created in 1435-37 and 1442-43 differ from those made two centuries later, probably because physical degeneration of the host caused the marks to be interpreted differently.[181] This devotional print was placed at the front of Boulier's 1646 *Remarques historiques…*

ACCURATE REPRESENTATION OF THE SANCTIFIED MIRACLE HOST OF DIJON
All good things came to us together with that [host]
Hence thou keepest the ancient beauty of the name, Excellent City (left/right)
"And he was clothed with a garment sprinkled with blood." Revelations 19:13
[The eyes of the Lord are upon them that fear him,] he is their powerful protector, and strong stay, a defence from the heat, and a cover from the sun at noon, a preservation from stumbling, and a help from falling; he raiseth up the soul, and enlighteneth the eyes, and giveth health, and life, and blessing.
Ecclesiastes 34:19-20 in the Latin Vulgate/Douay-Rheims Bible, with the first line of 34: 19 excised

To the left of Christ is a cockerel on the pillar of flagellation, a reminder of St. Thomas' betrayals, and to the right instruments of the Passion, including a flail and three knouts. Centuries earlier these markings on the host were interpreted as a cross with a crown of thorns, and the darkened circle of its perimeter was streaked like a crown of thorns.

The host also appeared in early prints of the gold ostensorium constructed for it in 1454, and carried in procession from 1486 onward, after a religious confraternity had been formed devoted to the Precious Blood.[182] The host's image spread widely in pictures, like other religious icons reproducible from description alone. Without a detailed story of origin, its fame was the result of a unique visual formulation, which conveyed a sense of its presence. It was enshrined as a wonderworking object of pilgrimage in a place where it did not originate and as an object of personal devotion in printed books and popular prints.

The Dijon host's abuse was the work of "an infuriated man" according to the pope's message. That the man was a Jew became attached to images of the host during the decades after its enshrinement in Dijon. Illuminations of the host were inserted into at least four separate Books of Hours during the 15th to 16th centuries.[183] Accompanying them was the text of "O salutaris hostia," one of the hymns to the host Thomas Aquinas composed for the Feast of the Holy Sacrament, along with another poem specific to the Dijon host.[184]

Ung juif mutilait jadis
l'hostie du Saint Sacrement
par frapper des coups plus de dix
fait sortir sang abundamment.

A Jew once mutilated the
host of the holy sacrament
By striking blows more than ten
Making it bleed abundantly

The remaining three quatrains recount the Pope Eugenius' donation and the duke's reception and enshrinement of the host. Nothing further on the Jew and the response to his actions.

Hughenin de Brégilles, a courtier in the train of the last Duke of Burgundy, composed a poem some time afterward with essentially the same structure.[185]

When the cursed and miserable Jew
With criminal intent and hateful courage
Had wounded the venerable sacrament
An event befell, both piteous and miraculous
As real miraculous blood spurted from the wounds

A member of the knightly Ordre de la Toison d'Or (Order of the Golden Fleece) founded by Duke Philippe le Bon, de Brégilles summoned the host's protective grace to "be our shield and large and advance/against the Turks of the infernal advance/without the grace we are disabled" in another poem included with the manuscript text of a morality play he had written.[186] The Jews were the internal enemy of the faith and the Turks the external.

A record places de Brégilles as quartermaster with the current duke in Brussels in 1466, where he no doubt took advantage of the indulgences extended by Pope Eugenius IV to those who visited the shrine of the Brussels hosts.

Besides their historical links, the Brussels hosts and the Dijon host were complementary. One was multiple, divided between two churches, with a strongly wrought origin legend that encompassed several confiscation and execution-worthy perfidies of the Jews. The other was singular, located in one place, a blood libel that could be disseminated pictorially, with a non-specific tag of a single Jew's violence. They both partook of features of the Paris miracle, especially of the bloodletting frenzy that generated pictures for Paris and Brussels, and the host itself for Dijon. Jewish authorship lingered about the Dijon host as an incised mark. "Tradition bears that he was a Jew" Boulier whispered in italicized parentheses in the 17th century.[187] Paris and Brussels displayed their hosts in Jewish property Christianized for that purpose. Dijon's host was in the Sainte-Chapelle of the Burgundian dukes that passed to the French monarchy after 1477.

The Paris and Brussels hosts, after a period of suppression, were revived in the 19th century before their material disappearance. The Dijon host was transferred to another church in 1792, where in 1794 it was destroyed together with its ostensorium. Unlike the other hosts, its story of origin was amplified in retrospect. A report given at the 10th International Eucharistic Congress in 1897 attributed the damage to the (no longer existent) Dijon host to an Italian Jew, who was executed after his deeds were discovered.[188] The author of that report also held the 450 year preservation of the Dijon host to be an even greater miracle than its bleeding. For the previous 100 years the only trace of the Dijon host had been the many prints and paintings, which did attest to its preservation.

With the erasure of the Dijon host came the end of the system of complements and oppositions that existed among it, the Paris and Brussels hosts. There was freedom to extend its story of origin during a time when other Eucharistic miracles with anti-Judaic stories were being revived. In the 20th century, when such stories were suppressed and relegated to the history of Jewish-Christian relations, there was freedom to invent an entirely new story of the Dijon host's origins.

According to this version a woman in 1430 Monaco purchased a used ostensorium and tried to pry out the host with a knife, causing it to bleed in the image-making manner.[189] This is strictly a web-based version. The faint presence of a Jew in the making of the now image-only Dijon host has called for his replacement by someone more salvage-conscious, in keeping with the times.

Notes

[162] Bério (1999: 235-37). The *exemplum* had been extracted by another priest for a collection found in Bibliotheque Nationale Latin ms. 16482 1-38va.

[163] Marmursztejn (2001: 51; 57). Latin original and French translation of *Quodlibet* XIV, 15. Bibliotheque Nationale Latin ms. 15358.

[164] Rodríguez Barral (2009: 200-01). The retablo is now in the Museu Nacional d'Art de Catalunya.

[165] Baron (1967: 173); Rubin (1999: 110) give contrasting views of the affair.

[166] Rodríguez Barral (2009: 187n179); de Espina (1487: Liber 3, Consideratio 9)
[167] Ydens (1605)
[168] de Cafmeyer (1720)
[169] Griffet, et al. (1770)
[170] Kumler (2011: 188)
[171] A brochure printed by the Belgian *Imprimerie Nationale* in 1790 gives details of the hiding of the hosts.
[172] Smet (1839: 140). Wine spilled on the corporal cloth during a service at Notre Dame de la Chapelle reportedly turned to blood.
[173] Liber (1874: 8-9); Navez (1790)
[174] Bruyn (1820: 24)
[175] Rahlenbeek (1870); Liber (1874) originally published in 1870 in the *Revue de Belgique*. Contains an appendix with transcriptions of critical texts and a thorough epigraphic analysis questioned by later writers.
[176] Le Fèvre and Praem (1953: 395;398)
[177] Le Fèvre (1931)
[178] Academy (1897: 776). The compiler of the list is the antiquary Joseph Victor Le Clerc.
[179] Boulier (1Ac646: 18). The Latin text is less expansive.
[180] Kumler (2011: 186)
[181] Wieck (2007a: 386n4)
[182] *Histoire de la sainte hostie conservée à la sainte chapelle du roi à Dijon, 1739: frontispiece.* d'Arbaumont (1863: Plate V)
[183] Izbicki (2010: 229-30). The Hours of Mary of Burgundy; Ogier Benigne Book of Hours; British Library MS 31240 and the manuscript noted in fn22. Wieck (2007b) surveys more examples, not all with the texts.
[184] Original text and painting of the host with crown in the John Work Garrett Library of the Johns Hopkins University Library. http://digitalassets.lib.berkeley.edu/ds/jhopkins/images/MdBJ-G.0000199D.jpg
[185] Merback (2012: 210)
[186] Roy (1903: 446)
[187] Boulier (1649: 20)
[188] Voillery (1898: 393-94)
[189] Only online at www.therealpresence.org/eucharst/mir/english_pdf/**Dijon**.pdf

12.
The Mystery Plays

The nine lessons of the miracle were recited annually as part of the Office of Reparation on the Sunday after Easter in the Chapel of the Miracle from early in the 14th century, and in both the Chapel become the Church of the Billettes, and St. Jean-en-Grève every Thursday from the mid-14th century onward.[190] Camille Salatko Petryszcze observed that "the monotonous reading of the offices and the immobilized images on the walls of the churches" had been the only representation of the miracle. Preachers strained for drama never realized in their readings, and the processions that accompanied the feast of the miracle were an invitation to public display.

What may have been enactments of the miracle were documented a few times in association with the Eastertime processions in Paris. Based on internal evidence of a 16th century text of the play, these enactments were authored or commissioned by members of the confraternity of the miracle.[191]

A Paris bourgeois noted in his journal entry on the May 15, 1444 procession that after the sacred relics a Jew passed bound on a cart as if being led to be burned, followed by the justice with his wife and children, and there were scaffolds set up for "very feeling mysteries."[192] On January 29, 1534 the records of the Hotel de Ville recount a platform set up at the end of the bridge of Notre Dame (across the Seine at the Place de Grève) where a number of very fine stories were told, including that of the canivet used by a Jew to pierce the host later enshrined in St. Jean-en-Grève.

The knife, one of the relics of the miracle, came to the fore of the story for the writer of those lines, which suggests attention-getting stage action. This story may have been a performance of a mystery play already in print. Between 1512 and 1519 and again between 1530 and 1537 the Paris press of Veuve Trepperel and its successor issued the text of *Le mistere de la saincte hostie*. Between 1547 and 1566 Jehan Bonfons, printer of his own Paris guides, produced a third edition of the same text with few modifications, *Le jeu et mystère de la saincte hostie, par personnages (The play and mystery of the blessed host, by characters)*. The word *jeu*, play, added to the title distinguishes it from its own earlier editions and from other religious dramas printed in the 15th-16th centuries. It is now theatre with a separate list of characters and a few stage directions. It almost has the form of a printed script.

Mystery plays were fashioned and transmitted orally and in writing to celebrate many different events with a place in the Christian liturgy and sacred calendar. They represented constant themes-the passion, death and resurrection of Christ, the machinations of demonic figures such as the Jew-while appealing to local and national loyalties with peculiar circumstances. Eucharistic miracles in which the host substituted for Christ were among the offerings. A miracle represented in one locale might take shape in other locales and languages through the medium of the Eucharist and its antagonists.

The mystery plays are known from manuscript and printed texts, and from accounts of performances, usually by observers rather than performers. Scholars of mystery plays have adduced some details from the written record, and there have been modern restagings. The plays were reenactments of events of transcendent significance bound to recur eternally more than they were dramatizations of past happenings.

They were meant to stimulate faith that might be flagging, like the miracles they often were made after. The shift to a theatre frame without forsaking the religious base meant that the entertainment purpose, always present, had become the guiding principle in performance. The plays were made to forward the interests of shrines, churches and religious organizations.

The displacement of violence in the readings of religious ritual and secular chronicles was (seemingly) restored to blood in the play of the holy sacrament.

The Bonfons edition has on the front page a woodcut that does not illustrate any scene in the play but conveys a redemptive message.[193] Christ is seated at a table set with plates, knives and bread, a man at his right, the chief secular authority, the Provost, and a woman at his left, Martine, the virtuous rescuer of the host.

On the floor before the table a woman grovels: the Evil Woman who bartered the host for her pawned gown. The hand gestures of Jesus, and the book he has closed under his arm, indicate that he is instructing the audience through the play, which should bring their repentance.

The Jew is not pictured in the front woodcut. In the play he is burned at the stake after having been refused (forced) baptism, and after being examined by inquisitors and declared a magician by the bishop. He dies clutching at his magic book, calling on the Devil and is fully consumed, soul and all, by the flames. The Jew's children and wife have been baptized; the Evil Woman is the only one left with a possibility of redemption. The play ends with her death while begging Christ to forgive her.

The Jew is named, Jacob Mousse, but only in one dialogue title, and the members of his family are given Christian names where their Jewish ones are not used. Sites specific to Paris are mentioned: St. Merry, St. Jean-en-Grève, St. Croix, the pig market where the Jew is burned. The "children of Paris" carry the report of the Jew's attack on the host related by his son, who with his mother and sister had tried to stop him and then left ("saved themselves") when his destructive rage reached a fever pitch.

The strophic language of the play is set in rhymed couplets declaimed by the 26 characters, making recitations or in dialogue with each other. Besides the two women, the Jew and his family, the street children, Paris bourgeois, inn host and hostess, ecclesiastical and secular officials, two male sergeants, *Maigredos* (Skinnyback) and *Affamé* (Famished) appear and utter a few lines at the time of the executions. They personify the hunger for punishment and the lust for vengeance soon to be satisfied. The characters remain static as they speak-they do not physically interact-but the Jew's family's descriptions of the host's bleeding, flight and transfiguration give ample room for stage effects, as does the Evil Woman's murder of her child ("The Evil Woman holds the likeness of a small child," reads the stage direction).

The words of the characters are concrete and transactional, always corresponding directly to action being carried out or planned. By repeating the words the actors project the deeds. The Evil Woman begins the play with her request to redeem her fine clothing which she has pawned with the Jew, whom she calls "Jacob." He will return the dress, which a stage direction indicates he holds out and examines, for 30 sols. His wife thinks it is worth more.

The Evil Woman does not have the money, or anything else of comparable worth, and pleads with the Jew to let her have the dress to go to Communion at church on Easter. At the culmination of their fairly long dialogue the Jew horrifies her by asking her to bring him the host. She says it is like the treason of Judas to bring him the body of Christ in payment of 30 sols. The Jew threatens to sell the dress if she doesn't agree. As she recoils, his wife says:

> How mad it is to be firm
> In your wicked, puny faith
> And receive the host in your mouth
> And with your tongue not touch it
> And place it afterward in your hand
> Where will you put it in your breast
> And hold it coming back all undetected

The woman (not wearing her gown) arrives at St. Merry greeted by Paris bourgeois, who praise her piety. She is given Communion by the priest, and next is back at the Jew's house exchanging the host for the gown. The wife has verbally summarized the woman's unseen progress in her abstraction of the host. The chief fear driving the drama, that the Eucharist itself has become an article of commerce, is succinctly sounded out.

The daughter of the Jew
Oh, Mother, how white and soft it is.
Let me have it a while.

The son of the Jew
And me, let me have it.
And, on my life, it is very pretty.
It is as white as an angel.

The wife of the Jew seeks the woman's dress
Speak low for your father.
If he hears you, you will be beaten.
Leave it there, put it down.
Your father will blame me.

The daughter of the Jew
And on my life you could never
See anything more beautiful.
Look brother: its color
Is finer than crystal.

The son of the Jew

Ah, you speak true.
There is nothing more beautiful in the world.
Ah, my sister,
We will be rich.

The dialogue of the brother and sister while their mother seeks the woman's dress is a grasping appreciation of the host's material splendor that culminates in the brother's final line making it clear that the apparent admiration of the host is wonder at how rich it will make them. The Jews have no values other than to negate good Christian values. They share this with the Evil Woman, who is awaiting her payment. Their father is a child- and wife-beater who will respond with anger if he hears them speak covetously about his new acquisition.

The Jew urges the Evil Woman to leave quickly once she has received her garments, lest the neighbors notice. She reciprocates as she leaves by warning the Jew not to draw outside attention to their business transaction. He declares that he will test if this is the god the Christians babble about, and calls for his family to gather around the table. There is no better time than the present to see what it is about the host that moves Christians, adds the Wife.

Canivet verbally poised over the host, the Jew says he will now know if this is human flesh as a virgin woman. What blasphemy, cries the Wife, by Mahomet, he really means it! Both daughter and son beg him not to carry out his plan, but he threatens to beat them if they do not silence themselves. He applies the bloody scourge, and the host bleeds from all sides.

The daughter of the Jew

Alas, my sweet father, I see
The blood flow from all sides.
And for God's sake do not kill him.
Your face is too fierce

The Jew growls in his rage as he knives, scourges, nails, lances, cuts, tries to burn and boil the host. He appeals to demonic forces to drive himself onward, and calls his wife and daughter whores when the urge him to stop. The dialogue and stage directions express the emotions of rage and pity for the host, and monitor the visible results of the Jew's drive. Why would he want to kill "such a child."

Takes the host and nails it with a nail to a panel, and the blood flows to the ground.

The knifing, hammering and stabbing are intended and pleaded against in the dialogue, and manifest in the stage directions as is the consequent bleeding. After the Jew tosses the host into the cauldron his Wife calls him a tyrant and a very perverse persecutor, and tells him to ask pardon for his deeds. The appearance of the crucifixion spurs the Jew to admit he is at fault, but it is too late. The Son and Daughter see their savior on the cross, are converted, and the Son curses his father. The Wife flees the house with the Daughter, leaving the Jew on his bed beside himself with anger and fear.

The good Christian woman Martine, about to enter the nearby church of Ste. Croix with some children to pray before the altar, learns from the Jew's son that the host is not in the monstrance but in the Jew's house. She enters (stage directions), makes the sign of the cross and the host leaps onto her plate. The Jew cries out from his bed that he is destroyed, that he didn't know when to stop or how to accomplish his wish. For tormenting the Son of Mary he will lose his life.

However else it might be taken
For this you see me clearly.
Empty the water of my cauldron.
What god is there? Made of what?
It is white, red or black.
And my house, green like a pear.
This is good for losing your mind!
I'll throw it into the toilet
In the rooms out back.
So that neither the deed
Nor its date can be known.

The Jew's deranged plan of concealment is foiled by Martine, who brings the host to the Priest at St. Jean-en-Grève, and initiates a chain of official response. While the priest places the host on the altar a bourgeois present brings word to the Provost, who pronounces it a miracle. Another bourgeois relates the trials of the host to the Bishop, who orders an official to summon an assembly of clerics. The Jew will burn for this.

Guided by the Jew's son ("this little fool of a Jew"), the Provost, a Bourgeois and a Sergeant enter the Jew's house. They discover the evidence of what the Jew has done: the bloody water, the bloody lance. "We will take of this wash," interjects one of the children who has come along.

If it please God who made all
For there is no holy water
That would be more blessed than this.

The Jew accuses the people who have entered his house of robbery and planning his murder. The two bourgeois then find the canivet and the cauldron, which they say will become a relic, to announce to the world that the miracle is authentic.

The Provost introduces the Jew's son and wife, the Bourgeois and the good Christian woman to the Bishop as witnesses of the crime. The Bishop asks the Jew to give his account. A woman "worse than a [female dog]" gave him a host to ransom her overdress. In order to see if the host is alive he subjected it to tests, and was convinced. Now he asks that the Bishop spare him and allow him to convert to Christianity, quoting in Latin the words of Christ: "I do not wish the death of a sinner, but that he convert and live." The Bishop asks the opinion of the others present.

The Provost
No, no, he should be sentenced to death.
This is nothing more than a strategy of escape.
He can do worse again
Than he did before.

The Bourgeois agrees but asks that the Children and Wife be baptized, which they accept, denouncing the father.

The Bishop exposits church dogma to the Jew's wife and children. On their assent he baptizes them and gives them Christian names. The Priest exhorts them to observe their faith

Do not be negligent
Who before your eyes have seen
The goodly miracle not at all a play (*jeu*)

Though this is a performance, the miracle actually happened.

The following section is set off by a title: the condemnation of the false Jew; how he was set afire and burned inside Paris walls at the pig market. The Bishop consults with an Official on the inquiry then sends a Sergeant to the university to bring the authorities and the Rector, and to the Provost to come with the Jew who has been imprisoned. The punning Provost in turn orders his two jailers, Maigredos (Skinnyback) and Affamé (Famished) to conduct the Jew to him. They roundly abuse the Jew as they bring him along.

Affamé
Come out! Let the gibbet
Be dressed with your accursed body!
Blast of hell! Let your soul
Be knit with a knot today!

Maigredos
Look! What a gross wicked man!
May his line be cursed!

Jacob Mousse, Jew
Many words you've said to me.
This wish that comes out:
I'll die according to high Jewish law,
Not yours.

The Jew is brought before the Bishop, Inquisitor and Provost. The Bishop asks him if this is the host. The Jew responds that it is-in 5 pieces. The Rector advises him to confess. Why not believe in Jesus? "I hold it all as fantasy. The devil with this rotten bread," returns the Jew. For all you did to the host, the Inquisitor asks, can't you see its power? The Jew's evocation of Jewish law causes the Bishop to condemn his "magic art." The Church says put an end to evil-doers. In answer to the Provost's blunt command to convert, the Jew says "Never." He will burn, the Provost responds, bring the Executioner. Maigredos goes to summon him, and he arrives ready.

The Jew calls out for his book as the Executioner builds the pyre around him. He is still defiant, denying the power of Jesus. The Provost, asserting that this is a chance to disprove the power of the Jew's magic, orders Affamé to fetch the book, which he quickly does. "Is this the book," the Provost asks the Jew.

Yes, it truly is.
This is it. Now I have no refuge.
O Devil, it seems I am catching fire.
Devils, devils, I burn and catch fire.
I catch fire, I burn on every side.
I am taken up in fire and in flame.
My body, my spirit and my soul
Burn and catch fire too ardently.
Devils come quickly
And carry me off at will.

The Jew full of evil arts is burned with his book, the Provost concludes. He and the two guards form a chorus of the end of the Jew. Cursed be his nation; his house will be made into a monastery. This is an exemplay story; the Jew has paid his dues.

Now the protagonist, the Evil Woman, returns to the stage. She announces her misfortune having sold the flesh of Jesus. She has left Paris and now seeks employment in a hostelry in Senlis. The Host and Hostess hire her because she will work for little pay. The Hostess warns her about Gillet, the Valet, but assigns him to show her around. [Seven years pass] The Woman finds herself pregnant, which the Hostess notices but the Woman denies.

Holding the figure of a small child, the Evil Woman says
Alas, I am a great martyr
How could I hide it
So that news of it will never be?
I think the Devil tells me
How I will now hide it.
Beneath a dung heap I will bury it.
I think no one will know.
It's done.

The Hostess asks her what happened to her large belly. The Woman denies she was pregnant, but the Hostess insists. The Woman asks her and the Host to help conceal the crime, but the Host doesn't want to be blamed for the deed and tells the Bailiff that the Woman served for seven years but has "come to an adventure" and killed the child. The Bailiff sends his sergeant to bring the Woman. Maigredos makes the arrest, and the Woman begs for the mercy of God. Affamé warns her not to lie. She makes her farewells to the Host and Hostess.

The Bailiff accuses the Evil Woman of killing and burying her newborn. The Woman assents and confesses to selling the Blessed Sacrament to the Jew, who was later burned in Paris. The Bailiff says he remembers the crime and pronounces the Woman equally culpable and deserving the same punishment as the Jew, and condemns her to burning. He calls for the Executioner. Maigredos tells the Executioner "You have to burn a woman. Bring your tools." The Executioner responds, "I'll make her grow teeth a foot long [become a skull]. No doubt about that." The Woman falls to her knees:

Oh, my Creator! Oh, my Redeemer!
Oh, my Savior! Jesus, my friend!
I cry out for mercy in this world.
Alas, I sold you to the cursed Jew.
This cruel crime, Oh sweet Jesus Christ!
My child murdered, for which I make repentance.
Having in you faith always
In your grand highness.

To which the Executioner replies, "I don't understand these fine points."

The Bailiff urges the Executioner to make haste. He advises the Evil Woman to think only of God. The Woman pleads with Jesus for mercy and in a Latin quote commends her soul to God. The Executioner says the sentence is carried out. The Bailiff makes a final statement.

Our execution is finished.
We have nothing else to do.
Each one goes about his business.
We ask Jesus the fruit of life
That is the true and sacred host
Of which one makes each Thursday of the year
In Paris at St. Jean-en-Grève
The Grand Solemnity of the Sacred Host.
Each woman with child is blessed
As are all people great and small.
Jesus give us paradise in the end.
Amen.

The play and mystery ends with this notice of the blessing of pregnant women at St. Jean-en-Grève during the weekly ceremony. Promoting this may explain the extension of the traditional plot of the miracle to include the woman's infanticide in Senlis.

The Evil Woman is the protagonist of the play. She initiates the action by seeking the restoration of her dress for the Easter church service, in order not to appear less grand than she feels she should. This introduces the theme of economic status which the broadening exchange economy has made achievable and tenuous. Her antagonist, the Jew, who is both named and unnamed, pressures the woman to pay back the loan for which the dress stands as collateral. He demands thirty sols, the amount of the loan, which the woman doesn't have, and he threatens to sell the dress his wife believes is worth more than that sum. The woman's status depends upon the Jew's willingness to accept something of equivalent worth for redemption of her property. After the woman brings up how her self-display at Communion on Easter will suffer if she is not properly (competitively) dressed the Jew asks her to bring him "her god."

His purpose, deplored by his wife, is to demonstrate that this is not a god at all. His has no belief system of his own, only an urge to discredit beliefs if it favors commerce. The Jew plans to make the host into an article of exchange and nothing more than that.[194] The woman cooperates and, stealthily abstracting the host from the sacrament of Communion, delivers it to the Jew, who completes the exchange by returning her dress. The Jew's wife further materializes the host by speculating on the method the woman must have used to conceal and transport it. His children are impressed by the precious appearance of the host and, seeing its value, desire it for themselves.

The Jew's increasingly furious sequence of armed attacks on the host, projecting the Passion of Christ, demonstrates its resistance to commodification by introducing the only supernatural (special effects) features into the play. The Jew only succeeds in leaving marks (blood, breaks) that can later be used to identify the host. His instruments are collected as relics. Ignoring the pleas and arguments of his wife and children that he stop, he induces the crucifixion from the boiling water, leading his son to give him away to Christian children in the street. Despite the Jew's plan of concealment, a devout woman rescues the host by sheltering it and transferring it with no hint of a commercial transaction to the church where it will be restored to public view.

The chain of secular and religious authorities is activated by the host's discovery. With the help of his son the Paris Provost and other officers enter his house where they find him in his bed, defiant and accusing them of robbery. The evidences of the miracle, the household tools the Jew used, are gathered; even the bloodied water in which it was boiled has become sacramental. The miracle is now over and must be memorialized by a judicial procedure. There must be reparation for the Jew's treatment of the host.

Brought before the Bishop, the Jew's family and the good woman serve as witnesses as the Jew explains his test of the host. The revelation that it is alive has caused him to seek conversion, which request the bishop submits to the secular officials. The Provost opposes conversion; he doubts the Jew's sincerity and believes he will repeat his actions or worse. The Bourgeois agrees but asks that the wife and children be allowed to covert. They assent to the doctrine the Bishop expounds and are baptized. A priest preaches to them about their responsibilities. Thus begins the next phase of the play, verification of the miracle through violence now directed against the Jew.

In the next section the Bishop summons a conclave from the university to sit in judgment of the Jew, who is brought before them by a pair of warders whose names signify the hunger for vengeance. Their prompts and buffets bring the Jew, named for the first and only time, to invoke Jewish law. The urgings and reasonings of the University Rector and the Inquisitor do not persuade the Jew to embrace Jesus and convert. His second invocation of Jewish law causes the Bishop to disparage his magic arts and put him in the hands of the secular authorities for execution. Conversion would not have saved his life, but it would in the view of the Christians at least save him from damnation.

The Jew calls out for his book as the Executioner builds the pyre around him. The book arrives but provides him with no protection as it is reduced to ash along with him, just as so many Talmudic texts were on the same Paris square. All that is known of Judaism in the play is a law and a book that do not help the Jew in this life or the next. The wife's invocation of Mahomet is one alien god name indiscriminately associated with Jews. The Provost and the jailers announce his end, body and soul, and the monastery that will be made of his house.

The Jew's attempt to commodify the host has only resulted in its becoming the charter for a ritual performance of the attempt, profitable to the performers. The Christians have taken over the Jew's possessions and business to their own sanctified profit. This in in the same vein as the kings who become the creditors of debtors owing loans to the Jews whose ledgers they have seized.

The Evil Woman does not escape inclusion in this business. She flees Paris and the trial of the Jew, a single woman who summarily is made pregnant by a servant at the hostelry where she works and rejects the shame of raising a child out of wedlock by killing the newborn and disposing of it ignominiously. Her employer detects her and she confesses that crime and the sale of the host, for both of which she is executed not by burning as a heretic, as the Jew was, but by hanging as a murderer. Her final pleas for divine mercy only reach the indifferent ears of the executioner. Her life's drama adds a category of people, expectant mothers, who will benefit from attending the weekly service of the miracle at St. Jean-en-Grève.

The play gained its local magnetism from the Paris landmarks woven into a novel cultic topography enacted regularly in religious ritual, a recognizable characterology and value system. The Jew's bloody rampage was an opportunity for acting and theatrical ingenuity which could be an object in itself.

Performances of the play or one like it in French cities are recorded as early as 1444, over 150 years after the events it dramatizes. By 1513, when a Metz bourgeois, Philippe de Vigneulles, attended a performance staged on a city plaza as part of Pentecost celebrations, the effects machinery (*secrets*) captured his attention, and at the same time lightened the moral onus of the play. de Vigneulles wrote in his daybook that the blood spurting from the host stabbed by the Jew was like the stream of piss curving up from a recumbent infant.[195] This dirtied and bloodied the Jew and the performer made a good show of it. The host flew up from his attempt to burn it in the fire, and spurted out more blood after he stabbed it with a blade. When he affixed it to a pillar with nails and lanced it with a spear so much blood poured out that the stage was covered. A radiant child appearing over the kettle of boiling water followed the Jew's final attempt to destroy the host. The burning at the stake of the Jew and of the repentant woman merited only a passing notice. The blood torrents stayed with de Vigneulles because they promoted a state of religious awe and antagonism against Jews, and as a stimulating diversion.

This play and the stirring stage work de Vigneulles describes were likely the source of the lasting imagery of the Paris host miracle. If this play or one very like it was being performed in Metz and Laval,[196] provincial towns at crossroads, the histrionics of the enraged (and caged) Jew left its imprint. The Rouen stained glass windows, the St. Jean-en-Grève tapestries and the paintings and postcards based on them, and a mid-18th century Paris print[197] all contain the same theatrical sequence of the Jew trying to dismantle the host.

The Jew pierces it with a lance

This section of the Paris play, the miracle itself, was the vehicle for its spread where other parts did not find an audience. The Croxton Play of the Sacrament has five Mohammed-worshiping Syrian Jews (again the prophet of Islam made into a Jewish divinity) torturing the host one of them, Jonathas, has purchased from a reluctant Christian, Aristorius, in an imaginary Spanish city.[198] The date is given as 1461. The characters of the evil Christian woman, her travails and final repentance, and that of the good Christian woman, are not present. Instead the focus is on the Jews, their explicit attempts to disprove transubstantiation, and their ultimate repentance and conversion. The torture sequence includes the elements of piercing, burning, and boiling resulting in massive bleeding with the added refinement of Jonathas' hand becoming attached to the host and being immersed in the boiling in oil just the same. After a quack doctor fails to provide any more than comic relief, Jesus appears and heals the Jews of their wounds and religion. The torture scenes would have played with a slapstick quality, but there is no record of the play ever having been performed in the East Anglia of its composition and language, and the text exists in only one manuscript copy. It did not have the pictorial resonance in England that *Le jeu et mystère de la saincte hostie* did in France.

One of the Italian plays of Jewish host profanation, *Uno miracolo del corpo di Cristo*, starts with a didactic message from an angel, then news of the Bolsena miracle and the institution of the *Corpus Domini* feast.[199] The Jew, named Manuel, obtains the host by offering to return the woman's *cioppa*, a dress gown she needs for the coming Easter, which her husband has pawned to pay gambling debts. He claims to need the host to heal his ailing son, but on receiving it from the woman he puts it on a pan over the fire and stabs it, releasing such a flood of blood that two officers of the king entering the shop think that a murder has been committed and rush to report it to the authorities.

A constable who enters the shop recognizes that the blood flows from the host. The King and the Bishop learn of the host's plight and go together to rescue it. The Jew, who does not accept conversion and denounces Christian beliefs, is burned. Thomas Aquinas appears to the King in a dream and conveys Christ's command to spare the woman, who begs forgiveness. The woman tells the king that she wants the money she received from the Jew to be used to build a temple called "The Boiling Savior." The Jews in town, including Joseph the Glutton and Joseph Squareballs, are brought into the court and beaten until they flee.

This play was performed, though there are no details about the staging. Bolsena, where a Eucharistic miracle took place in 1263, Thomas Aquinas and his Corpus Christi hymn *pange lingua* and the dedication of the temple constructed (not from the Jew's house, but with the money he gave the woman) and two references to "The Boiled God"(though the host isn't boiled in this play), and the absence of place specifics all make this play a catch-all for the Jew-tortured host miracle. The stabbing-lancing-burning-boiling fury of the Jew is concentrated in one act of tossing the host on a cooking pan and knifing it. In this one instance the blood on the floor gives the crime away, bringing retribution and rescue. The blood does not cry out as in the Cain and Abel story; it gives a sign of desecration and murder. The Jews suffer as a community.

This arrangement of themes is visible in a woodcut that accompanied the manuscript text in Rome's Biblioteca Corsini Incunabula. The woman redeems her coat from Manuel seated at his table to the left marking his ledger as his assistant hands over the pawned garment. On the right Manuel stands over the host in the pan on a tripod over the fire, dagger poised for a downward thrust while an assistant manages the long handle of the pan and another throws up his arms. The men are all dressed in *camicia*, doublet and hose in the manner of the time. They are marked as Jews by the round badge on the right breast. They are collectively singled out as sinners, usuers and committers of sacrilege, in the illustration as they are in the play. The blood has not yet begun to flow.

The Paris miracle was exported in the drama that brings the Eucharistic dogma in line with the ambitions of the Jews to increase their possessions even to include the body of Christ. This aspect of the play was most compatible with other miracles of the bleeding host passed to England and to Italy while other aspects were left behind. Not in service to promote a specific church and its related ceremonies, the play became generalized to faraway, mythic locales where the Jews pursue their all too transparent aims and provoke the wrath of God and the authorities.

Blood violently released from the deathless sacred body identifies the desecrator, and associates him with an entire community. It reaches the floor and marks the place of its release, but unlike the Bolsena altar stones the floor of the Jew's house does not become sacralized by the blood. There are no relics of blood falling on ordinary things in the world of this play, only a Jewish blood crime, like others imagined for the Jews and harshly punished. In the Italian play the moneylender's theft of the host and attempt to destroy it places his entire community at risk. Blood is confined to the Jews' locale, and the "boiled God" phrase is imported.

Notes

[190] Attested by papal bulls granting permission.

[191] Petit de Julleville (1880: 576)

[192] Petryszcze, n.113.

[193] This was the latest of the three known 16th century editions of the play. The previous edition also was prefaced by a woodcut, of a priest kneeling at the altar. Petryszcze mounted the transcribed 1512-19 Trepperel text alongside the 1547-66 Bonfons text in her online edition of the play. I also consulted a copy of the 1547-66 Bonfons text online in the original 16th century printing at gallica.bnf.fr.

[194] Goldstein (2004: 161-62)

[195] *"comme se ce fut ung enfant qui pissait"* de Vigneulles (1852: 244)

[196] "This year (1533) at Laval: The Blessed Host was played before the Cimitière Dieu the day of the Feste Dieu and the day of Saint Gervais (June 18 and 19)" *Annales et Chroniques* of Guillaume le Doyen quoted by Petit de Julleville (1880: 120)

[197] *Histoire miraculeuse de l'hostie outragé par un Juif l'an de grace 1290*. Collection Michel Hennin. Bibliothèque nationale de France. gallica.bnf.fr

[198] Sebastian, editor (2012)

[199] Newbigin (2009: 74-97) is the original Italian text, and Newbigin's translation into English is in the online collection *Early Italian Drama in English Translation*. http://english.cua.edu/faculty/drama/italian.cfm

13.

Predella

At around the same time that Antoninus and Fregoso were composing their written versions of the miracle and the mystery plays were being performed in France and Italy, Paolo Uccello painted the predella of an altar commissioned by the Confraternity of Corpus Domini of Urbino, Italy for their church in that city. Uccello worked on this strip of three double-sectioned paintings between 1465 and 1468. A large panel placed above it, the Communion of the Apostles by Joos van Ghent, completed the altar in 1474.

The subjects of main panel and predella, unusual in Renaissance painting, were occasioned by the commissioning confraternity's devotion to the Body of Christ. The unique painting dedicated to the miracle, and the form it took, were due to historic circumstances in Urbino at a time when interest in the Eucharistic miracle was reawakening.

The commission for the large panel was first offered to Piero della Francesca, who would have completed a perspective piece quite different from the late Gothic style of the Flemish painter. Uccello used a perspective in the individual sections of the predella that allows for the distortion possibly encountered viewing separate space constructions together. The history progresses horizontally from left to right without strain. The two parts of the altar were separated and the predella now is on exhibit in the Galleria Nazionale delle Marche in Urbino.

The first double section of the predella corresponds to the beginning scenes of the Italian mystery play and the woodcut that illustrates Biblioteca Corsini manuscript text. The Christian woman presents the Jew with the host shining atop a holder (she is not touching it) in exchange for payment (no garment is visible) at the counter of his shop. A set of shelves adjacent to the counting table holds a thick ledger placed at a slant, and nothing else. The Jew and the woman are the only people present. On the triangular flue projecting from the far wall of the shop a *scudo* (shield) with a *testa di moro* (Moor's head) is placed between an arms crest and the scorpion crest. These symbols used in heraldry were brought together to form imaginary family crests for the Jew, connoting his foreignness and perfidy. The thick metal-strapped door of the business room is visible edge on.

The right hand side of this first section is a cutaway of the interior of the Jew's house. He stands in the center of the floor looking toward the door as do his wife with infant clinging to her and weeping older girl slightly apart. In the distant perspective a pan on the fire under a flue emits a tangled leaping red stream that makes its way across the floor to a drain hole in the wall. Such a drain carried floor-cleansing water washes and cooking boilovers into the street but here the blood pouring out gives away the bloodletting inside.

Outside a group of soldiers in dark doublets are battering and jimmying the front door, their assault as much a source of the family's terror as the blood-spurting host. In the Biblioteca Corsini woodcut the Jew in the company of others is about to stab the host in the pan. In the predella he has already done so and the blood gushing onto a public thoroughfare has revealed his crime. The predella recalls the scene in texts and in the miracle play *Uno miracolo del corpo di Cristo* where the blood flow in the Jew's shop alerts the officers who have come for a loan.

In the next predella section a procession including the Pope in tiered tiara and holding a ciborium containing the host lines up behind a woman and the standard bearers to an altar where a priest is folding a corporal. Past the divider the woman stands beneath a small tree a ladder extending into its branches some lopped to clear a space for the hanging. Ropes dangle downward. A group of mounted soldiers faces toward her, one of them holding aloft a staff flying a pennant printed with the Roman S.P.Q.R. lettering. Soldiers on foot surround the woman shrouded all in black. Only one of them looks upward at an angel who hovers above them arm extended toward the woman.

The Jew and his entire family are tied together burning at a stake between two standing groups of soldiers. A soldier with bicolor leggings takes a bold stance. A Tuscan campagna unfolds in the rear perspective.

In the final scene, only found in this representation, the woman lies on a bier two demons grasping her legs and positioned to pull her suddenly while two angels in more stately stance hold open hands over the woman's head. In an angel's right hand is a pyx used to carry the host for Communion given away from the church. Over the woman's open mouth flutters the white body of the host.

The outpouring of the host's blood onto a public street is punished by the destruction of the Jew's entire family. The French original makes the exposure of the Jew's procurement of the host and sequential attack a slow, circuitous process, and his death the result of his resistance to repentance and conversion. The Italian form of the play had the exposure happen more quickly, in keeping with the international humanist account of the miracle.

The predella does not exhibit the communal beating of the play, but expands the Jew's lethal punishment to his entire family.

The greater emphasis on Jewish mendacity and sacrilege in the predella was the product of preaching against the growing population of Jews in Italian cities by itinerant Franciscans. Marilyn Aronberg Lavin connected the interests of the Confraternity that commissioned the altarpiece to Christian banks founded to give no-cost loans to the poor victimized by Jewish usurers.[200] The annual procession on the Corpus Domini feast day, evoked in Uccello's painting, required expenditure on candles that in part was subsidized by the Christian bank.

Ducal policy in Urbino was to accommodate the Jews and to prevent attacks upon them and their property.[201] The harshness of the punishment in the painting, the Jew's entire family burned, displaced onto fictive Jews communal anger that could not be visited on the Jews. The free flow of Christian blood out of the Jewish house and the resulting punishment directed against all its inhabitants was an imagery to encourage solidarity in the Urbino Christian community against the alien moneylenders. The same terms had been used to justify persecutions elsewhere.

The good Christian woman who retrieves the host in the miracle stories and the French play has no role in the predella. The pope himself in procession returns it to the altar standing behind a woman who may be a memory of her.

The woman who precipitates the action by the sale she makes to the Jew is the subject of two panels. The last section is an unusual representation of a common theme: the psychomachia, or struggle between good and evil for and in the human soul. As in the other sections of the predella a single moment is evoked. Either the host will enter the woman and she will gain absolution with the prospect of salvation or it will not and the demons will drag her off to hell.

The French play had reintroduced the evil Christian woman after the execution of the Jew and extended her culpability with the mortal sin of murder-infanticide. Her pleas for mercy as she is about to be hanged seem to be dismissed, so great are her crimes. In the Italian play she is spared death through the intervention of Christ's agent Thomas Aquinas, and devotes her ill got gains from the Jew to the foundation of the "boiled god" monastery where the Jew's house once stood. That much of the original Paris story returned to provide a good deed for the woman, who did not add the death of the illegitimate newborn to her burden.

The predella picture reset the eternity of the woman once again and though not a murderer she still hangs in the balance between salvation and damnation depending on the flight of the host. Unlike the severe punishment meted out to the Jews the end state of the woman in the predella does not seem to be a historic artifact of the era in Urbino, nor a means of introducing women's expected and contested social roles into the miracle. It is an exposition of doctrine in the manner of a theatre piece. What can shift the decision of divine forces in favor of or against a soul? The unbearable uncertainty of that moment on which a soul's eternity depends is grounded in an almost invisible floating wafer.

At least one piece of evidence from the painting itself suggests that a viewer tried to intervene.

The demons were partially scratched out, to weaken them in their contest with the angels for the woman's soul and in any other mischief they might be about.[202]

The predella was a restaging of the Paris miracle in a theatre of paint. Themes were added or dropped to meet the ideological requirements of its commissioning patrons, their own annual and periodic celebrations of the Holy Sacrament, and to achieve a singular dramatic tension.

Another Italian drama that drew upon the Paris miracle for a peculiar local effect was composed by Bernardo Cungi of Borgo San Sepolcro over a hundred years later, in 1578.[203] This brief excursion begins after the Jew has bought the host from a Christian, who then loses the money gambling and flees into the forest, becomes an unsuccessful highwayman only to be devoured in short order by a lion. This is witnessed by a group of Capuchin monks, as is the arrival in the forest of the Jew, who has left his house in order not to arouse suspicions when he stabs the host with a dagger the Christian also sold him. It sticks to his fingers when he tries to throw the host into a spring, then flits away and causes him to stab his own hand which becomes trapped between rocks. The only blood present is already mixed with the waters of the spring. The Jew repents, promises to be baptized and appeals to the Capuchins to pray to Christ for him. They ask Christ to "bring the Jew home."

This play quickly enacts several of the themes of the Paris miracle. A Christian sells the host to the Jew, who plans to test it and has a dagger. The host sticks to his hand and then flies away when he tries to toss it into already bloody water. He stabs his own hand, repents and asks to be baptized. There are some features-the male Christian host seller, the wilderness setting, the Capuchin monks-not present in any version. The Jew sees blood in the water though the host is not shown to bleed. No women appear in this play.

The play most resembles the Croxton Play of the Sacrament, in the sticking of the host to the hand, the conversion-healing of the Jew and the lack of women characters. By its brevity it seems to be a comic interlude. Little is known of the author, Bernardo Cungi. Vasari mentions two 16th century painters with the same surname, Lionardo and Battista Cungi, from Borgo San Sepolcro, which was within the domain of Florence. Vasari included Battista among the technical crew who assisted him constructing a scenic apparatus for a *commedia*. Battista and another Borgo San Sepolcro painter Christofano Gherardi were taken for Jewish, Vasari wrote, because Battista's eyes were prominent and Christofano's eye had a speck in it. A shoemaker who came to their dwelling to deliver shoes commissioned by the Jewish painter Dattero insisted they were Jewish, until Christofano dismissed him announcing, "Wait till you see how we paint like Christians."[204]

At least one Cungi family member from Borgo San Sepolcro constructed theatre machinery, and by the physiognomic criteria of 16th century Florence was taken for a Jew. Not every Jew wore the badge or lived in the quarters expected. Bernardo's play was meant to express the arbitrariness of Jewish identification in a society where Jews might slip out of their stigmatized role if there were no sure marks to distinguish them. The miracle could serve as a vessel for this change as well.

Notes

---

[200] Lavin (1967: 9-10)

[201] Katz (2008: 17-32)

[202] Gallagher and Greenblatt (2000: 95)

[203] *Rappresentatione d'un miracolo del Sagramento,* Italian text and translation by Nerida Newbigin in *Early Italian Drama in English Translation* http://english.cua.edu/faculty/drama/italian.cfm.

[204] Vasari (1792: 141-42; 144) Life of Christofano Gherardi

14.
Proof, Doubts and Symmetry

It took decades to construct the Paris miracle to seem to take place on one day in one place. As its initial form was developed in the consolidation of buildings, religious order, relics, services and processions it spread abroad by rumor and in writings which influenced the formation of other miracles that joined to make categories incorporating the original miracle. During the period from the Paris miracle (1290) to the Brussels miracle (1370) to the Dijon papal gift of a miraculous host (1433) a pattern dictated by the Paris miracle enabled the religio-political containment of Jewish populations through stories of attacks on the Eucharist.

The Jew's rage imagined and imaged in the Paris miracle was assumed to be motivated by the same animosity that had led to the Passion of Christ, and by a desire to demonstrate that the host was nothing more than a wafer: a heated round of torture combined with a rational test. The miracle is the consequence of not accepting the real presence on faith, of demanding tangible proof. The permanent heresy of the Jews, their resented material prosperity and the dogma of transubstantiation drive the story forward. The Jews must be forced to profess faith or they must be eliminated. On acceptance of the proof encapsulated in the relics and *imago* hangs the ability to master the Jews and assume control of their assets. The proximal fabulous of the host is always at hand ready to encompass other examples at variance with the received truth.

Acceptance of the proof depended upon the position of the believer in relation to the Jews and their assets. The mediators in the miracle narrative-the Christian women in Paris, the wavering converts in Brussels, the shadowy Jew of Dijon, the confraternity of Urbino-are both inside and outside the charmed circle of compelled belief. They both disregard and embrace the miracle. Doubt is built into the miracle itself. The first printed critiques of the miracle came from people similarly positioned in the historical world of Western Europe. These positions developed by the 18th century.

The Calvinist clergyman Jacques Basnage de Beauval was introduced early as the author of a challenge to the miracle that precipitated a written history of the Billettes. He was the eldest son and heir of a lawyer and landowner in Rouen. The revocation of the Edict of Nantes in October, 1685 made it discrete for him to leave a France no longer guaranteeing the safety of Protestants and take refuge in Holland, where after a period as a pensionary he was appointed pastor at the Walloon church in Leiden. Basnage's exile was not a complete separation from his home country. He served as a diplomat in negotiations between the government of Louis XIV and Protestant powers, and for this purpose he returned to France several times with or without official leave.

Basnage was a prolific author of multi-volume religious histories, of the Christian churches and of the Jews. The promotion of Eucharistic miracles to support the real presence had been frowned upon by Christian theologians, including Thomas Aquinas, from the mid-14th century onward as opportunities for the unscrupulous to debase the Blessed Sacrament for gain.[205] Basnage wrote of the Paris miracle in this tradition, with a further strain of skepticism about the miracle itself. "The reader is fully at liberty to reject these fabulous miracles, but they figure too often in the History of the Jews to pass over them completely in silence."[206]

The church of St. Eloi in Basnage's home city of Rouen held a series of stained glass windows dated 1540-50 that illustrated phases of the Paris miracle.[207] The author did not refer to them in his account but cited the Latin universal chronicle compiled by the 15th century jurist Johannes Nauclerus.[208] In this chronicle and Basnage's retelling the Jew offers the Christian woman her pawned dress for Easter Sunday in exchange for "the Body of Christ." He throws the host into boiling water, slashes it with a sword, causing it to bleed. Christians arriving at his shop to borrow money see the host leap from the boiling water and fly. The Jew's property is confiscated and the church of Saint-Sauveur is constructed from his house. Basnage does not include the burning of the Jew and the processional enshrinement of the host mentioned in Nauclerus' chronicle. He emphasized using a presumed miracle to take Jewish property.

A similar miracle that took place in Paris fifteen years after the first spurred the expulsion of the Jews from France. There were not as many Jews as the chroniclers claim. The Jew purchased a host from a Christian woman and threw it into a cauldron of boiling water. This time a child of great beauty appeared above the water and eluded the Jew who chased him around the cauldron with a knife. The Jew's own children ran to tell their mother and she opened the house to outsiders. The child disappeared when the people and clergy entered, but the host remained, and the bishop came running when word reached him. The condemned Jew's Talmud was burned with him in flames all the hotter for its presence.

When they learned of this the population of Paris rose up and besieged the king until he acted to expel the Jews. The fugitives were allowed to leave with their clothes and enough money for the passage. They fled to England, or converted and remained in French towns. The pope, when consulted by the Queen, recommended that a moral employment of the gains from confiscating the Jews' property would be to conduct a holy war, thus masking avarice with religion.

Basnage cites several chronicles as sources for this sequence of events. The continuation of the chronicle by Cardinal Baronius[209], Villani and others provide the familiar outline, but the Jew chasing the child around the cauldron, the tattletale children, the burnt book named Talmud and the condition of the exiled Jews have their unique origin in the third book of the *Fortalitium Fidei* of Alphonso de Espina. The Protestant historian admits bewilderment in finding the Jew's 1290 host pursuit used to justify the expulsion of the entire Jewish community of France sixteen years later. Ill coordinated accounts given by different chroniclers have led him to suspect that this a fable malleable to the purpose of a greedy monarch and his clerical enablers. This makes it unnecessary for him to question the veracity of the astonishing host behavior.

Basnage's exposé stung the keepers of the miracle through the layered volumes of his history. His is the first name the Carmelite Theodoric de S. René abjures in the Preface to his grand compilation of miracle proofs.[210] He has gathered these proofs together in the face of the derision "Minister Basnage" conducts, to keep uninformed Catholics from being misled by the mockery. He leaves it as a twice-told tale with variations and moves on to other fables of Jewish perfidy.

Further in his *Remarques*, S. René engages with Basnage's objections to the miracle. Like other host miracles it is a fable, Basnage claims, which only have been heard since the promulgation of the doctrine of transubstantiation in the 13th century. Why did the Jews want to profane the host? Basnage asks. It didn't benefit them and certainly exposed them to harm. The Protestant repeated the history of the miracle "impertinently," the better to deny the real presence of Christ in the host.

S.René's rebuttal confronts Basnage with his failure to examine the proofs readily in view. Host miracles are not all new. They go back to the early history of the church. The Carmelite cites a single example. There always have been complaints against the Jews abusing the Holy Sacrament, with a passion that gave them little latitude for reflective caution. What is "impertinent" about the miracle? Here S. René rolls out the list of chroniclers and recounters from Villani to Spondanus and the more recent Moreri.

To Basnage's associating disparate miracle accounts with the venal interests of monarchs S. René only asserts that all the authors writing on the miracle concur with each other. S. René rehearses the disjuncture between the historical view and the spiritual view of events and gives the spiritual view pride of place. Variations in reportage are not so important as the underlying undeniable truth.

The Paris miracle was unique and yet it was one of several closely resembling it or one of many manifesting the Body of Christ in the Blessed Sacrament. One of these contentions was asserted against the others, or in support of them. Whether the multiplicity of host miracles was the result of the spread of the same story taking on local colors, or a sign of an underlying truth asserting itself in many different places was the driving question. The defenders of the miracle were tripped up by the number of miracles in the category to which it belonged.

The Jesuit Claude-François Nonnotte identified himself only as the author of the *Erreurs de Voltaire* on the title pages of his multi-volume *Dictionnaire philosophique de la religion* (1772). In the long entry on miracles he cites as evidence of the truth of miracles the processions of the miraculous host of Dijon, which bled after being pierced with a canif (he doesn't mention the Jew) and the miraculous host of Dôle, which survived the flames intact.[212] Processions celebrating the host were themselves sufficient proof of the miracle.

His chosen antagonist Voltaire recurred to this citation in a historic commentary. Nonnotte did not show any signs of knowing that there were over sixty towns in which Jews had knifed hosts and caused them to bleed.[213] The miracle of the Billettes in Paris was one of these. Fourteen years earlier (1762) on a visit to Brussels he had heard the song:[214]

Rejoice, good Christians, in the punishment
Of the vile Jew called Jonathan
Who had on the altar, with great malice,
Murdered the Most Holy Sacrament

These were not innocent miracles, as Nonnotte pretended, happening by the grace of God for the edification of the people. They were replicated instances of sacrilege attributed to the Jews who were punished to the rejoicing of the crowd. Voltaire did not question the happenstance of the miracle. It was enough to point out that there were many, and they resembled each other in the role of the Jews, which resemblance their believers did not acknowledge. A few similar miracles might be God's grace working in the same way; so many miracles with the same outcome seem more like human transmission of stories than divine intervention in human affairs.

After a distraught look at blood libels, a Chinese sojourner in Paris, Sioeu-Tcheou, continues a letter to his home country correspondent Yn-Che-Chan epitomizing his reaction to an episode of host abuse: "You would have to be-I'm not saying an imbecile-but at least obtuse to believe in a fable like this."[215]

Both writer and recipient were personas of Jean-Baptiste de Boyer, Marquis d'Argens (1704-71) in his *Lettres chinoises* (1739-40). The episode, supposedly set down by Thomas, Patriarch of Barbarie, is the de Espina miracle variant, wherein the Jew throws the host into boiling oil only to have it transformed into a beautiful boy he chases around the cauldron with a knife. His children cry out, the people come and the Jew is burned with his Talmud. This variant is readapted to the Paris miracle with the introduction of Paris locales.

Sioeu-Tcheou, a civilized stranger in a strange land and a literary device of the free-thinking marquis, objects to the fable on the grounds of human character and plausibility. If a host actually became a child the Jew would be paralyzed with mortal terror. He hardly would be in a frame of mind to chase a lively child around a cauldron of boiling oil. Jews understand the host to be made of water and grain. Why plunge it into boiling oil?

> Is it natural for the Jew to perform such an action before his children? Is it natural
> that they would make this marvel public when keeping it secret was a matter of life
> or death? I repeat, you would have to be obtuse to place faith in fables like this.

For the first time a writer asked the audience of the miracle story to consider that the Jew's behavior in the story was contrary to nature. That is not how human beings such as Jews can be expected to respond. The Confucian Yn-Che-Chan could nod sagaciously on reading this, as could d'Argens' fellow *philosophe* Voltaire, who admired *Lettres chinoises*. Humanizing the Jew foregrounded the made-to-order distortions in his character that only someone not quite an imbecile would let pass.

d'Argens, the descendant of a line of jurists in the regional parlement, was the heir to an estate in Aix-en-Provence until his father disowned him for his vocal criticisms of the Catholic Church. He removed to Holland, where his books could be published and distributed abroad. *Lettres chinoises* coincided with *Lettres juives* (*Jewish letters*, 1738-42), and like them were in the literary tradition of an intelligent, cultivated outsider commenting on the peculiarities and injustices of European culture to international correspondents. d'Argens did not himself convert to Protestantism, and kept a commentator's distance from religion in general. *Lettres chinoises* was translated into English within a year of its publication, and was reprinted in augmented editions during d'Argens' lifetime.

From the first edition onward, Letter 123 continues with the Jew-chasing-the-child version of the miracle (no longer situated in Paris) to engage in a review of host abuse stories. A further dimension is added: d'Argens' Chinese surrogate sees all of these stories, like the blood libels, as ploys developed by clerics and rulers to take advantage of the Jews. He uses contrasting sources to demonstrate this.

The explicit criticisms of the Paris miracle equate it with others all fabricated to make the Jews seem inhuman and unyielding, deserving to have their property confiscated and their lives forfeit if they fail to convert. This grouping of the miracles had been a long time in the making. The repeated proofs made room for doubt.

d'Argens instances Simone Maioli (1520-97), the Bishop of Volture in Italy, who included several stories of host abuse by Jews in the *De perfidia iudaeorum* (On the perfidy of Jews) section of his *Dies caniculares* (*Dog days*, 1597).[216] Unable to pierce and break the host with his knife, Salomon dares it to show that it is the true God. The host splits into three pieces with bloodied edges. Jacob does cause the host to bleed with his stabs, staining the wooden table so indelibly that he has to cut it apart. Majer presents the host to his daughter-in-law on her wedding day to his son before he and other Jews set upon it with daggers.

These fables gave the authorities of Brandenburg an excuse to seize the Jews' property and to condemn to the fire thirty-eight Jews despite their earnest protests that they were innocent of wrongdoing. Maioli wrote that he would not believe the Jews' response if had not seen it with his own eyes. On hearing their sentence the Jews began to laugh, and raised their arms in a sign of joy. For Maioli, however, this meant that on being consumed by the flames they rendered their souls to the devil. "Cruel, pestiferous, blind, malicious, obstinate, slanderous Jews" Maioli calls them,[217] using words often applied to Jews, in a passage that d'Argens doesn't quote. The Italian bishop judges only evil and resistance to the true faith in the Jews d'Argens finds firm and unwavering by Maioli's own account.

The Jews' steadfast denials in the face of persecution and damnation renders needless any questioning of the miracle of the host. Their laughter before doom, bewildering and disgraceful to their persecutors, underlines their firmness. d'Argens' final example "makes the hair stand on end."

His Chinese correspondent gives a French translation and the Latin original in a footnote of a passage from *Historia Reformationis Polonicae* (*History of the Polish Reformation*, 1685) by Stanisław Lubieniecki.

Lubieniecki (1623-75) was a Polish theologian and astronomer of the Socinian persuasion. He was a follower of the Italian religious reformer Fausto Sozzini, who taught an anti-Trinitarian theology, and he was a member of the Protestant community, the Polish Brethren. His posthumously published *Historia* was especially sensitive to the moral bases of rifts in the Roman Catholic Church and among Protestants.

The passage from the *Historia* in Letter 123 is on a Catholic churchman's invention of a host miracle to serve a purpose.[218] A papal nuncio in Poland, Aloysius Lipomano,[219] beset by the success of the Protestants and the doubt being cast on the mystery of transubstantiation, sought a way to strike terror into the hearts of those considering separation from the Roman Communion.

Lipomano hit upon the widely disliked and defenseless Jews as the most likely means. He arrested three Jewish men and a Christian woman named Dorothea. He suborned witnesses with cash payments to say that Dorothea had taken Communion and delivered the host to the Jews, who drew blood from it with needles. The blood was collected in a vial to be used to treat the wound of circumcision. Lipomano thus built an accusation that combined host abuse and the blood libel without needing to prove that a Christian child had been abducted to supply the blood.

Armed with an order from the sovereign, he had them condemned to burn. As they were being readied for the fire they protested their innocence to each of the charges, and declared that they do not believe that the host is the body and blood of Christ or that the Messiah is a god but rather that he is the anointed of God and an envoy. They said they had no need of blood. The infuriated Lipomano acted to prevent the accused from persuading the people that they were telling the truth. He had molten lead poured down their throats to assure their silence as the fires rose around them.

The king was enraged against Lipomano when he learned of the horrors unleashed in his name. "The anger of the king did not restore life to the Jews, but it served to make known to all of Europe the case one should make of the criminal imputations on which the Jews were so often persecuted." The blood libel and host abuse allegations claimed to be miraculous should be scrutinized before Jews were burned.

A miracle story like this was usually told up close, as a sacred history which God controls. In d'Argens' retelling of Lubieniecki's narrative through his Chinese traveler the frame is widened to make the chief witness into an actor. To Lubieniecki and other ecclesiastics Lipomano's prosecution of the Jews serves the interests of the Church by issuing a warning against apostasy. This is what you lose communion with if you discard the faith.

The bleeding of the host is not a manifestation of doctrine but a natural fact the Jews want to utilize to heal the results of their circumcision ritual. They pierce the host not to abuse it and disprove that it is the Body of Christ, as in the Paris miracle story and its counterparts. They want to use Christ's blood for their own selfish purposes. Lipomano had used this accusation to obtain the writ of the secular authorities, allowing him to silence and kill the Jews.

This is the final variant of the miracle story, its viscera exposed three narrators deep. Rather than entertainment, which it became in the stage bloodied "plays" of the 16th century, it is a device to keep power in the hands of the Catholic priests at the expense of innocent Jews. As Sioeu-Tcheou concludes his letter, "little is lacking that I would want not to be born human, and so shameful as to resemble certain Europeans, that I might wish to be born the vilest brute creature."

In the next *lettre chinoise* Sioeu-Tcheou determines to search Jewish customs for what makes the Jews so hated by Europeans. The customs were not the ritual sacrifice of children or the theft and abuse of hosts.

d'Argens' critique was a sign that the miracle had reached information phase lock in Europe. Its workings, the power struggle between religious and secular authorities, the clinging expulsions of the Jews, the useful incredibility of the real presence, were as visible as they ever were going to be. A small literate elite traded in revealing the miracle's inside relations by manipulating them for their own benefit using the growing variety of discourses available, from rigid belief to outright cynicism.

Removed, disbelieving narratives of miracles that made them out to be fabrications for gain usually applied to miracles in general, with perhaps a mention of the Paris miracle or others derived from it. They were countered by assertions of belief in the transcendent truth of miracles in numerous faith versus irreligion controversies. Truth and falsehood became poles of a field with no stable center.

The Paris miracle appeared in a few universal histories as a primary event in God's dispensation. The late 17th century saw the arrival of Paris histories in which the miracle was treated as an event at the origin of institutions and relics. Matter-of-fact statements of the miracle placed it among other events mundane and miraculous in the making of the city. Stating the miracle in this way, with or without substantiating documentation from earlier periods, made it an article of faith and a story told about buildings and people of an early period. Presentations of the miracle preserved its faith and fable quality by itself and for inclusion among other miracles.

The editor of a collection of the letters of St. François de Sales added a set of documentary proofs of the Dijon host miracle as an appendix to a brief letter of the saint which mentions his mother's thwarted wish to attend a devotion of the Dijon host.[220] At the end of the Dijon documentation he appends a paragraph on the miraculous host of Paris as another example of survival and the continuing devotion of the faithful perpetuated by religious orders. The proofs of one miracle carry over to another, and the saint's mere mention of the Dijon host triggered a history that includes them both.

This history is a tradition examined and verified in Jean-Baptiste Renou de Chevigné's *Recherches critiques, historiques et topographiques sur la ville de Paris (Critical, historical and topographic researches on the city of Paris,* 1773). This multi-volume study divides the old center of Paris into *quartiers,* the eleventh of which is *La Grève,* where the Carmes Billettes were established.[221]

> A constant tradition, founded on the testimony of contemporary Authors, the admissions of the Jew, and the most authentic records that certified the miracle, do not allow any doubt. It happened Easter Day, 2 April of the year 1290. Our Historians, in accord on all these deeds, differ among themselves on what followed these events.

Renou affirms the consolidated tradition of the miracle with as much certainty as St. Francis de Sales' editor or Theodoric de S. René, yet also recognizes that the record is disputed among historians when the outcome is reached. He spends the following pages passing through named accounts beginning with the *Chroniques de St. Denis* and Corrozet's 16th century antiquarian opus, in search of what occurred when human agency took over after the divine had acted. Renou (1710-80) was the king's cartographer charged with laying out the official map of the monarch's domain in space and in time. The Paris miracle was pinpointed and flickering in place.

The 500th anniversary of the institution of the procession and adoration of the Blessed Sacrament, Fête Dieu, in Liège, France was marked in 1746 by the publication of the history of the institution by the Jesuit Jean Bertholet. This was not a defense of the real presence, Bertholet stated at the beginning, but of how the annual feast was instituted. The bishop of Liège was inspired by the visions received by a local woman to initiate the celebration, which was expanded to the entire Church in 1264 by papal bull after the Bolsena Eucharistic miracle. The Paris miracle took place not long afterward, and Fête Dieu was on the annual calendar for the Thursday after Quasimodo, the day of the St. Jean-en-Grève celebration of the Paris miracle.

Bertholet brought the Paris miracle together with other host miracles in a later book of his history added at the urging of friends. His brief account of the Paris miracle follows Léon de St. Jean's 1664 *Histoire* with some modifications.[222] Léon's Christian woman on receiving the host at Communion places it in a handkerchief for delivery to the Jew; Bertholet's Christian woman spits it out after receiving it. For Léon the Jew is "the cruel enemy of Jesus Christ" who has the body of our Lord in his power, does not see the species within the host and, quoted speaking his wrath, takes up the knife. Bertholet wrote of the same episode, "As soon as this cruel enemy of the Christian Religion had the Body of Our Lord Jesus Christ in his power, he took the knife, put the Host on a table and pierced it with several strikes."

Bertholet omits Léon's reference to the Jew's blind spiritual state and other deficiencies in favor of action, which he maintains through the entire section. He places the Paris miracle with other miracles in the context of the ceremony of Fête Dieu, the Adoration of the Blessed Sacrament, plainly visible in an engraving that precedes the text.

Adoration du St. Sacrament.
Miracles 1. à Bruxelles. 2. St. Hildeprand. 3. de Paris.
4. d'Amsterdam.

In the center the host is in an ostensorium on an altar engraved with the christogram IHS. Both male and female clergy kneel on the altar steps, heading a crowd of kneeling laypeople on both sides and in the front with backs to the viewer. Prayer beads dangling from the hand of a girl signifies the prayer of the adoration. Vignettes of the four miracles are numbered in the four corners of the illustration. On the lower left the crucified Christ emerges from a cauldron over a fire while a woman kneels before it and a bent, black-clad figure, probably the Jew marked by the dog racing at his feet, stoops with his hands raised. The Brussels miracle on the upper right is the Jews gathered at the table knifing the hosts. The two on the right, Herkenrode and Amsterdam, are miracles of the host bleeding when touched by a layperson and surviving fire.

This is the Paris miracle as an instance of the adoration that surrounds Fête Dieu on all sides. A practice of formal adoration had been instituted for the miracle. Printed memorial brochures record a "miraculous and royal adoration of the Most Blessed Sacrament of the Altar" held in 1604 and 1718 at the Chapel of the Billettes in Paris.[223] This was not the miraculous host, which was kept at St. Jean-en-Grève, but an adoration of the host in the place of the miracle attended by members of the royal family.

Making the miracle into a performance of an institution that existed apart from it and shared its subject was carried forward with its inclusion in Bertholet's history. The qualities of its story and services that could be transported into any context was a sign that it had attained staying power apart from its personnel, architecture, even its relics, which it would outlast.

Notes

[205] Macy (2012: 395)

[206] Basnage (1707: 1817)

[207] Listed in the 19th century catalogue of the Rouen Musée des Antiquités, and still on exhibit there today. Photos and study at Des traces de l'antisémitisme médiéval à Rouen, https://pierrickauger.wordpress.com/2014/01/30/des-traces-de-lanti-Semitisme-medieval-a-rouen

[208] Nauclerus (1614: 2,975). The Paris miracle is the very first event Nauclerus describes for Generation 44 (since the Creation), the year 1290. Excerpted in Chapter 4 Selection 4-3.

[209] Spondanus (1612: 416)

[210] S. René (1725: 1, Preface and 434-42)

[212] Nonnotte (1772: 52)

[213] Voltaire (1832: 396-97)

[214] d'Argens (1838: 236) gives a slight variation of the same song.

[215] d'Argens (1769: 65-66)

[216] d'Argens (1769: 67-68); Latin original Maioli (1609: 36-8). d'Argens referred to the French translation, Les jours caniculaires.

[217] Maioli (1609: 37) "iudaei crudeles, pestiferi, caeca, malitiosi, pertinaces, inverucundi"

[218] d'Argens (1769: 70-74)

[219] Lipomano (1500-59), a Venetian priest and later the Bishop of Verona, was the author of a set of saints' lives composed as anti-Protestant polemics. In words not quoted by d'Argens, Lubieniecki (1685:76) denounces him as "cruel" and born of an unknown father.

[220] de Sales (1758: 574-90) note to letter 71, to Mlle de Villiers, March 24, 1605.

[221] Renou de Chevigné (1773: onzième quartier, 13)

[222] Bertholet (1746: 256-68). Bertholet cites Léon's book by title at the end of the section.

[223] "A whole literature on this miracle…"

(1) Toute une littérature sur ce miracle. Cf. l'*Adoration miraculeuse et royale du Très Saint-Sacrement de l'Autel dans l'église des R. R. P. P. Carmes du couvent du très Saint-Sacrement des Billettes de Paris, pour faire amende honorable à Jésus-Christ de l'outrage commis au très Saint-Sacrement de l'Autel par un juif dans les caves de ce lieu…* Paris, 1714. La 1ʳᵉ édition est de 1665. Le titre du frontispice est aussi à retenir : *Le sacrifice de la Croix représenté en l'Eucharistie par l'hostie miraculeuse de Paris.*

Bremond (1932: 220)

15.
Revolution

Bertholet's list of conserved relics of the Paris miracle included the knife, the cauldron, the lance and the vessel in which the host came to rest "and other perpetual marks of this second Passion of our Savior."[224] The entry on the Paris miracle in the "corrected" third edition of his book one hundred years later (1846) did not list these objects.[225] The annual service of the miracle at St. Jean-en-Grève on the octave of Fête Dieu was still celebrated in 1846, according to Bertholet's history, though St. Jean-en-Grève itself no longer existed then. This was not noted.

This discontinuity and mistaken continuity reflected the effects of the French Revolution on stories and institutions. The miracle passed through the turbulent final years of the 18th century outlasting the destruction and loss of some of the personnel and material that had anchored it. Its consolidated story, now an artifact itself, also made the transition detached from the matter and ceremony, to which it later became reattached.

The National Constituent Assembly secularized church property by a series of acts in November-December, 1789. The government operating as a constitutional monarchy with an elected legislature replaced the Catholic Church as the largest property owner in France. Over the following year a series of legislative initiatives removed the clergy from their position as an estate of French society. Monastic vows were abolished on February 13, 1790, which released thousands of monks from the state of social death they had entered when they took the vows. The Civil Constitution of the Clergy of July 12 subordinated the Catholic Church to the government, completed the dissolution of the monasteries, and required all priests to take an oath of loyalty to the Civil Constitution. On October 8 of that year a census of religious by institution was mandated, and individuals were required to state whether they would continue to live communally, or reenter secular life.

The laws and implementing regulations affected monasteries, abbeys, and churches at a varying pace, with responses from the affected populations ranging from comradely compliance to outright revolt. A week after the monastic vows were abolished, Brother Cyrille, the prior of the Carmes Billettes, supplied the municipal administration with a count of those living in the convent.[226] There were 22 total: 13 priests, 3 clerics and 6 monks. He gave the full and religious names of four of them: he was Jean-Baptiste-Pierre Marquis; Father André, the sous-prior, was Charles-Pierre Nicolle.

Brother Cyrille also recorded the revenues of the convent. A total of 26,475 *livres* 15 *sols* 10 *deniers* –broken down into rents collected on houses and hostels inside and outside Paris, farmed land outside the city, and an array of feudal arrears and fees. The average of over 1200 *livres* annual revenue per Billette placed them among the relatively affluent, especially since they did not have the residential expenses that exacted a large portion of wages in the city. The typical manual laborer earned 320 *livres* for 230 working days by the end of the 18th century, housing not provided.[227]

The standard of living of the Billettes at the time of this account-making helps explain their reaction to the requirement that religious from divisions of the same order wanting to live communally gather in single designated *maisons de reunion* (houses of consolidation).[228] The Billettes and other Carmelites living under the Carmelite rule were expected to move into the house of the austere Discalced Carmelites on the Rue de Vaugirard.

Charles-Pierre Nicolle, now the prior of the Carmes Billettes, joined with ten others in his convent to compose a measured plea addressed to the department administrators.[229] The destination house, the Billettes wrote, was large and capacious as the Assembly required, but the cells for dwelling were too small to hold the *couchette*, table and chair indispensable to their living arrangements. The absence of chimneys in the cells would prevent them from having their customary fires. They requested larger rooms with chimneys and enough space for their furniture.

On moving to the new quarters the Billettes would face a shortage of the necessities of worship. The Discalced Carmelites have only two chalices for 30-40 priests, two ornaments of each color, no bell for assembly, no ostensorium, no censor, and no processional cross. They ask to be allowed to keep two chalices from their store of silverwork, a ciborium to bring the host to the sick, songbooks for chants, a bell, a soleil or ostensorium, a processional cross and candles for the altar. If granted these concessions they were prepared to set an example of submission before the law.

The concessions were not granted. The state archives contain entries describing the cataloguing of the Billettes' library (May 13, 1791) and a mob breaking into their convent, where they found, as they were led to believe, a mass of pikes, and a few guns, which they carried off (June 21, 1791).

The remaining Billettes put up such resistance to the state taking possession of their ceremonial silverwork that officers forcibly entered and broke the lock of the sacristy. The next day, August 1, 1791 the priests and monks gathered and made a solemn declaration: "that they neither should nor could in conscience take part in the proceedings of the municipal officers, reserving for themselves legal recourse and before whom it is appropriate, against the illegal removal, made invasively, of their sacred repositories and other pieces of silverwork, proper to the celebration of divine worship, and against the irreverences, profanations and sacrileges committed in their church."[230] A note remarks the presence of a reliquary enclosing the "Deicide knife" of the Jew of the rue des Jardins. Its final disposition is unknown.

An "active citizen" named Vial wrote a letter dated December 9, 1791 to the president of the legislative Assembly protesting the judgement that put up for sale in a block five houses formerly belonging to the Billettes and now national property.[231] Vial advanced the view that the block sale of the property on the Rue de la Bretonnerie-Rue des Billettes was contrary to the spirit of the Assembly's decrees, which was to create numbers of small property owners. The speculators and entrepreneurs who were likely to buy up the five houses were less attached to the Constitution than small holders. The president should encourage an increase in propertied supporters of the new state.

That Citizen Vial would be moved to write such a letter foreshadows a conflict between private aggregation of public property and the redistributive values of the Revolution. The clearest track of acquisition was traced by the church of the Billettes, which was secularized and sold in 1793 and again in 1795. After being vacated by the recalcitrant Billettes, the church first became a salt depot.[232] For the next sale the cloister was occupied by woodworkers (*menuisiers*) who used it as a workshop. This was an association drawn from the history of the church: the *menuisiers* were patrons of a guild chapel to Ste. Anne in the church while it was active.

The Billettes were no longer distinct from the other Carmelites gathered at the Rue de Vaugirard residence. That building was the site of mass executions of priests and others assembled there on the first days of September, 1792. No Billettes or Carmelites were listed in the martyrology compiled after the Terror.[233]

The city of Paris repurchased the church from its private owners in fulfillment of a decree signed by the Emperor Napoleon on July 20, 1808.[234] The narrow street was daunting, but the Lutheran community (Augsburg Confession) in Paris, who had been offered a church of their own by the imperial government, chose the structure always called the Eglise des Billettes, the Church of the Billettes, for its central location and the open building next door which could serve as a presbytery. Napoleon's August 11, 1808 decree instituting a Consistory and establishing positions for two pastors gave the Lutherans a state-approved administrative structure. After more than a year's work the structure that the Paris prefect had wanted to have demolished was the site of an inaugural service on November 26, 1809. Many years of modifications followed.

Eglise des Billettes before street widening. Weber (1908: 32)

There were no traces of the Jew's house or the miracle in the Lutheran church. The origin of the place was recalled in its name Eglise des Billettes used to this day. In 1908 Auguste Weber, a pastor who reintroduced services in both German and French after they had been abandoned during the Franco-Prussian conflict decades earlier, published a centennial history of the Evangelical Lutheran Church in Paris. He summarized the story of the miracle, and identified several representations of the miracle still visible in Paris churches. Above the entry portal of the Eglise des Billettes was the inscription "*S.S. dicata*," "Dedicated to the Blessed Sacrament," which had been placed there when the church was reconstructed in 1756.

Weber also noted that in St. Jean-St. François, a church neighboring the Billettes, was annually celebrated a novena, nine successive days of prayers, in commemoration of the miraculous event.

At a May 10, 1790 meeting of the *Bureau Municipal* of the Paris Commune, a delegate assembly which had been set up to govern the city after the storming of the Bastille (1789), M. Champion conveyed the interest of the curés and marguilliers of St. Gervais parish that they be given custody of the miraculous host and the ostensorium in which it is sealed, kept at St. Jean-en-Grève.[235]

> They base their request on the fact that the territory occupied by the [original] St. Jean chapel belonged to St. Gervais parish, when that chapel was elevated to parish in 1212, a time when St. Gervais shared with St. Jean its revenue and ornaments. M. Champion also said that this same ostensorium was requested by the curé and parishioners of the new parish of St. Francis of Assisi, which they base on their not having any, and on this parish encompassing in its jurisdiction a large part of the territory of St. Jean parish.
>
> The Municipal Bureau, after having deliberated upon it, decrees that the miraculous host will be remitted to St. Gervais parish, and that, as for the ostensorium, it will be delivered to the curé of St. Francis of Assisi, for the service of this new parish.

The situation of St. Jean-en-Grève in close proximity to the Hôtel de Ville, and its parent church of St. Gervais, made it a candidate for demolition, preceded by the relocation of its most precious possession, the miraculous host. At this time in May, 1790, it appeared to the clergy that the newly empowered municipal authorities were making practical decisions to relieve the redundancy of church buildings in the city, and that the churches slated for demise would give up their goods to others. The St. Gervais clergy might feel confirmed in this opinion by being granted the St. Jean-en-Grève host on May 10, and the following day being designated the repository of the St. Jean-en-Grève baptism, marriage and mortuary registers by the Corps Municipal of the Paris Commune.[236]

The Convent of the Capuchins in the Marais had been established in 1623 not far from the church of St. Merry. With the suppression of the monastic orders in 1790 the twenty-four monks living in the convent were released and the convent building was refitted to serve as a parish church. The baptismal fonts, the eagle of the pulpit, the confessional stalls and the ornaments from St. Jean-en-Grève were transferred to the new church, initially named St. François d'Assise.[237]

The curé of St. François d'Assise, likely to have been Marc-Louis Royer, a Sorbonne doctor of theology who had been the curé of St. Jean-en-Grève, joined with his parishioners also making the transfer from old church to new, to request the miraculous host of their original church. The Bureau Municipal granted them the ostensorium, but it appears from later records that the host came with it. St. Gervais already had a miraculous host, the Lendit host of 1274, not the object of pilgrimages like the 1290 host. The influx of St. Jean-en-Grève into St. François d'Assise occasioned an amalgamated name, St. Jean-St. François.

Royer seems to have had confidence in the restoration of his cure in a new venue when he appeared before the Assembly on June 2, 1790 to invite the representatives to join the Fête Dieu procession, which they accepted.[238]

Royer did not belong to a suppressed monastic order, and as a priest he was called upon to swear an oath of loyalty to the civil constitution of the clergy. He declined. He was a leader among the nonjuring clergy arrested and interrogated at the Carmelite convent, and was executed on September 2, 1792.[239] He was the most prominent member of the St. Jean-en-Grève nonjuring clergy to have lost his life during the Terror.

St. Jean-St. François was closed the following year, remained vacant until sold in 1798. In the environment of conditioned restoration of Catholicism following Napoleon's July 15, 1801 Concordat with Pope Pius VII, St. Jean-St. François was repurchased by the state and reopened in 1803, the sole remaining repository of the Paris miracle.

St. Jean-en-Grève's slow process of demolition, finally completed in 1800, became the subject of paintings. Pierre-Antoine Demachy's oil of around 1800 takes the perspective looking aslant the church's vacated ambulatory, again populated by vendors and country figures. The 77-year old Demachy had painted many ruins over the course of his career as an architectureal landscpe painter, including the ruins of the Bastille, and the ruins of Rome, which he had never seen. His younger rival Hubert Robert (67 years old) took a view that same year looking through the collapsed apse of St. Jean toward the towering portal of St. Gervais nearby, the human figures fleeing a cloud of falling debris.

Aged painters with a practice of picturesque ruins under the ancien regime adapted their skills to meet the devastation of the Revolution with an imagery of the persistence of the church. The apparatus of the miracle had been in part transferred to a new church, and its *imago* and liturgy remained in paint, ink and glass. Of the fallen St. Jean-en-Grève a Communion chapel remained, and was attached to the nearby Hôtel de Ville, where it served as a meeting room under the name Salle St. Jean.[240] The personnel of the miracle, the Billettes responsible for reciting the reparation service, were dispersed, and the St. Jean-en-Grève clergy who survived no longer had their original church.

Notes

[224] Bertholet (1746: 268) This is a maximal list; the lance was seldom named as a relic.
[225] Bertholet (1846: 100-01)
[226] Archives Nationales S 3.707, No. 342. Delarc (1801: 217-18). The archival entry is accompanied by the titles to the properties owned by the Billettes. Listed by Lebeuf (1863: 380-81)
[227] Roche (1987: 87)

[228] Pisani (1891: 231-32)

[229] Sorel (1864: 26-28)

[230] Lebeuf and Cocheris (1863: 379) Quoted from an archival document catalogued on the following page.

[231] Tuety (1902: 515 no.3833)

[232] Deneev (1922: 185)

[233] Peltier (1797)

[234] They paid the sum of 73,000 francs, considered a modest amount. Weber (1908: 33)

[235] Lacroix,ed. (1905: 220)

[236] Lacroix,ed. (1905: 205)

[237] Delarc (1801: 216)

[238] La Croix,ed. (1897: 637-38)

[239] de Salamon (1896: 71-74)

[240] Lebeuf and Cocheris (1863: 361)

16.
Continuities

"Their church was constructed on the place where there once was the house of a Jew named Jonathas, whose history everyone knows."[241] The enterprising historian Luc-Vincent Thiéry wrote in the brief entry on the Carmes Billettes in his guide to pre-revolutionary Paris soon after the Revolution, in 1795. At that time he was correct, but in the following century public knowledge of the miracle flickered on and off, with a few flares.

The human means of its continuity persisted.

Fifteen St. Jean-en-Grève clergy did not take the oath swearing allegiance to the Civil Constitution of the Clergy; five of them endured incarceration, deportation and concealment to return as clergy of Saint-Jean-Saint-François when it reopened after the Concordat in 1803.[242] Marc-Louis Royer, the curé in 1790, had been executed in 1793, but Pierre Greuzard, first vicar of St. Jean-en-Grève, second in rank only to the curé, returned from Ghent to become curé of Saint-Jean-Saint-François.

Greuzard was "replaced" in 1805 by Philippe Cantuel de Blémur, a nonjuring exile who had not previously been associated with St. Jean-en-Grève. The four others continued to serve in the church for decades, from 1814 to 1837. Several priests familiar with the traditions and services of St. Jean-en-Grève carried on at St. Jean-St. François through the Directorate, the First Empire and into the Bourbon restoration.

The continued ritual life of the miracle during these years can only be inferred from the presence of the priests and ritual instruments transferred to the successor church. The host either disappeared or was hidden to avoid destruction. There is no remark on its presence or absence until later in the century. The Feast of the Miracle on the Sunday after Easter (Quasimodo) ceased to be celebrated.

The two feasts of reparation, during Advent and Lent, were perpetuated until the introduction of perpetual adoration of the Blessed Sacrament at St. Jean-St. François. Archbishop Marie-Dominique-Auguste Sibour, who drove the spread of the perpetual adoration in Paris churches, determined that the reparation feasts and the adoration had the same aim, and cancelled the nearly concurrent Advent service.[243] The Lenten reparation was the only active liturgical remnant of the miracle at St. Jean-St. François by mid-century.

The miracle's most pronounced reappearances were not liturgical.

Douglas Loveday was an English barrister and long-term resident of Paris who left his two daughters and a niece in the care of Ernestine Reboul, owner of a boarding school, when he left the city in 1819. Two years later he returned to discover that his daughters and niece had converted to Catholicism and would not rejoin him as he wished. Complaints, demands, attempted seizures and legal maneuvers brought him custody of the younger daughter and the niece, but Emily, now twenty-one years old, eluded his grasp. Loveday asserted that the young woman experienced a *rapt de seduction*, and should be returned to him, and to his family's Anglican faith.

That phrase *rapt de seduction*, which Loveday used in both the French and English versions of petitions and responses, had a specific legal meaning in 19th century France.[244] It signified the carrying off of a young woman by a man with a hope of marriage but without paternal (that is paternal, not parental) consent. The rape that the French wording hinted at in English was a separate violation, taking by force against the will of the victim. Loveday used the figuratively to imply that his charges were drawn into the Catholic religion through the vehicle of a superstitious story.

Both conservative and liberal parties in the National Assembly, to whom Loveday's petition was addressed, respected paternal authority, especially in this restoration period when women were being sequestered again after a bout of liberty during the Revolution, but Emily's conversion to Catholicism trumped her father's approval. Religious differences, national rights, women's position in society, and the priorities of nature and culture stirred a pamphlet war in which the principals, including Ernestine Rebouf, Emily Loveday, and Loveday's brother, a colonial governor in India, and father of one of the girls, defended their prerogatives and attacked their opponents.[245] English, French, Dutch and German editions of the pamphlets were printed and disseminated.

The Catholic monarchist party did not bring up the Paris miracle in the controversy over Mr. Loveday's daughters; they ignored that it even had been evoked. Loveday and William Hone, the London publisher of one of the pamphlets issued in the controversy, printed a translation of Léon de St. Jean's account of the miracle, with the illustrations in Léon's book reinterpreted by George Cruickshank, who provided engravings for Hone's antiquarian publications. Loveday's purpose in this salvo was to expose the rank superstition that had befuddled his daughter, and to stir up his sympathizers with the suspicious speed and irrationality of her defection.

"It is the history of a Jew and a protitute tormented by the apparition of a bleeding host over their heads."[246] Loveday's description of the miracle is loose to the point of caricature. Cruickshank's rendition of the illustrations follows suit. The configuration of the host stabbing scene is the same as the original in Léon's book, and the faces are similar except for The Jew who in profile now has a long hooked nose, in keeping with the Jewish type developed in popular prints and book illustrations.[247] Cruickshank imposed the received English iconography on Radot's etching to suggest that this was how French Catholics saw Jews.

Loveday's party opposed the anti-Semitic expressions in the miracle stories and evinced by the illustrations. Catholics driven to favor Emily's conversion to their religion over the demands of paternal authority they would otherwise support, also supported "the priestcraft that sacrificed a helpless Jew." The Jew and bleeding host were equally one of the "absurd and lying fables, which told for centuries in a hundred different ways, are a disgrace alike to human nature and religion."[248]

Emily Loveday was not lured away by this fable or by others Loveday claimed had turned her away from faith and family, but by the liberty she attained escaping her father's hold as taskmaster. In 1838 Niccolo Paganini wrote a public response to Douglas Loveday's claim that Paganini owed him a sum of money for lodging and for piano lessons his daughter gave to Paganini's daughter. Among other detractions, Paganini questioned Loveday's ability to speak French, and thus to communicate directly with his opponents.[249]

That Loveday could use the Paris miracle to stand for the superstitions that drew his daughter into Catholicism implies that it was well enough known to be held against the French in general, now that they had returned to Catholicism as the state religion supporting the restored Bourbon monarchy. "Odious superstition, which seems destined to plunge France once more into the gloom of ignorance and the horrors of fanaticism!"[250] Loveday conceded that "the enlightened followers of your religion reject [such superstition] with indignation and contempt." The Terror and rule by superstition in the miracle stood opposed to the Enlightenment in French history.

Loveday did not know or did not care that the miracle was stripped of its locations and most of its relics during the Revolution. He and his publisher Hone promoted awareness of its continued seductive presence in the renewed regime.

Part of the miracle's attraction was the potential since the days of Guillaume Duchesne and John Calvin, of viewing the miracle skeptically while keeping a distance through oblique language. Jacques Albin Simon Collin de Plancy (1793-1881) was a writer, publisher, compiler of tales and demons, a nephew of the executed revolutionary leader Georges-Jacques Danton, who recounted the tale of the Paris miracle in the person of Paul Bérenger, a voyager returning to Paris after a forty-five year absence.[251] Following a summation of the miracle, he commented

> But how could all the particulars of this sacrilege be known? The Jew was alone. Could it be possible that this horrible story was invented only to have a miracle and make a Jew burn? If the host could bleed, couldn't it flee? Another particular, is that at the same time, the same profanation was committed at Brussels, by a Jew equally named Jonathas…

Collin's surrogate Bérenger, like Collin's master Voltaire, did not give the lie to the events of the miracle. He suggested inconsistencies and nonsequiturs within the story itself. No witnesses besides the perpetrator; no life in the host besides what leaves traces. The co-occurrence (from the viewpoint of the 19th century) of another miracle with the same general features was a sign of imitative invention. Not that it didn't happen, but that it couldn't under the conditions given.

Collin made Bérenger's comment the whole of the entry on the Paris miracle under "miraculous hosts" in his 1821 *Dictionnaire critique des reliques et des images (Critical dictionary of relics and images)*-without identifying himself as the author of Bérenger's *Voyage*.[252] He thus took one step closer to an avowal of his skepticism without attaching his own name to an already oblique questioning of the miracle. The passage in the *Dictionnaire* was footnoted to historians' straightforward descriptions of the miracle and to Calvin. Collin's 1822 edition of Calvin's *Traité des reliques* added Guillaume Duchesne's Latin comment on the idolatry of the canif exceeding reverence for the host. Skepticism of the miracle's gross aspects had a pre-Protestant foundation.

This assemblage carried forward in a post-Englightenment, post-Reformation publication the package of oppositions that the miracle had become. The historians' stand-aside narrative of the accepted belief without comment suspended its unverifiability through written records in a scrutiny that employed logic without outright disproof. Collin's position was like S. René's a century earlier, only with doubt in the place of proof.

Collin's subsequent career clarified the preparation for the revival of the miracle in the background of these writings. In 1818 his best known work, the *Dictionnaire infernal*, appeared. It is a categorical demonology of the kind that had been issued by priests and scholars for centuries: the names, ranks and powers of demons were laid out in a listing that was amplified with time to include anecdotes and illustrations of demonic appearances and encounters.

Collin underwent a conversion to Catholicism in 1830, and the subsequent editions of *Dictionnaire infernal* betrayed greater adherence to Catholic doctrine concerning the infernal hordes. The 1863 edition featured sixty-nine illustrations of demons by Louis Le Breton, who drew scenes of ships and natural history for accounts of marine voyages. The demons Le Breton realized visually had something of the vessels and sea creatures he pictured in his illustrations. This was in keeping with the faintly recognizable, uncanny figures. Collin's final vision of demons was the congruent with his vision of the miracle, chronicled belief emerging in a critical dialectic with superstition.

Citations of the miracle during the same period that Collin's demons evolved into view, together with the French Republic, photography and the internal combustion engine, had the same quality of grounding confirmation of faith in remote proofs with a decided valence. The perfidy of Jews lurked beside the real presence of Christ in the host as a historic proof. The purgation of the material objects of the miracle during and after the Revolution served this development.

The spiritual director Marie-Joseph Favre (1791-1838) retold the story of the Paris miracle as a exhortation to the frequent taking of Communion.[253] The animation of the host in the hands of the Jew authenticated the life it brought to the faithful. Favre's 17th century sources (Leblanc, Dubreuil, Dubois, Labbé) recounted the story from bleeding host to apparitional crucifix. For the continued display of the vase and canif relics at the Billettes and the host at St. Jean-en-Grève he turned to the Napoleonic First Empire church historian Berault-Bercastel.[254]

This was superfluous given that his other sources provided the same information. Favre wrote that the host was still to be seen at the church in the 17th century, while the historian he cited said it was still on view in his time (1809). Favre assumed that the host disappeared at the time of the Revolution as other miraculous hosts did, and that the most recent testimony of its presence came from the 17th century writers. Some 19th century historians used the assured accounts of miraculous host survival from previous centuries as the sole evidence that it remained where the Christian woman brought it.[255] The vitality of the host in the basic story was his point of reference; the other elements were embellishments.

Favre's program of frequent Communion did not meet with a positive reception among other clergy, who considered it excessive dependence on that sacrament for spiritual development. His revitalization of the Paris miracle was an abstract association between miracle story and the always current act of receiving the Holy Sacrament. Adoration of the miraculous host itself was not a consideration. Restoring the connection between the relic and the present required an environment favorable to the specifics of its origin. Otherwise the story might be told and retold for merely contemporary purposes without contact with its present-day custodians.

The story was told and retold for contemporary purposes in the years between the revolution and the Second Empire. Favre was only one of several writers who looked back to urban and church historians of previous centuries for the miracle story, and therefore treated both the chapel of the Billettes and St. Jean-en-Grève as still extant, though it would have been easy to verify that they were not. New histories of Paris composed in the 19th century (Dulaure, Belin, de Gaulle) and updated old ones (Lebeuf-Cocheris) added a few lines on the chapel of the Billettes becoming a Lutheran church and the demolition of St. Jean-en-Grève, but nothing after. As sanctified structures they existed for the devout in an eternity not affected by political upheavals and natural disasters, like St. Augustine's spiritual Rome.

The eternity of the churches of the miracle, the host and the other relics was not the same eternity as that of Rome, Mecca or Benares. The eternity of the Billettes and St. Jean-en-Grève was a French national eternity that had been broken with the transfer of the host and personnel to St. Jean-St. François, and the extinction of the church building, other personnel and relics. The story of the miracle and the services lasted, and in forms that serve as the nucleus of a revival.

The historian and antiquary Jacques-Antoine Dulaure (1755-1835) had been writing critical histories of Paris and of France since the 1780's. A would-be architect who turned to civil engineering, Dulaure switched professions when he nearly fell to his death while testing the integrity of the dome support columns of the church of Ste. Genevieve. His sense of the shakiness of the ancien regime was physical, civil and moral, which was the title of the multi-volume history of Paris he published in the 1820's. That vision had been grounded by his inquiries into the bits and pieces of the Roman past and later he uncovered and analyzed while working on projects of demolition and reconstruction before, during and after the revolution-when he was not in flight from arrest for his radical politics.

The miracle was one of the curiosities of Paris Dulaure turned up in his 1787 *Nouvelle description*.[256] He did not engage with it until well after the Revolution, when the clergy were regaining some of their former position during the restoration.[257] A retelling of the story of Jonathas according to "an anonymous author and reproduced exactly by other authors" (the *Chroniques de St. Denis*) begins immediately after the title Carmes Billettes, followed by a commentary:

> From this piece and its copies, it should not be doubted that Jonathas, who, as it appears rejoiced in a large enough fortune, had he not been accused of this

sacrilege and punished by the ordeal of fire, but was he legally convicted? The absence of legal protections, the wealth of the accused, the bad faith, the avidity of the clergy, the inveterate hatred of the people against the Jews, the vested interest of the curé of St. Jean-en-Grève, principal accuser, who, becoming possessor of a famous relic, stood to attract numerous offerings to his church; the consensus then set among the priests, who agreed to consider impostures profitable to them as permitted actions, as pious frauds; tortures that extract false confessions; and finally the guarded silence on means of exoneration for the accused, more than suffice to raise doubts, and these doubts are fortified by the shocking unlikelihoods contained in the relation. How did prodigies as strange as those recounted not immobilize with fright the Jew who caused them?

Dulaure asked all the questions already asked from Basnage and Voltaire to Collin de Plancy and added a few of his own. He fell only just short of stating outright that the miracle as transmitted and repeated was a pious fraud. His rhetorical mode was to raise doubts about the criminal process against the Jew, from its legality to its moral legitimacy.

Each aspect had another meaning if considered separate from the drive of the narrative. The Jew's wealth is a trait of his character according to medieval typology, but it also is a temptation to the greedy priests, who took advantage of the hatred of the people to feed the relic-generating potential of a presumed miracle. If the host's bleeding and transformation is in doubt (the Jew being the only witness) then it can be seen as an imposture crafted to benefit the priests. An imposture the Jew was forced to affirm under torture.

Dulaure's was the most scathing critique of the miracle to be printed, but it remained a critique of doubts and suggestions. Elsewhere in his volumes, where for instance he addresses the career of an early 17th century magician held to be strangled by the devil while imprisoned in the Bastille: "All these absurdities were received by the courtiers and the bourgeois of Paris as incontestable truths."[258]

The forgotten tradition of the drama had already answered one of Dulaure's questions-why wasn't the Christian woman punished? She was, by execution following other crimes. In the version all historians recognized, however, the Christian woman ceased to exist after she left the Jew's shop with her gown. The psychological leverage provided by conscious fiction was abandoned for the sake of accurate reporting of the myth itself. But not forever.

Dulaure finished the section on the Billettes with the sale and rededication of their church to the Lutherans, and nothing afterward. His only mention of St. Jean-en-Grève was to locate the church and say that it was torn down. St. Jean-St. François was not mentioned at all. The miracle for him lived on only in the scandal of the story, not in the miracle-related services still going on.

At least ten editions of Dulaure's history were published during his life, and others, with additional notes by Paris advocate and publisher Jules-Léonard Belin, appeared in 1839 and 1857, preserving Dulaure's comments on the miracle story in each successive printing.

Historians of Paris writing after Dulaure were compelled to take his considerations into account. Jean de Marlès listed on the title page the earlier historians he drew upon for his *Paris*

Ancien et Moderne, ou Histoire de France (Ancient and Modern Paris, or, History of France, 1838) and pointedly added "and the most estimable modern historians." At the outset he signaled his intention to raise three historiographic issues: ancient versus modern accounts; whether the history of Paris is the history of France; and which modern historians are "estimable." That would include Dulaure, from the number of times de Marlès cites him with colleagueal comity.

de Marlès' section on the miracle is not one of those times. Under "the Carmes Billettes, today the Lutheran temple," he starts with the building's origins, gives a brief run-through of the miracle without references, and remarks:[259]

> Assuredly nothing is impossible for he who holds the entire universe in his hands; also, it's not the miracle in itself that astonishes us; what confounds our reason is that the Jew, witness to prodigies that he was bringing about, would not have abjured his errors and fallen terror-stricken before the omnipotence of the God he was at that moment offending. Or if he was so blinded by rage that he pushed the unconscionable a thousand times farther than the executioners who crucified Jesus, how did he suffer an outsider woman and of an enemy religion to become the witness, later to be the denouncer of these horrible sacrileges? For the rest we do not intend to make any inductions from these circumstances; we do not want to make proselytes or unbelievers: we make to observe besides that doubt, even on this occasion, and would not know to injure religion either in its dogmas or in its morality.

de Marlès restored the craven, sacrilegious Jew that Dulaure had made the victim of priests. Dulaure's wonder that the Jew was not frozen by fear questioned the veracity of the miracle narrative. Far from questioning its truth, de Marlès asks how depraved a man must be not to be awed by what he has caused to manifest. The Jew's unfeeling state is magnified by his inability to prevent a believer in the Jesus he has crucified a second time from seeing the tortures and carrying away the host itself. None of the doubts like those Dulaure and his predecessors entered can shake the dogma of transubstantiation and the real presence. Both Dulaure and de Marlès may begin from the same premise of asking why the Jew didn't have a more humanly credible reaction to the bleeding host but reach the opposite conclusions, the one skeptical about the miracle itself, lending humanity to the Jew, the other reasserting rigid belief not subject to reason, to the great detriment of the Jew.

A later historian, Amédée Gabourd, staked out ground somewhere between Dulaure's skepticism and de Marlès' dogmatism. Gabourd treated the official handling of the report of the miracle as a historical event of the reign of Philippe le Bel, and the foundation of the Billettes as a separate event happening in the aftermath of the miracle.[260] The rapacity of the monarch Gabourd confirmed by instancing the contemporaneous exaction of property from Italian merchants at his orders. Philippe's eagerness to use any means at his disposal to lay his hands on the goods of foreigners (including Jews), and the sanctimonious founding of the chapel of the miracle on the site of the Jew's house set aside once again the heady question of the miracle's ontology.

Gabourd reflected one of de Marlès' bemused asides, that the transfer of the Billettes' church to the Lutherans was an ironic donation of the site of a Eucharistic miracle to members of a religion that denied the Eucharist.[261] Gabourd's language is more florid, but both imply that the Lutherans taking possession was a curious disjuncture because the miracle actually took place in the Jew's house become Billettes church. Which may be why Dulaure never broached the subject. He did not imply that the miracle actually took place.

Degree of acceptance of the miracle's reality determined the sources a historian cited for the story of the miracle. de Marlès began with "it was recounted" ("*on recontait*"), a truth handed down not requiring an original, despite his preoccupation with fixing sources. Hurtaut's *Dictionnaire* entry just related the tale without references. Gabourd cited "church historians" without naming any. Dulaure, who attributed the persecution of the Jew to fabulating priestcraft, turned to the Latin text of the Billettes' cartulaire (Appendix) as printed in Labbé's *Bibliotheca*.

The most frequently given source for the miracle story was the *Chroniques de St. Denis*, usually noted without specifics. This practice continued from the 17th century historians up to the 20th century.[262] Julien de Gaulle quoted a portion of the *Chroniques* entry in the original Old French with explanatory definitions of obscure words in parentheses. The text was taken from the printed edition of the *Chroniques* edited by Paulin Paris and published two years before de Gaulle's history.[263] At least one other historian reproduced the same passage.[264] The orientation toward the *Chroniques*' French rather than the Latin sources was nationalistic, an assertion of the Gallican church and uniquely French miracle under the Concordat still in effect. This would have a strong role in the revival of the miracle to follow.

Suspended in time and out of sight as it was for Parisians, the miracle did not exist at all for visitors. The guides for English-speaking strangers in Paris produced by the Galignani company in numerous editions were guides to its absence. The 1822 edition only contains a mention of the "chapel of St. John" remnant of a church in the Hôtel de Ville with no further explanation. Neither St. Jean-en-Grève nor St. Jean-St. François is named in any edition of the guides. In the 1837 guide "The Lutheran Church (Eglise des Carmes)" is located and given a history that begins with its construction in 1754, and use as a Carmelite priory until the suppression of the order in 1790. In 1808 it is bought by the city and given to the Lutherans four years later. The 1842 guide adds "Billettes" to "Eglise des Carmes" in parentheses. A sentence or two on the interior fittings and paintings, and the occasional visits of the Duchess of Orleans for Lutheran services complete the entry for the entire history of the guides. A guide not shy about the lurid details of Paris history for tourists did not delve into the Jew's house and the chapel of the miracle .

The prominence the miracle was returning to in Paris and France was not the same prominence it had before.

Notes

[241] Thiéry (1795: 567) "Carmes Billettes. The Convent of these religious gave the name to the street in which it is situated. Their church was constructed in the place where once was the house of a Jew named Jonathas, of

whom everyone knows the history. There in the sacristy is conserved the canif this Jew used to outrage the blessed Host, as well as the wooden bowl in which it as received..."

[242] Grente (1903: 329-31)

[243] Gaultier de Claubry (1889: 447-48)

[244] Fuchs (2008: Chapter 1)

[245] Ford (2005: 37-39)

[246] *The Miraculous Host Tortured by the Jew, under the Reign of Philip the Fair in 1290; being One of the Legends which Convinced the Daughters and Niece of Douglas Loveday, Esq. under the Reign of Louis XVIII in 1290.* London: Wi liam Hone, 1822.

[247] Cruickshank's Fagin in his illustrations for *Oliver Twist* (1837) is similar, and his Oliver Twist is not unlike The Jew's son in the 1821 Paris miracle picture. See Eisner (2013: 124-26) for a collection of early 19th century portrayals of Jews with the same characteristics.

[248] Bates (1876: 17)

[249] Prod'homme (1911: 38)

[250] Petition to the Chamber of Deputies by Douglas Loveday, *The Kaleidoscope; Or, Literary and Scientific Mirror* January 22, 1822: 226. English newspaper translation of the French petition separately published that year.

[251] Collin de Plancy (1818: 2,15)

[252] Collin de Plancy (1822: 289)

[253] Favre (1837: 167-70)

[254] Berault-Bercastel (1809: 120-22)

[255] de Gaulle and Nodier (1839: 32n1) "where it actually is" citing Hurtaut and Magny (1779: 64) and others

[256] Dulaure (1787: 110-12)

[257] Dulaure and Belin (1857: 355)

[258] Dulaure and Belin (1839: 67)

[259] de Marlès (1838: 82-83)

[260] Gabourd (1864: 24-26 (miracle); 82-86 (Billettes))

[261] de Marlès (1838: 83) "Strange destiny this church would have. Constructed at origin in expiation of an outrage against the blessed host, it was delivered to a religion of which the primary principle is to reject the dogma of the Eucharist, and to negate the real presence." Gabourd (1864: 85-86) "Catholics might have wished that a place where one of the most astonishing miracles that attested the sanctity of the sacrament of the Eucharist might not have devolved to the enemies of their dogmas, to those who recount, a smile on their lips, the abominable profanation to which Paris was witness in the thirteenth century."

[262] Loth (1894: 333)

[263] de Gaulle and Nodier (1839: 319); Paris (1837: 100)

« Quant le juif l'ot par devers soy, si mist ladite oeste (hostie) en plaine chaudière de yaue chaude, le jour du vendredi aouré (le vendredi saint) ; et quant ladite oeste fu en l'yaue bouillant, il la commença à poindre de son coustel , et lors devint l'yaue ainsi comme toute vermeille (2). « L'hostie n'en reçut aucun dommage. Jonathas la

(1) *Hist. litt. de la France* , t. XVI , p. 20.
(2) *Chron. de Saint-Denis*, édit. de M. P. Paris, t. IV, p. 100.

[264] Meindre (1855: 463)

17.

Billette, or the daughter of the Jew

Eugenie Foa (1796-1852) was the first Jewish woman, and one of the first writers of Jewish descent to publish fiction in French. She was the descendant of two prominent Sephardic families in Bordeaux. She moved to Paris after the death of her father and departure of her husband, and turned to writing to support herself and two children. Escape and independence from patriarchal domination were recurrent themes in her fiction.

Like other writers arriving in the metropolis bearing traditions not well known or understood by the main of urban readers she made her background the subject of her early works. With time she extended her reach to include French history in general, and expanded her genre from romances to children's literature and biography. Her life of the young Napoleon combined them all.

Her fictionalized version of the Paris miracle, *Billette, ou la fille du Juif (Billette, or the daughter of the Jew)* was first serialized in a Brussels literary periodical, *La Macédoine Littéraire* in 1843, then published in 1845 in the same volume as another of her novellas.[265] It was a "Scott-inspired historical fiction"[266] first published in a journal with many other pieces of fiction inspired by the style, and success, of Sir Walter Scott. Foa fastened the miracle onto the framework of a romance that allowed her to make some pointed changes in the characters, amounting to a critical revision of the miracle for anyone with prior knowledge of it. That would include at least some of her contemporary readers.

This revision begins with the first word of the title. Billette, a name which led to much fruitless discussion among scholars, is conceivably a woman's name. In Foa's novella it is the name of a 15 year-old girl "dark and mirthful" who appears ashore on the Ile de la Cité on Holy Thursday, 1290, in the view of an 18 year-old University of Paris scholar, Ranier Flaming.

Foa set her scenes with historic detail. Flaming must return to his student hostel very soon, but is stymied by the need for water transport back to the right bank of the Seine, the bridge having washed out some years before. The girl agrees to carry him back on her launch. When they encounter a young man dressed in a horned hood Flaming recognizes as a Jew ritually insulted at Eastertime, Billette responds to Flaming's interest in seeing her again by disclosing that the hooded Jew is her fiancé, causing him to coldly withdraw.

The "slapped" Jew is Daniel, Billette's cousin and fiancé. She denies him the familiar "*tu*" form of address, as he picks up the mass of wild herbs she has gathered to perfume the house for the Sabbath. Daniel reminds her that according to the *kidouschim*[267] he can prevent her from marrying anyone if she doesn't marry him. She in turn tells him that if it was her she would have returned the slap he received that morning. Then they would have been massacred me, Daniel replies. I would have regretted your passing, she rejoins, as I disdain you alive.

They reach Billette's house, where a servant in answer to her knock reminds Billette to go to her mother who will give her the Sabbath candle to light. Daniel descends the stairs to the office, and Billette crosses an interior courtyard leading to the dwelling of her family where only intimates and other Jews can enter, and where all the paths lead to gardens bordering the Seine. The office located on the street side is accessible to anyone.

Billette's three young siblings precede her father, Jonathas, in his 40's, bent from habits of obsequiousness, something of the eagle in the arch of his nose and of the fox in the look of his eyes. "Like Daniel, he wears on his brown clothing a tongue of yellow cloth." Billette tries to smile and lowers her forehead, suppressing the troubles crossing her face as he raises his arms to bless her.

Jonathas asks her what has compromised her usual gaiety. "Everything," she answers. He then asks if she has had consoling words for Daniel who has been affronted by the Christians in their temple. Daniel, just entering the courtyard, says that to the contrary she greeted him saying she never would be his spouse. "That is neither just nor generous on your part," replies Jonathas. Billette insists that she will never marry a publicly dishonored man-an unfortunate man, Daniel interjects-unfortunate, so be it, Billette finishes, and marches past Daniel preceded by the children and followed by the two men to the section of the house where her mother is setting the table for prayer. Sephora ignores the children's message that Billette won't marry Daniel and praises to her husband the silver lamp and vessels her father sent from the Levant. The Christians may despise us but they eat from plates of wood while we have plates of silver. Quiet, says Jonathas, looking about him warily.

"The Christians are poor, but powerful." Billette enters, "They may eat from wood but without fear that someone will come seize their wooden bowl and the food it contains. They lie down on straw but the roof that shelters them they have from their father, they will bequeath it to their children. An edict won't come and take it away from them, burn it or hand it over to others."

Such astonishing words, Sephora reacts, God of Israel pardon me that she would wish to be born a Christian. Billette shivers with discomfort and asks her mother if she thinks the Jews are fortunate. Jonathas pronounces her words blasphemous but curtails further exchanges by declaring it time for prayer. A side panel opens and ten men enter, some attired like Jonathas and Daniel, others with the long beard and turban of the Orient, a Polish bonnet and an Alsatian bicorne.

The prayer is at Jonathas' house rather than at the synagogue because of the misfortune that has befallen a member of his family. The Christians are rude persecutors, Jonathas sighs. Luckily that chaplain who administered the slap was not a wicked man, Abraham says. Not exactly a dead hand either, Daniel touches his jaw where he was struck.

Another rabbi recalls his grandfather's reminiscence that in 1003 or 1004 the chapter of St. Etienne in Paris in order to honor a visiting viscount charged the viscount's chaplain with slapping one of the rabbi's ancestors, which he did with such frightening zeal that the man's eyes and brain were knocked out of his head.[268]

All shiver with the thought. Jonathas reflects that the Jews must have sinned greatly for God, who is so good, to punish them down to their descendants.

We are dispersed, pursued…Manassas observers, but in spite of it all and everyone we will not be destroyed, we will exist forever.

"Ah," says Jonathas with one of those smiles that reveals an astute finesse and hidden sorrows that are only the better for it, as much as the profound assurance of his self-esteem. "We are for the kings what the water is for the earth, we are cursed, exterminated, driven away when we are in too great a number, we are recalled as soon as the need for us makes itself felt."

To Manassas' counter that the Jews are sent away as well as restored only to be ruined-we are charged a *truage* tax to return and a *chenage* tax to stay-Jonathas delivers a brief history with dates of the expulsions and readmissions of his family in France from being despoiled and expelled by Clotaire in 633 only to return flourishing under his successor...to Jonathas himself, forced to leave by Louis XI to be called back by his son Philippe le Bel, "which doesn't prevent my coffers from always being full, he adds casting about him a look of somber defiance."

He calls upon Billette, standing in a corner in a kind of lethargy, to bring him his *talad* (prayer shawl) and book. "It is as if we never met," passes through her mind awakening in a somersault, as she recalls Ranier passing her by, her sister shaking her arm to call attention to their father's command, which she fulfills.

During the prayers of the persecuted men rising to the recesses of the house "grave, slow, pure, severe, and sweet at the same time," joined by the women and the servants there is only one voice silent, that of Billette, which only her sister Anne notices.

After the prayers, the repast and the prayers following it comes a loud knock at the exterior door. The curfew, which Jonathas scorns as an imported English practice, has since sounded. With a second knock Billette accompanies a servant to the door to determine if the visitor is Jewish and must be received or a Christian who must be sent away. Billette recognizes the voice of Adeline, the young daughter of an impoverished poet, Gautier de Metz, living next door. The two girls, sharing neighborliness, greet each other affectionately, and when Adeline asks to see her father Billette conducts her by the hand from the somber entranceway to the luxurious family quarters surrounding the garden. A pity you are a Jewess, Adeline exclaims on entering the palatial apartments, because rich as you are you might marry my cousin, Ranier Flaming. Billette dissembles her surprise, and denies knowing Ranier.

Adeline in turn is taken aback by the company surrounding Jonathas, who reassures her and asks her to state her business. On the next day Adeline will receive her first Holy Communion and she wants to recover the white dress she pawned with Jonathas the past month, -for thirty sols, he reminds her. Jonathas tells her that the Sabbath has begun and no business can be conducted until it is over. Adeline is aware of the custom and has not brought money; she requests the loan of the dress for her Communion. Such a sacred ceremony requires that she be dressed in white, to receive the body and blood of Our Lord Jesus Christ.

"Receive it? Where and how?" Billette asks.

"In the host that we consume," says Adeline.

"I would like to see one of those hosts," says Jonathas.

Jonathas, giving his wish simply to see a host as the motive and overcoming his wife's objections, offers Adeline her white dress that evening and free of the debt of thirty sols if she brings him a host. Exhilarated by the concession, she agrees to take the host "lightly" so the priest does not notice and bring it to Jonathas the next day.

174

"Adeline, poor, thoughtless child, did not think of the gravity of the sin she was going to commit, an immense sin in her religion, and which all conventions disapprove."

Jonathas' wife anticipates the misfortune that this "fantasy" is going to bring upon them. Jonathas dismisses her qualms: the king protects our commerce. The same way we protect the geese in our courtyard, his wife rejoins. He lets us fatten the better to devour us. One day we will prevail, Jonathas insists. Perhaps one day when religions are effaced and all form one family, perhaps then, says his wife. *Effaced* and not *illuminated?* Billette asks.

And the children are getting involved, Jonathas finishes, and ignoring a final remark by Adeline gives her the dress and asks Billette to conduct her to the street since the lights must soon be extinguished. Before parting Adeline tells Billette that she is not rich enough to marry Ranier Flaming but that she loves him with all her heart. Billette watches to see that Adeline reaches her home door in a leap before closing.

There follows an almost operatic interlude in which Jonathas and family make their way to the synagogue, one of the two remaining in Paris, in the street the Christians call *"Pet-au-diable"* ("Devil's fart"). The cries of vendors, artisans, mendicants and lamenters surround them, and as they approach the synagogue Ranier Flaming, indifferently glancing at Billette, approaches Jonathas to ask when he will be in his office to make him a loan. After sunset-Flaming will be there.

"Although a story-teller," Foa inserts, "and little obliged, by this title, to tell the truth, I am forced, however, to avow here that the poor Billette felt her soul go off after the student." She spends the day going over her first meeting with him in her thoughts, his openness followed by coldness when he learned she is Jewish, rehearsing in her mind that same sentence, later, it was as if we never met.

Her mother notices that she does not seem to be attentive at prayer, and as she gazes into the space of the synagogue she catches hints of Ranier Flaming's brown cape and blond hair. "She even seemed to feel upon her cheeks the fire of the gazes of the student fixed upon her." Never was a Sabbath day so long as she waited by the window watching the sunset. A knock at the door, and footsteps were coming toward the room where she was!

Adeline in her white cotte and veil has come from Communion bearing the host, which she places on the family table set for supper. No one suspected she took it. Father Bertrand was looking down and hardly saw her lips as he placed it, allowing her to put it in her hand. As Jonathas raises it to examine it his wife pleads with him to throw it into the fire since it can only bring misfortune. Jonathas does as she asks, but a sudden draft carries the host away from the fire and deposits it at Jonathas' feet. He picks it up and resisting his wife's entreaties unfolds a knife and pierces it to separate the layers and see how it is made. "As several persons affirm, blood flowed and several clots fell to earth."

"At the cries of his wife, of his daughter, of the young Christian cause of the sacrilege, of a new person who entered and had seen the strike of the knife, and of the children, who ask no more than to cry without knowing why, and above all at the sight of the blood that flowed, Jonathas, to get rid of the host, threw it into the water boiling on the fire."

Shouting "sacrilege," the new person entering rushes to the boiling water, plucks out the host riding on the waves and deposits it in a wooden bowl. Jonathas explains to madame Ferron, the mother of Adeline who has just entered, that it is no sacrilege. He only was trying to satisfy his curiosity about the host.

If I were wicked, she replies, I could make you out to be bad.

Sephora takes madame Ferron's hands in hers and declares her husband a good man who has never harmed anyone. Madame Ferron will not hold it against him, Sephora declares, and if she stays silent Sephora will return the silver cup her husband pawned before his death as well as the golden ring and Sunday cotte, everything her family has given in for loans, without her having to pay a single coin.

She accepts the proposition in her poverty and the responsibility she has for an aged father and a daughter who would rather sing than work. She is sure that though they are Jews, they are honest people. Do you think Jews are rascals? Jonathas asks. That is likely a lie, but at present they are not much esteemed, she replies. Billette, whose pride is revolted whenever her people are accused, exclaims that the Jews will be esteemed when people are enlightened enough to judge and understand, and stop persecuting them.

Why don't they all become Christians? the woman inquires.

Quoting a commandment, Jonathas ascribes Jewish unwillingness to convert to honoring the memory of the father and mother rather than just to adhering to a religion. Billette, almost in spite of herself, says that persuasion, forthrightly accepted, is better than persecution, lazily endured. Where do you get this talk, Billette? Sephora then turns to address Jonathas, God of Israel pardon me but she already sounds half Christian.

Before any more words can be spoken Ranier Flaming enters the room, and madame Ferron slips the bowl with the host under her cotte and leaves. As she passes, she reproaches her nephew Ranier Flaming: "Doesn't your father give you enough money, that you have recourse to Jews?"

Billette stands transfixed at Ranier's presence and needs to be prompted twice by her father's request for his pen and writing desk. Ranier's gaze has passed without seeing her, causing her to feel like death.

Jonathas asks him his business, and he says he requires a round sum for a purpose Jonathas doesn't allow him to state. He deflects Jonathas' denial that he has money to lend, and assures him he has not come to pillage or to spy on him. He requires 1000 *ecus* of August 4 coinage with the *Sit nomen Domini benedictum* legend. And will you give the diamond ring on your finger as collateral? Ranier Flaming proclaims that his word and honor should be sufficient. In love it may be, Jonathas responds, but in business we require more security. Jonathas is not sure that he has reached the age of twenty for his initial on a document to be valid, and to Ranier's challenge repeats that on his word he will not give a loan but on his ring he will.

Ranier leaves refusing to stake the ring that came to him from his mother. As he crosses the moonlit courtyard a portal opens and Billette appears and standing before him hands him a purse, saying that she accepts his word, before disappearing.

The following day while Billette's parents are closeted together calculating accounts, the children are off playing in the neighborhood and Billette is passing the time reading, Adeline comes to her with the diamond ring Ranier refused her father. He has told her to give it to Billette in surety for the loan. "He does not love me, because he loves you." But that is impossible, I am Jewish, Billette protests. That agonizes him, Adeline says, and he is Christian, Billette continues, to which Adeline responds, for he wants very much to love you.

Adeline and her mother lived with Flaming's wealthy father, her brother, until the mutual attraction between the two cousins became apparent and the father ordered them to leave. When Ranier brought her the ring to give to Billette he no longer spoke to her of his love or told her she was pretty. He said to her, marry who you will, I am entering into religious orders. "Why couldn't she be Christian?" he sighed as he left.

Billette works the diamond out of its setting and placing the ring on her finger gives the diamond to Adeline to return to Ranier as "the surplus." You haven't loaned him enough silver for this to be the surplus, Adeline remarks.

Jonathas and Sephora enter with their son Benjamin, who on being questioned, discloses that he told Christians leaving Notre Dame: you adore your god in vain, my faith boiled him yesterday evening. In proof, the neighbor Ferron burned her fingers taking it from the water, and removed it in a wooden case which she has not returned. Now a crowd has gathered at Ferron's.

To Sephora's exclamation that the child has killed his father, Jonathas is confident that it is a matter of little importance. When one wants to harm someone, everyone turns against him, she says, and he cannot say he lacks enemies because everyone who has come to borrow money whether successful or not is his enemy. "No enemies…a lender for interest?"

Suddenly noise erupts outside and the house is full of enraged people. Sergeants at arms at their head command Jonathas to follow them in the name of the bishop of Paris. He casts a sorrowful look behind him and complies.

An accusation of an act of irreligion, amounting to sacrilege in this period, and for a Jew, was a capital charge, as the family knew. Sephora descends into uncontrollable grief while Billette and Adeline stand, the children beside them. Adeline whispers into Billette's ear that her uncle Ranier Flaming senior is a close friend and counselor of the king, who mistrusts the great men of the kingdom and fixes his amity on someone who is not of their caste. Billette divines Adeline's plan to go to him and renounce marriage to his son, thus gaining the uncle's support. Adeline advises Billette to cover her face with a veil so children in the street don't recognize her by her pallor, and denounce her, as she accompanies Adeline to her uncle.

At the exit they encounter Daniel, who has learned of Jonathas' arrest and come to offer his support. Sephora laments the possible outcomes, including ruination, but Daniel says that would be the least harm since he has enough fortune for all. Billette pledges herself to him, but when she tries to rouse him on behalf of her father he warns that the least mistake can compromise them. There you are all over again, says Billette, capable of a generous act but not of a courageous act. She has another mission…

Billette asks her mother's blessing. As she grants it Sephora says by the God of Israel Billette is the strong woman of scripture while Sephora herself is the weak one. God will bless both of us. As they leave, Adeline tells her that she loves Ranier but is going to renounce him while Billette does not love Daniel but has made her pledge to him. It is not the same thing, Billette replies.

Part of the fortifications of Paris established by Philippe Auguste in 1222 are the great and small Chatelet where tolls and rights of passage from north and from south are collected. The toll for a monkey is relaxed if it dances, the source of an expression. In the time of Philippe le Bel the chatelets have become the jurisdiction of the provosts and viscounts of Paris, and notaries have established their households there.

Adeline warns Billette that everyone down to the least dog has to be addressed properly. An aged servant, Isabeau, answers Adeline's knock and tells them that Ranier Flaming has been summoned by the king on hearing that a Jew boiled a host that Adeline provided to him, and her mother retrieved it from the water in a case. Only her great aunt is present and she also is distressed, because she has been given a book containing beautiful things she cannot read. Adeline gains admission for both of them by volunteering Billette's reading skills.

Adeline's great aunt Madeleine, seated at the foot of her bed in an antique wooden chair, is puzzling over a book her grandson gave her which she believes is a guide to the art of the toilette and how to appear beautiful. Billette determines to read it to gain an ally, and perusing its pages sees that it is verses counseling women to be modest in speech, avoid pride, not be hasty on the way to church and always to greet those she meets, among many other admonitions.[269] The set of readings on the proper deportment of women ends with the arrival of Ranier Flaming father and son.

Approaching her uncle, Adeline agrees to do as he wishes and marry his colleague the notary Robert Hennequin, under a condition. Leading Billette forward she asks that he take pity on her friend. Ranier Flaming senior says that his purse is open to her but Billette has no need of money, her father has wealth by the bucket. Billette knows that the wealthy are more likely to be protected than the poor. Naming her father causes Flaming to recoil. He recalls the host boiling and admonishes Adeline that if she were not of his family she and her mother would be locked up with the Jew.

Save my father, Billette implores, and I will give you his treasures, more than enough to fill this room.

His son, after a flash of recognizing Billette, has withdrawn into a corner with a look of indifference yet unable to take his eyes off her. For a moment indecisive, Flaming forms the plan of having his son accompany Billette to his godfather the minister Enguerrand de Marigny whom Billette will try to interest in her father's favor. Madeleine is apprehensive that Ranier walk the streets with a Jewess, but Billette offers to follow behind him wearing a veil.

At present Ranier senior orders his son to conduct the two women back home. During their walk arm in arm Adeline confirms to Ranier junior that she will marry Hennequin. She has divined her uncle's intentions toward Billette, who has rooms full of coins, which her uncle covets. He will have his son marry Billette who will be made a Christian with words and holy water. Billette has already received the ring. When Billette says that she has sent the diamond back to Ranier she asks for the ring as well. Adeline passes it to him, and enters her mother's house. Accompanying Billette to her door, and setting a time for the next day's meeting, Ranier says that if she were not Jewish (why is she?) his father would unite them.

"Your father only wishes my fortune," says the daughter of the Jew.

"Yes…but I…Billette…do you think it is your ecus that please me about you?"

Overcome by the tenderness of these words, Billette asks for a souvenir of a service rendered, and Ranier, slipping the ring onto her finger, says it is a souvenir of me, not of a service rendered. She calls out his name twice as she slips into her house. When Ranier arrives home his father expresses the plan that Adeline anticipated, what a good Christian wife for you this pretty Jewish girl will make.

The following morning Ranier arrives to meet the veiled Billette, who walks behind him as they go on their errand. Billette is carrying a carved wooden box that contains a relic of the true cross left with her father as collateral for a loan. She will offer it to the queen as a present for her infant son Louis. Ranier confesses his love to her, and after his challenge, she confesses her love to him. She asks what he will do with this love. Marry you, is his response. "Me, a Jew," she cries out. "You, a Christian. If you love me you must love my God," says Ranier. "It's true, I love your God, Ranier." "Then you should serve him, and for this end marry me."

Billette then speaks to him in such a stern tone it causes him to quail. I am only a poor girl without thoughts fixed on any religion. "…my father is Jewish; I love the God of Israel; you come, I love you; you are Christian; I love the God of the Christians." If you tell me to I will become a Christian if only to avoid the fatal look of disdain you cast upon me when I made you understand that I am Jewish." As for marrying you I can't expose my past life, the religion of my father and the beliefs of my mother, to that same disdain. I can become Christian but not the wife of a Christian.

Billette reveals that she is sworn to Daniel, but also that she has sworn to herself that she will not marry him. Using the familiar form of address, Ranier assures Billette that his father wishes their marriage. "Make Billette a Christian and I will make her your wife." Billette knows his father wants her fortune and says he will have it. Ranier takes her arm: he will not let her marry any man but him. With that they enter the Palace of Justice.

Seeking to break Ranier's expression of tenderness, Billette requests that he review the history of the building and institution as they pass through its imposing atrium and mount the stairs to the great room, encircled by the effigies of kings, where vassals and ambassadors are received, public festivities and the accession of the heirs of kings are announced. There Ranier sees his godfather, Enguerrand de Marigny, and on Billette's advice, approaches him with news of the gift Billette has to offer the queen, Jeanne de Navarre.

Ranier instructs Billette, in preparation for Enguerrand conducting them to the queen's presence, that the queen is young, rich and very pious. It is best to give her the impression that she is ready to be touched by grace, and to accept the counsel that she will believe can draw a soul from Hell. A favorable glance in Billette's direction and the minister is leading them to the queen's apartments.

Billette approaches the queen with downcast eyes, and presents her with the relic, which is suspended as the pendant of a necklace of large pearls. The queen notices from the cachet of the beauty of her face that Billette is a member of the accursed and detested race her husband the king scarcely tolerates in his realm. Billette appeals for the queen's indulgence and pity. How can she grant it to this race hardened by impiety, who neither wish to repent nor to accept the true religion?

By giving them time, Billette answers. They are driven out, ruined, killed, but does anyone take the time to convince them? No. Who will do this, the queen inquires. "Try, you will," Billette says raising her beautiful eyes to the young queen.

The queen is overjoyed at Billette's confidence that she can convert her and seize a soul from Satan. The queen seeks a gilded missal prompting in Billette the thought, how can she use the missal to speak to her father. Declaring Billette to be hers, the queen recites the Lord's Prayer and prompts Billette to follow her. The prayer completed, with the queen well pleased with Billette's conversion, Billette asks her a favor.

At first the queen is aghast that Billette asks mercy for her father Jonathas whose sacrilege is infamous, and tells her to seek another favor. "What do you want a daughter whose father has one foot on the scaffold to desire?" Billette rejoins. The queen gives Billette a ring and tells her that wearing it all the doors of the palace will be open to her. Billette should return the following day, when she awaits the arrival of the king in the next chamber.

Ranier Flaming senior, whom Billette encounters leaving as she reaches her father's house, warns her to try to get her mother to see reason. Sephora is like an enraged lioness, exclaiming that the Christian who has just visited asks a mere bagatelle to save her husband…he asks that they all be baptized Christians. To Billette's question, how did you respond? Daniel answers that Flaming said more than that, he said you love his son.

Billette evades further response and says that it is a matter of saving her father at any price. "At any price! You hear, God of Israel, at any price!" Sephora says, bringing her hands to her forehead in despair. "This child is half Christian, I told your father not wanting to believe it myself. Listen, Billette. I love your father more than my life; you are my daughter, you, I don't have to wonder if I love you. But rather than seeing your father a Christian I would better see him fastened to the pillory; rather than see you the wife of a Christian I would strangle you with my own hands."

Billette tells her that she never will be the wife of a Christian. Fearing another question, Billette relates her visit to the queen, who will speak to her husband on their behalf. "Words of the great, gone with the wind." In answer to Sephora's queries how she arrived at the queen she traces the path from Ranier Flaming to his father the notary to Enguerrand de Marigny to the queen's chamber. Billette evades her mother's questions: does she know the notary's son, does she love him? When her mother asks what she expects, she says she will talk to her father tomorrow.

The following day, on her way to meet young Ranier Flaming, Billette notices the despairing Adeline seated on a ladder inside her mother's house. Billette speaks to her and enters the house, but Adeline demands that she leave. Adeline is torn between her loss of Ranier's love and her affection for Billette, embracing her and pushing her away at the same time. "I love you; I hate you; I would give my life for you; I want to see you dead." The Jews and the Gypsies are the same, one look and he is yours. Adeline's reproaches over the loss of Ranier's love tear Billette's heart apart, but what tears at her more is the thought that having left Adeline for her Ranier might leave her for another. As Adeline demands that Billette renounce Ranier he appears outside and she joins him.

In the middle ages buildings were constructed down into the earth as well as up and the prison was extended in stages underground progressively deeper according to the nature of the crime.

Leaving Ranier at the entrance Billette shows the queen's ring to a jailer and following him enters the depths of the oubliettes section of the palace of justice. For three quarters of an hour they descend through archways past thousands of bolts and desolate grilles until the jailer stops before a door so dark it was difficult at first glance to distinguish from the black wall where it was set. The jailer introduces a key into a lock, draws the bolts and opens the door. Billette has a quarter hour. He will wait.

Barely discerning her chained father in the blackness of the cell, Billette says she will save him, the queen is for us. "Like God, my daughter," says the Jew with a despairing accent, "who lets it happen." The bishop has already spoken to him and offered him salvation at the price of uttering a single word, and of standing barefoot before the cathedral with a noose around his neck. He refuses to deny the God of his fathers to escape a quarter hour of suffering. Her father gives her his blessing. The Christians covet our daughters for their treasures not for themselves. To Billette's protest that Ranier loves her he says that to the Christians she is nothing but the envelope that holds the fortune.

Jonathas senses from the trembling of her hand that she doubts his belief that the wolf will not join with the lamb or the vulture with the dove, and that misalliances do not favor the weak. He cannot prevent misfortune from coming to her. He gives her a small key that escaped the attention of his jailers and instructs her to use it to open a plank in a recess in the garden where his Muscat wine is kept by inserting it into one of the letters of an inscription. There she will find his legacy divided into five lots which she must distribute according to his will. Do not marry a Christian, and take these kisses to your mother, brothers, sister and yourself. With this the jailer separates them and conducts her back to Ranier, whose love for her causes her to forget her burden.

At the palace the queen has left her a note commanding her to go to the Cordelières in the faubourg St. Marceau, rue de l'Oursine number 95. "Let's go," says Ranier to Billette."Let's go,"says Billette with no other comment.

Billette's spontaneous echo of Ranier's word was the mountain echoing the valley. Total love, total submission, like the myth of the nymph Echo, a being without form suddenly reassembled at a lover's call. "The woman who loves. What is she but the reflection of the one she loves? Thus with Billette. Her father in irons! Her mother in tears! All was forgotten before the powerful gaze of the one who dominated her." Ranier leads her to a house into which she follows him. He says a few words into the ear of a nun, and tells Billette to remain. She stays for days regaled by the delights of the Catholic religion, the delights of a union formed by love.

Ranier visits her only in the parlor of the convent with a nun in attendance, whom she scarcely notices, so strong is the perfume of intimacy surrounding her beloved. Ranier's father and grandmother also come. So strong is the affection, the care, the respect for the formerly despised Jew that her head is turned and she agrees to be baptized, to marry Ranier and to surrender her father's treasures. She forgets father, mother, brothers, sisters, Daniel, Adeline, Ranier whom she promised she never would marry.

Billette is seated in the garden of the convent on the afternoon after her baptism and celebration with her new family, seeing before her a future of joy and consideration in Ranier's love, her father liberated from his chains, her angry mother seeming the only one in the world without a smile, when she hears from the street outside the proclamation of her father's upcoming execution.

She immediately shakes off the reverie of her bliss and requests permission from the convent superior to go to the queen and by persuasion or through gold gain her father's release. The superior does not oppose her plan: if she is not successful she can return and pray to Jesus for the repose of her father's soul. Accompanied by an elderly nun who takes errands outside the convent she sets out for the palace.

They enter a large crowd surging toward the Place de Grève, and Billette loses track of her companion as she is carried forward hearing cries of "the Jew, the Jew." Billette had never seen the trapezoid of the place de Grève, gibbet and pillory prominent, bordered on two sides by houses, on the others by the Hôtel de Ville and the Seine. At the center is a masonry monument ten feet tall the crude steps of which a man whose face she cannot see is mounting supported by two archers one behind and one ahead. Billette feels her soul separated from body and mounting the steps with the man, feels it in her arms when he is fastened to a horizontal wheel atop the monument and begins to turn driven by a mechanism inside. When his pale and haggard face passes her she sees it is her father and letting out a cry collapses into the crowd.

She awakens in the dark and deserted square propped up against a pillar of the Hôtel de Ville, and standing, begins to flee, as if one could flee one's self. Running aimlessly she finds herself outside the door of Adeline's dwelling, only a few paces from her father's house. She hears from inside the voices of Ranier and Adeline.

He pleads with her not to marry the old notary as his father wishes; she reproaches him for planning to marry the converted Jew, Billette. "Inconceivable mystery of the human heart," Ranier rejoins, "I cannot marry you and yet the idea that you will be with another tears me apart and transports me with fury." Billette has done me a wrong, Adeline accuses, and Ranier addresses her tenderly. I love you both, he says. But you can't marry us both, Adeline says, spite drying her tears.

Ranier continues his tender words, comparing his love for Billette with his love for Adeline: I would die for her but I would live for you. My father, who is not as rich as you think, wants me to marry her. If only I could have the dowry without the Jew. In a flash of feminine insight Adeline says, you don't love either of us; you're just ambitious for gain, that's all.

Ranier does not respond. Adeline has hit upon a truth he has not admitted to himself. While he is with Adeline he loves her, while he is with Billette he loves her and away from them both he loves neither. He stammers, trying to restore the illusion of love and Adeline, her hands in his, hears his words like a music that may not convince but does penetrate, her reproaches expiring on smirking lips.

Hearing this outside Billette suppresses an urge to enter and release the indignation boiling inside her into the face of the young scatterbrain. With the vision of her father on the pillory added to the grief caused by what she had just heard she begins to understand the religion she has just embraced, and broken, defeated, she leaves her soul and throws her body against the door of her mother's house.

The next morning Ranier Flaming is breakfasting with his son and mother-in-law, discussing the execution of the Jew Jonathas who was burned alive after the curé of St. Jean-en-Grève was unsuccessful in converting him. Ranier junior has not gone to visit Billette because he fears she will ask what is being done to save her father. At that moment a servant answers the door and the elderly nun who escorted Billette the previous day enters and reports that she lost Billette in the crowd at the time of the execution, and she has not returned to the convent. She is not at the house of her mother, who died an hour before the father's death. Only three weeping children and a young man equally desolate, who says he is the fiancé of our new sister.

The servant who goes to answer another hammering at the door returns to say that an elderly Jewish man has wheeled a tipcart into the courtyard. He is a servant of Jonathas. Yesterday evening as he lamented and prayed beside the corpse of the wife of Jonathas, Billette entered as white as the dress she was wearing and knelt before the corpse of her mother. She withdrew the covering and spoke a farewell, to her mother who died as she was born, Jewish. Billette told the servant Samuel to find someone to replace him at the bier and to meet her at the vault in the garden.

This was the place where his master kept his treasures. Billette said there were five lots each marked with the name of the recipient in the handwriting of Jonathas. Billette ordered Samuel to bring the portions inscribed for her sister and two brothers on the following day to Daniel, and to have him divide her mother's portion into two halves: one to be distributed among the poor of all nations whatever their religion and the other to be used to raise an expiatory chapel on the foundation of her father's house. Her own lot was to be delivered to Ranier Flaming together with a letter. She then gave the key to the vault to Samuel and returned to the house. He did not see her again.

Ranier Flaming senior takes the letter from him and reads it: "May God pardon you for the evil you did to me yesterday evening, Ranier, and may it happen as you wished. Here is the dowry of the Jew without the Jew. Marry Adeline. Adieu. Billette."

As Ranier enters the cathedral of Notre Dame for his wedding ceremony some days later he feels a piece of paper placed in the hand not holding Adeline's, and hears in his ear the words, "Here is your wedding ring, my lord." The voice bears the unmistakable timbre of Billette, but in the mass of needy poor, of pilgrims of all kinds, of pauper women each dirtier than the other he cannot not make out the elegant figure of Billette, who had not been seen her father's execution.

At the point in the ceremony when the ring is to be presented Ranier absently places it on the plate and the priest unrolls the paper and blesses it and gives it to Ranier to slip onto Adeline's finger. Both recognize it as the diamond ring from which Billette removed the diamond. The ceremony prevents Adeline from asking Ranier how he acquired it. "As for him, he was not at all present in his marriage: his spirit, his eyes, his heart even, if the chronicle must be believed, ran and galloped about him." The rest of the wedding and their return home proceeds without incident.

Four years later a chapel called "the house of the miracle" has arisen on the site of the Jew's house. In a footnote Foa gives a history of the chapel down to the 1812 rededication as a Protestant temple, and describes the knife and bowl enshrined as relics.

In the evening two women are alone at the altar, one richly dressed and the other in the simple sack of the Sachettes, a mendicant order. They both kneel, so absorbed in their sorrows that they do not notice the fall of night. The richly dressed woman rises and seeing the mendicant a few paces away does not want to leave the chapel without leaving her alms. When the mendicant sees the ring on the finger of the woman she rises and cries out her name, Adeline! She then parts the hair covering her face, and Adeline recognizes Billette. The two women embrace each other.

Adeline thought Billette was dead, and Billette says she is, in effect, the heart having left her body. How can Adeline, the happy wife of Ranier, be tearful and show such ennui. Ranier no longer loves me, she explains, and I still love him. How have you forgotten him? she asks Billette, who replies that she prays every day to the God he made her know, the God she has married, who does not deceive and who as remedy for all wrongs promises death, which can only be awaited. And you regret nothing, Adeline asks. Nothing, Billette replies.

At that moment Ranier appears. Billette sees that in the four years the young student has become a man. His forehead has become wrinkled, his eyes clouded, his lips pale and his voice has taken on a dry and rude tone. Why has Adeline lingered so long? Doesn't she know that she can be robbed by the thieves and brigands who are abroad while she lingers in the church?

She is giving alms to this woman, whose name is Billette. On recognizing her Ranier trembles, and Adeline sees that as a sign he still loves her. Not only that, says Billette, but he fears that I have come to reclaim my inheritance. No need to fear, the dead make no claims because they need nothing. Each evening at this time you will find me here, praying for you, praying for him, and for my two dear martyrs.

Saying that the Sachette slowly retires without looking back at the two left behind. "The heart of man, isn't it only regrets or desires?" Ranier observes, as the figure of Billette recedes, then adding, "Let's go, time for supper." And the church stands empty.

"Still to this day a house numbered 16 and 18 bears the name Billette, as does the street where it stands."

Foa naturalized and socialized the miracle story. She grounded the supernatural events in material and filled in social relations among the characters. The relics and the host itself are relegated to a footnote, and the transformation of the Jew's house into a chapel is through the agency of the Jew's converted daughter, who bears the name of the religious order historically charged with sustaining the miracle ritually. That religious order, the Billettes, does not exist in the novella. The house and street bear the woman protagonist's name. Not the abused host but Billette's shattered family and her disappointed love are being expiated in the chapel of the miracle.

The punctilious attention to the historical record, the details of buildings, streets and the cries of vendors, give way to allow the transition of the name from religious order to the Jew's spirited daughter.

The narrative drawing from and contributing to legends of the real presence of Christ in the host and meant to shore up the dogma of transubstantiation has lost all supernatural effect. The host does not fly, and when Adeline's mother, the Christian woman of the story, plucks it from the fire she burns her fingers. As a layperson, and a woman no less, she would never have touched the host, but here she handles it, as does Adeline herself when she pockets it before the bowed priest at Communion. Rather than taking the host to St. Jean-en-Grève in its vessel, madame Ferron negotiates with Sephora, gaining back her pawned property to keep silent about the incident and hide the host. The formal transfer of the host to the church is only in a footnote.

The central manifestation of divine intervention in the Paris miracle, the survival and bleeding of the host on being stabbed by the Jew, is plausibly naturalized. The host is carried away from the flames by the updraft and rides on the steam of the boiling water without damage. The Jew is holding it in his hand (another instance of profane touch) trying to pry apart the layers when clots of blood fall to the floor, "as several persons affirm." This is the one time Foa affirms a miracle event with witness testimony. At another point she casually mentions a chronicle.

None of the Jew's other host-bleeding actions are included (nail, lance, etc.) and here the only blood that appears falls from the Jew's hand, which may come from the host or from his hand itself nicked by the knife. There is no affirmation of what Adeline says Christians believe, that the host is the body and blood of Christ. On the other hand the doubts short of full denial introduced by Basnage, Voltaire, the early Collin de Plancy, and Dulaure are not given play. Only the visible fall of blood is seen, and the host is not said to be bloodied.

Foa's Jonathas is motivated only by curiosity about the composition of the host, not by hostility to Christianity, a wish to expose the Christians' god as a fraud or a compulsion to reenact the murder of Jesus. His action is later called an *enfantillage*, child's play, to contrast the gravity of the punishment with the lightness and thoughtlessness of the act deemed to be sacrilege. Whether the host bled or not it still is sacrilege, a mortal sin, to receive and handle the host as Jonathas did.

Adeline is similarly childish when she conspires to secure the host. The exchange of host for dress, which she initially asks only to borrow, is preserved in the novella, and becomes the first step of the deal ultimately made to buy her mother's silence with the other pieces of pawned property, now arranged by Sephora, who has urged Jonathas every step of the way not to bring the host into the house. She understands how Christians feel far better than Jonathas does.

If stereotypes of Jewish character and beliefs are not maintained in the novella (real beliefs are), the history of Christian treatment of Jews just as Jews (massacres, ruination, forced conversion) is reviewed by the men gathered for prayer, and forms a background of Jonathas' execution. He can convert and save himself, but resigns himself to a fiery death rather than betray the faith of his ancestors. This is the only time in any of the accounts of the miracle that Jonathas' avowal of faith in Judaism is introduced.

Billette does convert, at first in a delirium to win Ranier's hand and to enlist the support of the queen to gain the release of her own father, and later to stake out the independence she will have as a Sachette. The disillusionment she experiences is incorporated into the Christian eschatology she imbibes and accepts. Foa was entering upon her own conversion to Christianity at the time she published the novella, and her portrayal of the effects of conversion on Billette may correspond to her own.

The seizure of the Jew's property, confined to the house in the miracle narrative, is rechanneled in Foa's narrative. Neither royalty, who receive the True Cross relic in the form of Billette's gift to the queen, nor the Church, which receives Billette as a convert and a religious, is blamed for coveting the whole of Jonathas' property. The bourgeois Ranier Flaming and his son aid Billette because of the leverage she exercises with the property, and they do receive a portion of it in the end, as a dowry for Billette's marriage to Ranier that never takes place, and for Adeline's that does. Billette takes command of the hidden treasury and distributes it to her siblings through her former intended Daniel, uses it to make her father's house into a chapel (not Ranier Flaming's role here) and sends the rest to Ranier in a tumbrel. Royalty's word may be seeds in the wind, but the bourgeois only covet the gold.

The miracle story has a feature that overlaps with the novella, and which is fully developed in the novella: the precipitating role of women. The bad Christian woman, replaced by Adeline in the novella, initiates the action by seeking to recover her garment from the Jew and securing the host. The good Christian woman recovers the host and, in the story, brings it to the church of its enshrinement. Madame Ferron, who does the same less willingly, is clearly not the good Christian woman. There is no good Christian woman in Foa's *Billette*.

Women play the host-provider and host-retriever roles in the novella, but the male roles in the chain are reduced. Jonathas only prods and boils the host without going through the repertory of assaults; the bishop is mentioned, the provost is not. In the novella Billette organizes the core of the action. She goes to the house of Ranier Flaming to seek his assistance; she goes to the queen to seek hers; she goes to visit her father in prison; and she goes to the convent where she remains until she makes a final desperate foray which places her at her father's execution. At the convent she undergoes brainwashing meant to integrate her into the Christian family, which succeeds but on her terms, as a bride not of Ranier Flaming but of Christ. She is a fleeting but crucial presence at the wedding of Ranier and Adeline, and in the end she merges herself with the periodic expiatory prayers at the chapel, which have become prayers for individuals.

Billette's independent drive is mostly thwarted by males who resist her attempts to restore the familial order her father's rash inquisitiveness has terminally disturbed. The queen only offers Billette conversion and a chance to speak with her father one last time. Her father by his intransigence and the absent king through his edict undo her attempt to restore what has been lost. Even her young brother, childishly broadcasting his father's deed in the novella as he does in the miracle story, wrecks Billette's mother's arrangement to prevent Jonathas' sacrilege from becoming known to the authorities.

Unable to renew her previous life or begin a new one by converting and marrying Ranier, Billette uses her control of her father's fortune to engineer a new order. She carries out her father's wishes for the distribution of his estate with two revisions. With the portion due to her deceased mother she has her father's house made into a chapel; with her own she secures the marriage of Adeline to Ranier, and enriches their family.

Billette is the only character who keeps all the promises she makes. Her promise to Adeline that she will not marry Ranier, which she seems on the verge of breaking, she keeps, knowing better than Adeline how any marriage to Ranier will turn out. Being an unloved wife is Adeline's punishment for her sacrilege. Billette keeps her vow to pray regularly at the chapel for Adeline, Ranier and her parents. The dread of divine retribution for the abuse of Christ's body that impelled the construction of the chapel and the foundation of the Billettes in the miracle story is dispelled by the romantic melancholy of Billette's shadowy visits.

Entering into a Christian religious order offered women the only alternative to marriage, child care and the intrusive supervision that Ranier exhibits when Adeline lingers in the chapel. For a woman like Billette, breaking from the betrothal practices of her own community, the rule of the Sachettes dictated an identity that kept her safely to await death at the distance she sought from all familial, religious and trade entanglements. This was not an identity available to her in her own community of origin.

There was no miracle in the novella, only exchanges.

Foa drew upon a literary tradition of the young person (either man or woman), disappointed in love and threatened by the violence of society, withdrawing into the religious life. She used the miracle story to cast this theme in a medieval setting of Christian-Jewish relations more emotionally complex than the rages and retributions of the original. She also recognized that the miracle was undergoing a revival.

Notes

---

[265] Foa (1845: 205-396)

[266] Samuels (2010: 69)

[267] "sanctifications," rules of betrothal. The title of Foa's first published novel (1830)

[268] This story was derived from Dulaure (1789: 256n1) who in turn took it from Raynal (1759: 288). Collin de Plancy (1844: 288), repeating the story, called Dulaure a liar for writing that the Jews removed the body of the slapped man from the cathedral and buried it in their cemetery, though Raynal had attested to this in his 18th century history of Toulouse. "The truth of the matter, and we are far from excusing it, is that the blow toppled the Jew."Migne (1846: 907)

[269] The verses Foa sets down as read aloud by Billette are drawn directly from Dulaure (1829: 255-60), where in an exposition of the moral principles of the 13th century he describes and quotes the treatise *Le Chastisement des Dames* by Robert de Blois. This book was much quoted and cited during the debates about women's position in society in the mid-19th century.

18.

Revival

Eugénie Foa was born a French citizen (but as a woman a *citoyenne manquée*), a member of the first generation of Jews to be granted citizenship by the First Republic. The more assimilated Jews of her home region in southwest France gained that right on January 28, 1790 followed by those of Alsace-Lorraine and Paris on September 27, 1791. Her move to Paris was part of a general urbanization of French citizenry that accelerated during the 19th century, the Jewish population exceeding all others in the proportion living in cities, especially in Paris, which supplanted Alsace-Lorraine as the center of Jewish culture in France.[270]

Her exclamations about the unheard of state of being an author at the beginning of one of her earliest published novels (*La Laide, The Ugly Woman*, 1832*)* are about being a *female* author. She was one of the "bluestockings sometimes coiffed in red"[271] who attended meetings of the *Club des Femmes* that met in Paris during the heady days of the Second Republic. It was a gathering of socialists, mainly women, several like Foa established authors, at times literally under attack by reactionary (patriarchal, religious) forces.[272]

With Louis Napoleon's declaration of the Second Empire in 1852 and his fierce pursuit of political opponents, the *Club des Femmes* was dissolved. Foa's death in that same year coincided with a trend against the beleaguered inclusiveness the *Club* represented. Her life bracketed acceptance and rejection of Jews and women in the cultural life of France. Her novels and political writings reflect this. In the end Billette assimilates to Christian France not by refusing her betrothed, converting and marrying a Christian Frenchman but by converting and becoming a celibate religious, without the possibility of descendants.

Foa's life also brackets the maturation of French anti-Semitism. In "traditional" anti-Semitism Jews were hostile to Catholicism (specifically to Christ's divinity and the Eucharist) and its social values, and could only intermarry with Christians if converted. Foa's *Billette* revised the Paris miracle in the direction of reconciliation. In *Billette*, Jewish suspicion of Christians for past violence replaced belief in innate Jewish hatred of Christians. Jonathas did not deliberately attack the host; he overconfidently failed to respect Christian sensibilities, and rejected conversion when offered as an alternative to execution. He appeared to be the subject of traditional anti-Semitism.

Another vein of anti-Semitism arose in the cities with the rise of a Jewish bourgeoisie and an urban proletariat. The Jews became arch-capitalists conspiring to control trade, manufacturing and banking. Alphonse Toussenel, a disciple of the utopian socialist Charles Fourier, in natural histories and political treatises saw animal life as a reflection of human life and Jews as the parasites.[273] He singled out the Rothschilds as masters of this "financial feudality." Jonathas, a wealthy pawnbroker and moneylender at interest, was a precocious subject of this anti-Semitism.

Traditional anti-Semitism and socialist anti-Semitism were brought together in the massive compilation of history, folklore and news anecdotes, *La France Juive* (1886) by Edouard Drumont. The force of Jewish involvement in all areas of French life and culture made a Jewish France the likely outcome if no action was taken.[274]

Nothing has changed for them. They hate the Christ in 1886 as they hated him in the time of Tiberius Augustus; they cover him with the same outrages. Scourging the crucifix on Holy Thursday, profaning the host, sullying the holy images, such is the great joy of the Jew in the Middle Ages; such is the great joy of the Jew today.

Earlier in his treatise Drumont had cited several episodes of contemporary host profanation by Jews. In the illustrated edition of the book-it was a bestseller and went through hundreds of editions between 1886 and 1900-the "profaning the host" phrase in the passage above was footnoted with a paragraph on the Paris miracle and the establishment of the chapel of the miracle (per Pagniol de la Force). On the following page the nine engravings of the miracle which Drumont claimed were based on stained glass windows in the church of the Carmes Billettes were reproduced in a block.

Drumont promoted the conviction that Jewish hostility toward Christianity was timeless. The heading *"La Persécution Juive"* in Drumont's context means persecution *by* Jews, not *of* Jews.

Les anciens vitraux de l'église des Carmes Billettes, représentant la profanation de l'hostie par un Juif (d'après une gravure conservée au Musée Carnavalet)

In April, 1885 the fronts of Paris churches were posted with large yellow sheets reading[275]

Rétablissement de la fête solennelle
en l'honneur de la sainte Hostie (de 1290)

Reestablishment of the Solemn Feast
in honor of the blessed Host (of 1290)

From 14 to 16 April the church of St. Jean-St. François on rue Charlot was to be the site of masses and sermons restoring the reparation ceremony to the church where the remaining relics of the miracle had been tranferred together with the clergy from St. Jean-en-Grève. A cardinal and the Archbishop of Larisse, the coadjutor of the Archdiocese of Paris, were the ecclesiastical patrons of the revival, conducted by the Abbé Jules-Théodose Loyson, a theology professor at the Sorbonne. Abbé Loyson was brother of Hyacinthe Loyson, a Carmelite monk who had been excommunicated for marrying, denying papal infallibility and for his attempts to found a Gallican church, a purely national French church. The revival of the reparation ceremony offered a less divisive Gallican alternative within the Roman Catholic Church: a uniquely Eucharistic miracle recalled and ritually restored.

A revival of Fête Dieu with a papal procession in Rome in the early 1860's[276] had fondered after the capture of Rome in the Risorgimento of 1870. A remembrance of the two Paris Eucharistic miracles ceremonialized in churches-St. Gervais and St. Jean-en-Grève-in 1878 reported that the St. Gervais host had disappeared during the revolution but the annual festival was preserved.[277] The author recounted the miracle story of the Jew and host and the establishment of the two churches but made no comment on any contemporary continuation of the ceremonies. The church of the Billettes having been given over to the Protestants, a new venue was needed. The 1885 reestablishment was to fill a void.

That the void had an anti-Semitic shape was not lost on the Paris Jewish community in the person of Grand Rabbi Lazare Wogue. Rabbi Wogue had previously commented on Hyacinthe Loyson's anti-Semitic statements in an article in one of the oldest Jewish periodicals in the city, which he edited. He now focussed his attention on *"une fête intempestive,"* "a provoking feast," which once revived might continue to be celebrated until at least the 600th anniversary of the "legend" (he didn't refer to it is as a "miracle") in 1890.

Historians' accounts of the legend could fill his pages. He quoted one (from Frederick Lock) in full, and went on to consider the consequences of the story being aired again. All the more reason, we have seen with surprise, with chagrin, these reawakened memories it would be best to let sleep forever. In this time when disbelief on one side, anti-Semitism on the other grow apace, isn't it at least imprudent to revive a legend made of blood and tears, of superstition and hate, of ignorance and fanaticism; a legend which some don't believe at all, others believe too much, and of which the effect is to contradict itself? Because finally, if Jonathas sees in the host the true image of God, he an excellent Christian; if he only sees a common piece of wafer, he is not going to the trouble, like a madman, of jabbing it with stabs of a knife. Might it be to deride the Christians and insult their beliefs? Then he would do it before them. However, he shut himself up, according to the revivalists, in the depths of his quarters.

Rabbi Wogue recalled the other Christian tales aimed at the Jews, of disappeared children, of pious stranglings and Christian blood mingled with their bread, and appealed to the clergy to halt displays which had the potential "to taint" the multitude. He rightly perceived the revival of the story of the miracle and its ceremonies as a sign of rising mass anti-Semitism.

The consolidating anti-Semitism of the late 19th century was not the moving force behind the revival of the miracle ceremonies. It was rather a growing enthusiasm for Eucharistic displays that might feed anti-Semitism through the example of Jonathas. Wogue detected this in the host profanation narrative itself when he asked why Jonathas would stab the host if he was not already a believer in the real presence of Christ. He was not doing it to disprove that the host was Christ's body: there were no Christians present to observe his demonstration. He must therefore have been a doubting believer seeking confirmatory evidence.

Wogue made the Jew's performance out to be a cautionary tale aimed at Christians who would test the host for the real presence of Christ. The Jew remains a Jew because he is not converted by the bleeding host. According to Wogue, the legend tells Christians that they would do well not to have so little faith that they treat the host this way. Rather than instructing Christians, the rabbi fears, the legend would channel Christian rage of real presence denial against the Jews.

The reestablishment of the Solemn Feast in 1885 was part of a revival that touched on the sites of Eucharistic miracles whether they involved Jews or not. If the host abuse of Jews was visible in the history of a miracle it certainly was not ignored.

The Jesuit Jean-Baptiste Boone was a charismatic preacher and spiritual director to the Belgian aristocracy deeply engaged in charity work among the poor. He already was the author of a commentary on the Papal Index of Banned Books and a book of apologetics when he became the confessor and advisor of Anna de Meeus.[278] The countess had conceived an especial devotion for the Blessed Sacrament, and with the assistance of Boone founded l'*Association de l'Adoration Perpétuelle et de l'oeuvre des églises pauvres,* The Association of the Perpetual Adoration and the Work of Churches for the Poor. High society and ecclesiastical connections secured for them episcopal and papal approval, and a center in the all but abandoned *chapelle Salazar,* on the site of the synagogue where in 1370 Belgian Jews abused stolen hosts, one of the two establishments of the Brussels miracle.

Boone wrote a manual for the Association, providing an annual calendar of devotions, prayers and a history of the Association and its works. He relates the Eucharist to the Jewish ceremonial meal, the manna given in the desert, a sacrament and a sacrifice, but observes that the Jews took the words of Jesus ("this is my body, this is my blood") in too material a sense.[279] They thus found themselves among the heretics (including Protestants) and idolaters. The feast of the Blessed Sacrament of the Miracle is among the dates in his calendar, and he gives references to the story of the Brussels miracle but doesn't relate it himself.

A volume issued to celebrate the Association's fifty year jubilee in 1898 began with a detailed exposition of the 1370 theft of the hosts and their subsequent abuse by Jews at the Brussels synagogue later become chapel, illustrated with the old series of engravings, and with a print of a painting of the host-stabbing bloodbath.[280] During that fifty years the Association, now the Archiassociation, had become fixed on the Jews as malefactors conducting a campaign against the Blessed Sacrament.

1898 also was the year that the Eleventh International Eucharistic Congress met in Brussels, and held some of its sessions at the Archiassociation's chapel.[281] The Congresses linked Catholic clergy and lay votaries seeking to revivify and expand Eucharistic devotions and restore miracle sites. They were initiated by a Catholic layperson, Marie-Marthe-Baptistine Tamisier (1834-1910), who after an "unhappy" attempt at the religious life in the Servants of the Blessed Sacrament, sought in the town of Ars a "type parish for Eucharistic devotion."[282]

Under the spiritual directorship of Antoine Chevrier, the curé of Ars, in 1874 she planned a mass pilgrimage to a church in Avignon where hosts had been miraculously preserved from flood waters in the early 13th century and where perpetual adoration of the Eucharist had been instituted.[283] The following year a pilgrimage to another miracle chapel at Douai was extended to include Paris and the church of St. Jean-St. François, and followed by another to Avignon in 1876. The Eucharistic pilgrimages, which had the support of some local bishops and of Pope Leo XIII, were facilitated by the French railway network. The 1874-1876 pilgrimages to Avignon were connected to Lourdes, the village of the shrine of an apparition of the Virgin Mary in 1858, and linked into the national network in 1876.[284] There were accounts of traincar loads of pilgrims reciting the rosary according to a schedule dictated by railroad dispatches as they traveled from Lourdes to Avignon.

The pilgrimages began after France in 1873 completed payment of the heavy reparations exacted by the Germans for the Franco-Prussian War, precipitating the withdrawal of a Prussian force occupying northeastern France. The shrine at Faverney, where hosts had miraculously outlasted a fire, chosen for the 1878 national pilgrimage, was the Eucharistic miracle site closest to the territory France had been forced to cede to Germany (Alsace-Lorraine). Faverney was included with the other pilgrimage destinations in the exhortations of a handbook for pilgrims going through many editions from 1874 to 1886. Louis-Gaston de Segur, the prelate-author, called for a collective return to faith after the crimes of the revolutionary period.[285]

> The pilgrimages, especially the great ones, are a providential inspiration destined to revive a country bowed, suffocated for almost two centuries under the weight of public scandals of all kinds: political and social revolts against the Holy See; public outrages against the faith and Religion; terrible blasphemies of the voltaireans; public and secret sacrileges of the Freemasons and other secret societies; revolutions and negations of all authorities…

The Terror, the Commune, magazines and books, atheists, have contributed to this disrespect for religious authority. The Calvinists and Lutherans are indicted as well. Only in his section on the miracle of the Billettes does de Segur recur to the Jews, and there only as the community to which the host abuser Jonathas belonged. Eucharistic pilgrimages are a remedy for the disorder that has threatened the church hierarchy in France.

Those who joined together in the pilgrimages formed a planning body of church officials and laypersons who in 1881 arranged the first International Eucharistic Congress in Lille, France. de Segur, the chairman, and two other members of the planning committee sounded the alarmist note in their introductory letter, using the word "satanic" for the forces they combatted by bringing together French and other European Catholics for the days of pilgrimage, prayers and meetings.[286] A long list of participants in the Congress came before the Congress proceedings, which included brief mention of the Eucharistic miracles attributed to Jewish malfeasance at Brussels and Ratisbonne (Deggendorf), but not the Paris miracle.

At the Liège, Belgium congress in 1883 Matthieu Lecomte reported on the "priestly work" in Jerusalem.[287] This included an assessment of the Jews, reflecting their intransigence before missionaries.

> What does one encounter, in effect, in Jerusalem? At once the Jews, degenerate children of Israel; they are very numerous there, sixteen thousand in fact, and always growing. Now, gentlemen, the Jew of today, do not doubt that he still is the Jew of eighteen centuries ago: the one who denied the divinity of Jesus Christ, insulted his humanity, and refused to believe in the word of Our Lord Jesus Christ announcing the blessed Eucharist. "And how could this man give his flesh as nourishment?" The same are the dispositions of the Jews of today. Jesus Christ is neither their God nor their fellow man!

The Jews today (1883) are the same as at the time of the miracle.

The Paris miracle itself, prominent in de Segur's handbook, is absent from the proceedings of the Liège Eucharistic congresses and the others meeting annually in different cities until the congress in Fribourg, Switzerland in 1885. At that meeting Pierre-Almir Le Rebours, the curé of the church of Ste. Madeleine in Paris, reported on the heritage of perpetual adoration in Paris. Le Rebours announced to the assembled legates that perpetual adoration of the host was decreed by the royal patrons at the chapel of the Billettes (made from the house of the Jew), in the same year (1290) that the host of the miracle was transferred to St. Jean-en-Grève.[288] The Billettes and three other churches in the city carried on the adoration for centuries, as evidenced by documents.

Le Rebours neatly skirted the absence of both the Billettes chapel (then a Protestant temple) and St. Jean-en-Grève (demolished) from the miracle circuit, and reintroduced the Paris miracle as a property of St. Jean-St. François by mythically tying perpetual adoration to the foundation of the Paris miracle's chief relic reputedly handed over to that church. Not a representative of St. Jean-St. François himself, but of Paris clergy in general, Le Rebours needed to overcome the reputation of Paris as the "*Babylone moderne*,"[289] intensified by the anti-religious demonstrations of the Paris Commune of 1869. He accomplished this by placing the most revered rite of the Congress attendees in the historical context of the miracle. The documentary record of royal adorations in 1685 and 1714 at the Billettes enhanced his revisionism. Any extension of perpetual adoration, even to a time long before its historic beginning, was appealing to the Congress.

The Eucharistic Congress the following year, in Toulouse, was silent concerning Paris, but two years later the Congress was held *in* Paris, July 2-6. 1888. Perpetual adoration of the Blessed Sacrament was scheduled at several churches about the city, and on each of three days a separate church was selected as the center of activities. Saint Sulpice, on July 3, was to honor the clergy; St. Jean-St. François on July 4, in memory of the miracle of the Billettes (1290); and Notre Dame des Victoires, for the Virgin Mary.[290]

July 3

At 8:00 pm. Solemn salute, preaching and benediction of the Most Blessed Sacrament, at the church St. Jean-St. François, in memory of the miracle of the Billettes (1290)

At that time a bishop delivered a sermon at the church not specifically recalling the miracle, but its subject, the sacrifice of Christ in the Eucharist, meant that St. Jean-St. François was an accepted site on the pilgrimage circuit.

Among the oral reports in a plenary session at the outset of the Congress was a history of the Paris miracle, delivered by Henri Gaultier de Claubry, curé of St. Jean-St. François.[291] The miracle story was still current among the attendees, he noted, but he repeated it followed by the history of the chapel of the miracle and the enshrined host, up to the revolution. After that great dividing line, the chief remaining relic of the miracle, the host, was transferred from St. Jean-en-Grève to St. Jean-St. François. The two annual celebrations of the miracle during Lent and Advent were collapsed into one, the Lenten celebration, when perpetual adoration was introduced into the parish,

Gaultier obtained from the cardinal the restoration of the Eastertime feast of the miracle by introducing it as the third day of the perpetual adoration on the Thursday after Quasimodo (Sunday after Easter). Perpetual adoration had replaced most of the miracle liturgy at the church, but could also be a vessel for its recovery. Restoring a Mass unique to the miracle on the day of the feast was much to be desired.

The curé did recover the tapestries of the miracle that were the basis of the Léon de St. Jean engravings, but they were in a deplorable condition. He had succeeded in having copies made of two of them, which he invited the conferees to view on their visit to St. Jean-St. François. The remaining seven he hoped to have copied in new tapestries to adorn the church.

This was the beginning of a ritual and material rededication of the new church to the Paris miracle.

The proceedings of the Eucharistic Congress in Paris also conveyed the ambiguity of the attitude toward Jews. Jonathas is "transported by a Satanic joy" when he cries out that he will test the host to determine if it is Christ's body as the Christians believe. He is "frightened but not touched" when the host bleeds, and he flees to the most remote corner of his house at the sight of the crucified Christ emerging from the boiling water. Captured and interrogated, he is unwilling to abjure his religion and is quickly punished without further elaboration. His family and other Jews convert but he remains intransigent to the last.

This monster Jew whose investigation of the host is governed by diabolical spite is not to be found elsewhere in the proceedings of the Paris congress. Distributed throughout the pages are engravings based on paintings of Eucharistic events, several of them illustrating the Jewish precedents of the Eucharist.

LA PAQUE DES ISRAÉLITES
Partie d'un triptyque peint par Thierry Houts (xv° siècle). — Conservée au musée de Berlin.

"The paschal of the Israelites" based on a 15th century painting places four men and two women in the garb of that time around a table while one of the men arranges the body of the sacrificial lamb on a plate and the others, all holding staffs, intone prayers. "The paschal lamb is like a type in which the Eucharist is figured at once in the three states previously described."[292] The paschal lamb prefigures Jesus Christ who like the lamb is spotless, sacrifices himself and through the sacrifice obtains reparation for the people.

The rages of Jonathas over the body of the host are a mockery of the orderly Christ typology of the Israelites' sacrifice. Yet the resemblance was a balance point for Christian treatment of Jews. By referring to themselves as Israelites they were the people of Moses, from the time before the negative imagery of Christ-persecutors and usurious moneylenders took hold. The strategy of calculating anti-Semites like Drumont, whose compendium was first published two years before the Paris Congress, was to read the contemporary Jews back into the Israelites and claim that they never had changed and never could change, as he told his readers in the passage quoted earlier. Their paschal rites did not prefigure Christ's sacrifice but were a basis for denying it, and could spawn rampages like that of Jonathas.

The sixth centenary of the miracle in 1890 was celebrated with an octave of masses in addition to the three days of perpetual adoration culminating in the feast of the miracle on the Thursday after Quasimodo. The Vatican had not given permission to celebrate the distinct Mass of the miracle. Fifty of the sixty nine churches in Paris sent delegations each at a scheduled time. The entire Catholic city was drawn into the small church of St. Jean-St. François, which could not hold the capacity crowd.

The highlight of the centenary was the newly fashioned ostensorium, subsidized by subscription, on view in the church. Gaultier de Claubry admitted in his delivery at the 1890 Eucharistic Congress in Anvers, Belgium that the host the Jew abused no longer existed. The ostensorium would exhibit a host with no history. He described the new ostensorium at length.[293]

> For this centenary year, he had a rich ostensorium made representing in its features the whole history of this great event. In a monstrance in Renaissance style the Blessed Host, surrounded by rays, is raised as in the miracle above a cauldron recalling that where the Jew tossed it. To the right of the Blessed Host is the pious woman who receives it in a vase; to the left are the children of the Jew contemplating this marvel as a result of which they are converted. The crucifix that appeared is placed atop the ostensorium. At the foot are four groups representing: the Communion at St. Merry, the host brought to the Jew, Jonathas piercing the host, the host brought to the curé of St. Jean-en-Grève. And four medallions accompanied by inscriptions, representing the church of St. Merry where the sacrilegious Communion was taken, the church of the Billettes, built on the foundation of the house of the Jew, the church of St. Jean-en-Grève, where the miraculous host was preserved for 400 years, the church of St. Jean-St. François where the worship of the miracle now continues.

Saint-Elme Gautier engraving of ostensorium
Duplessy (1900: 361)

The central design is typical of a 15th century ostensorium placing the monstrance containing the host in a sun-like circle of rays, the general structure is that of an 18th century ostensorium surmounted by the cross over a columned dome. The 17th century ostensorium described by S. René included the original host in a second smaller soleil monstrance below the large monstrance with a few relief scenes from the miracle and a relic of the True Cross.

The structure of the 1890 ostensorium can only be for the perpetual adoration of the host as a sacrament that coincides with the reinstituted feast on the Thursday after Quasimodo. This is not the host of the miracle, which had been lost at the time of the revolution and not recovered, as a few had been (St. Aymé, for instance). The vessel compensates for the absence of the historic host with the presence of the species and a figural dramatization of the miracle.

That dramatization takes place on three levels: the appearance of the crucifix crowning the ostensorium from a model of the cauldron in which the host was tossed in an columned tier; the pious woman and the children of the Jew adoring the host in the monstrance soleil with four scenes of the miracle in relief encircling the base. On the bottom tier the four churches of the miracle are represented by sculpted scenes.

The sacrilegious Communion of the woman who brings the host to the Jew is repeated on the second and bottom level. The Jew's arrest, interrogation and execution, a major component of all representations of the miracle up to this point, is completely absent. That this is no accident is apparent from Gaultier's verbal delivery of the miracle story at Anvers. He uses the same text, including the same expressions to describe the emotions of the Jew: "transported by satanic joy," "frightened but not touched." The burning of the Jew was likewise absent from the miracle retelling in a contemporary report of the 6th centenary of the Paris miracle in the Reims diocesan bulletin.[294]

In his Paris presentation Gaultier invited the crowd to view the two newly copied tapestries of the miracle story based on those that had hung in St. Jean-en-Grève but were too seriously decayed to be exhibited. They were the same tapestries that formed the basis of published engravings from Léon de St. Jean to Drumont. At Anvers Gaultier told the audience that he had the tapestries reproduced for the revived miracle scenery in St. Jean-St. François.[295]

By "reproduced" he meant copied in paint. Duplessy's 1900 *Guide de Paris religieux* treats religious structures in Paris as artistic monuments, and provides a positional survey of the paintings and sculptures collected in churches such as St. Jean-St. François.[296]

> Below this last picture is found the first episode of a series of eight scenes, having for subject the "Miracle of the blessed Host in 1290," and reproducing the tapestries that adorned, before the Revolution, the church of the Billettes or that of St. Jean-en-Grève. We are going to pass in review these eight scenes, giving the details necessary to make known the history of this miracle, celebrated in the history of Paris, and of which the memory is perpetuated in this church.

Duplessy then follows the sequence of scenes down the stairway from the choir to the portal and up again, including in his book the second to the last scene, made into an engraving by his illustrator Saint-Elme Gautier, in an open Art Deco style. The "scenes" are painted copies of the tapestries.

The final scene in this sequence is the delivery of the host by the pious Christian woman. The ninth scene in Léon's canonical series, the burning of the Jew, is absent, as it is from Gaultier's Anvers retelling.

A 1921 tourist guide to historic Paris confirms that they were "painted copies of ancient tapestries," but does not enumerate them.[297] The strongest evidence that there were only eight, ending in the delivery of the host, is a set of eight postcards of the paintings that copied the tapestries, in the William A. Rosenthall Collection at the College of Charleston Libraries.[298] The Jew's punishment was the only part of the miracle that was consistently erased. But why?

Notes

[270] Graetz (1996: 42-43)
[271] "bas-bleus parfois coiffés de rouge" Claretie (1881: 22)
[272] Lucas (1851: 135-40)
[273] Toussenel (1845)
[274] Drumont (1886: 2,81)
[275] Wogue (1885: 499)
[276] Barluzzi (1862)
[277] Guérin (1878: 471-72)
[278] Suenens (2014: 251-53)
[279] Boone (1864: 7)
[280] Cartuyvels, et al. (1898: 2-19)
[281] Le Congrès Eucharistique de Bruxelles et la procession du Sacrement de Miracle, *Précis Historiques: Bulletin Mensuel des Missions Belges de la Compagnie du Saint Jesus* III ser. 7 (1898): 400-4.
[282] Musset (2000: 101)
[283] de L. (1926)
[284] Javel (1995)
[285] de Segur (1886: 13-14)
[286] *Congrès des Oeuvres Eucharistiques tenu à Lille les 28, 29, et 30 juin 1881.* Lille: Imprimerie Lefebvre-

Ducrocq, 1882: xvi-xix.

[287] Lecomte (1884: 611)

[288] Le Rebours (1886: 464)

[289] During the 1888 Paris session the Bishop of Liège had fulsome praise for the city as the center of world attention. *Congrès Eucharistique tenu à Paris* (1889: 517). Maurel (1895: 295) in a history of the Congresses at the Reims Congress six years later remarked that the whole Catholic world was present in spirit during the sessions in this "modern Babylon."

[290] Pastoral letter by the Archbishop of Paris. Richard (1889: 20)

[291] Gaultier de Claubry (1889: 441-49)

[292] *Congrès Eucharistique tenu à Paris* (1889: 179)

[293] Gaultier de Claubry (1891: 456)

[294] Hanasse (1890)

[295] Gaultier de Claubry (1891: 455) "He had reproduced the tapestries that previously served in the great ceremonies in honor of the miracle and recounted its circumstances."

[296] Duplessy (1900: 62)

[297] Wolff (1921: 76). Bicknell (1912: 266n1) stops at "it is suggested." Baloche (1911: 53-55) just says they were copied from tapestries dating before the Revolution.

[298] Lowcountry Digital Library. http://lcdl.library.cofc.edu/lcdl/catalog/lcdl:54331

19.
Absence

The Eucharistic Congress was held in Jerusalem in 1893, and among the many reports and presentations was one by Gaultier de Claubry adapting the telling of the Paris miracle to the Holy Land setting.[299] The curé of St. Jean-St. François addressed the European and "Oriental" Catholics at the gathering with an account of the Jew's host abuse divided into three parts, bringing the three stages of the Eucharist into line with the three phases of Christ's Passion: perfidious treason, bloody passion and glorious tomb. The taking of Communion under false pretenses was equated with Judas' kiss of betrayal. The Jew's treatment of the host was the same as the torture of Christ, an analogy already well established. And the receiving and transfer of the host to St. Jean-en-Grève was the same as Christ's entombment from which he rose again.

Gaultier did add that the Jew was arrested and, failing to convert, was condemned to the "final punishment" by the secular authorities. His family members did convert and save themselves. This part was the least consistent with the Passion analogy and given the least attention. Gaultier's presentation was the last time anyone told the full story of the Paris miracle at a Eucharistic Congress, and here it was almost completely assimilated to the Passion. This suggests one reason why the Jew's punishment disappeared from representations of the miracle: the suffering and death of the Jew, juxtaposed with Christ's, might offer an alternative Jewish passion in the same story.

The sufferings of Christ and of the host had to take precedence over anyone else's sufferings. Committed anti-Semites who did not hesitate to seek the punishment of Jews as fit revenge for their depredations on innocent Christians also sought to downplay the torture and execution of Jews in the immediate aftermath of the alleged deeds, the better to motivate communal assaults.

The Christians obsessed with the supposed Jewish obsession with Christian blood did not embrace the Paris miracle. Among the many avowedly anti-Semitic publications that appeared from Paris presses in the late 1880's there was a history of Christian blood in the rites of the modern synagogue, supposedly composed by a Greek orthodox monk who had converted from Judaism.[300] The actual author of this book, Henri Desportes, was a seminarian and follower of the anti-Semitic leader Edouard Drumont. In 1889 Desportes published under his own name *Le mystère du sang chez les Juifs de tous les temps (The mystery of the blood among the Jews of all times)*.

From the Jews conducting human sacrifices in Old Testament times onward, Desportes develops an imaginary cultural history of their abducting Christians to drain their blood for ceremonial and magical purposes. Desportes arrives at the life of "St. Wernher of Oberwesel."[301] Preferred as a sacrificial victim for his purity and innocence, Wernher had already caused one miracle before he traveled to the Rhine town of Oberwesel to work as a pruner in the vineyards (hence his iconographic pruning knife, used against him by the Jews). He was taken by the Jews after receiving the host during the week before Easter, and after he failed to disgorge it being suspended upside down from a wooden idol they keep for that purpose, was systematically drained of blood by young and old over a period of three days, then thrown into the river. Where his remains came ashore a chapel was built and the miracles began.

Desportes does not give any space to the miraculous host of Paris (or to any miraculous host). The Jews are denied the host Wernher doesn't spit out and Wernher suffers Christ-like tortures during Easter week. The body yields blood according to the host torture program without needing to enter upon the question of transubstantiation and the impersonality of the host. Christian believers of all strains were summoned to action by the cries of the innocent boy who died slowly under the knife. Desportes must have known, though he didn't write, that the finding of Wernher's body and the blame tied to the Jews led to pogroms in the towns along the Rhine after 1287.

Jewish responsibility for Wernher's death was a highly persistent rumor. Alfred Gottschalk, who grew up in the Jewish community of Oberwesel during the early 20th century, recorded in his memoir that Christian boys called Jews "Wernher-scourgers" and beat him up.[302] The removal of Wernher from the official list of saints in 1963 didn't erase those memories. Toward the end of the 13th century there were several blood episodes of the host, and a few that set the Jews permanently oscillating between perpetrators and victims as it suited the political economy of the time. Desportes inadvertently uncovered a mechanism for entrenching antagonism against the Jews in an account of deliberately bleeding a Christian body, probably a vague reflection of the Paschal lamb also abstracted into the bleeding host. The difference between the Paris miracle and the St. Wernher story is the absence of punishment of the Jews from the account of the St. Wernher story, leaving the community of the innocent victim to administer blows against the alleged murderers.

The removal of the punishment episode from the public representations of the miracle was a way to accomplish this with existing monuments. It had been noticed in peripheral sites of the represented miracle a little earlier than the late 19th century Paris revival occasions.

The sequence of stained glass windows of the *Miracle des Billettes* in the church of St. Eloi, Rouen were moved to the *Musée d'Antiquités* in that city, opened in 1834. The travel writer Louisa Stuart Costello made a tally of their sequence and tartly observed, "The sixth window, that only of the whole story which was true,-the burning of the Jew,-is wanting."[303]

A catalogue of the museum's collection was published the same year it opened, and grew in length and detail of the entries over the following decades. The earliest catalogue available (1836) lists three windows with two panels each, and quotes the inscription at the base of each.[304]

2nd window (in the museum's exhibit)-left side
How the bourgeois woman carried
Her dress to the Jew to pawn it
Then believing the evil talk
Of the Jew went out of her mind.

How the bourgeois woman seduced
By the Jew cursed by God
Agreed with him without protest
To deliver the host without delay.

3rd window
How the bourgeois woman without fear
The blessed Host to the Jew delivered
Who then after that delivered to her
The dress without payment or conditions.

How he placed it on the table
And struck it to the blood
And with his detestable dagger
Three times made it spurt out blood.

4th window
How the woman into the house
Of the Jew penetrated by stealth
At the time he slept senseless
And took the blessed Host.

How the woman by right complaining
Against the Jew, restored to her senses,
Brought the host no longer bleeding
To the Provost seated in his chair.

From these inscriptions alone the story told by the museum's windows departs radically from the typical miracle story by merging the bad Christian woman with the good Christian woman. The same woman is apparently carried away by the Jew's blandishments to obtain the host, and, coming back to her senses, recovers and delivers it to the Provost, not to the priest.

Comparing the inscriptions to the scenes shown in the stained glass windows adds a layer of dissonance: the woman who steals the host is not the same as the woman who recovers it. Different gown, different facial features, different color hair.[305]

The "sacrilegious Communion" episode and the crucifix appearing over the host thrown into boiling water are both absent from the ensemble, as is the punishment of the Jew. Several windows seem to be missing. Both Costello and the museum catalogue confined themselves to remarking on the absent punishment window, as does a more detailed catalogue published in 1868.[306] A presenter before the regional antiquities commission in 1915 advanced the same conclusion.[307] It seemed possible that the windows went missing when the set was transferred to the museum after the Revolution and before St. Eloi became a Protestant church under the Concordat in 1803.

No one explains why these windows in particular are missing. Costello's remark is a rueful reflection on the likelihood any report of a Jew being burned to death in the middle ages is truer than the supernatural events that allegedly led to the execution.

The consensus that there was a fourth two-panel window of the Jew's condemnation and punishment may be mistaken. No more than three windows were transferred to the museum from the church of St. Eloi. No account of the church itself, constructed in the 16ᵗʰ century when a few churches in France and Belgium were acquiring stained glass window sequences of the miracle, gives it more than three windows of the miracle. Three walled up windows, and no more, were visible to visitors to the Protestant temple that succeeded the church in the early 19ᵗʰ century.[308]

I argue that the St. Eloi Miracle of the Billettes windows exhibit an absence only when the whole story is expected, as in the longer written versions, the original tapestries and the published de Léon prints. Funding a full telling of the miracle in stained glass was beyond the means of the church founders and they abbreviated the story to retain segments with a single dramatic act at the center. Elision and omission of scenes is characteristic of all the stained glass accountings of the miracle, as will be seen in the following chapter. The punishment panel still is the most likely to be eliminated, but now from the original sequence, and the stabbing of the host the most likely to be included.

The most fiscally and symbolically economical aggregation of miracle scenes is in the one Paris church to retain a stained glass window of the miracle to the present day: St. Étienne-du-Mont, which holds the shrine (but no longer the relics) of Ste. Geneviève, the patron saint of Paris. The church was reconstructed and augmented during the 16ᵗʰ century. Among the windows placed in the ossuary in the early 17ᵗʰ century was one that at first sight appears to be a Crucifixion occupying the central axis of the window, surmounted by a standing Christ holding the host surrounded by the four evangelists above.

The base of the cross on the lowest level rises from a cauldron with the host hovering over its shaft. Disposed along the horizontal are scenes from the miracle, from the woman's Communion on the left to the Jew's rages and the good woman's rescue and delivery of the host to the church on the right. The stabbing is present but the judgment and punishment of the Jew are absent. This mild indirection, using a crucifixion to background the miracle, is a model for its preservation. The punishment of the Jew is missing from this representation as well.

The church of the Billettes, still known by that name despite being a Protestant temple since 1812, attracted renewed attention of the revivalists after the restoration of ceremonies and imagery at St. Jean-St. François. The disappearance of an image of the host from the pediment on the façade of the building in the course of restoration work in 1885-86 was widely noticed.[309] The site of the miracle had lost the one public reminder of its origins. At the same time the long-ago rivalry between the Billettes and St. Jean-en-Grève for primacy in the miracle and the pilgrim business was harmonized in an emphasis on the Eucharist in the miracle.

Pierre Coullié, the cardinal-archbishop of Lyon, in 1897 issued a pastoral instruction on the Eucharist that sublimates the miracle story.[310] The "poor woman" (alas!) forgot that the nuptial robe demanded by Our Lord is purity of soul, and made her deal with the Jew for her merely material dress and the cash of Judas. The purloined host receives the outrages only to multiply the miracles until it is in the vessel accepted by the priest. "The Christian people bring triumph to God living in his sacrament, and the blessed host remains incorruptible until the end of the last century, in the church of the Billettes. Now in our days a solemn ceremony of reparation perpetuates the memory of this miracle, in the parish that replaced that of the Billettes."

The cardinal takes it for granted that there once was a parish and church of the Billettes that included all relics of the miracle including the host which like many miraculous species was preserved intact until the Revolution and the Concordat. Still writing in parochial terms, he is reassured that the memory of the miracle is perpetuated in the new parish (St. Jean-St. François) by the reparation ceremony.

Gaultier de Claubry, speaking at the Paris Eucharistic Congress in 1888, was not willing to leave it at that. He referred to the nearly successful attempt by the Fathers of the Blessed Sacrament to recover the Church of the Billettes, which would have ended the scandal of a church "built to the glory of the Eucharist, delivered to the heretics." The host did not just disappear from the pediment, it was "made to disappear" by the heretics.

Unable to take possession of the building that in their worldview had been the center of the miracle,"some souls particularly devoted to the Passion of the Savior and the Eucharist" transformed a small chamber in a building just meters away from where the Jew's house stood into a chapel where the reparation service could finally be renewed after nearly a century's interruption.[311]

> But this private worship soon was not enough for the fervent reparationists. They did not delay in forming the project of an association that would increase those services. The sixth centenary of the miracle (Easter day 1890) augmented yet further their wishes, and finally on December 25, 1895, His Eminence the Cardinal-Archbishop of Paris capped their joy in approving the statutes of the projected association and giving them an ecclesiastical director.

Stimulated by the provision of papal indulgences, the membership of the association grew and the small chapel, "due to the protection of St. Anthony of Padua," was replaced within a few months by a larger sanctuary.

C.A.B. Delinotte, the seminary head who reported on the growth of the chapel and association, elaborated on the character and rites of the organization in his presentation at the 10th International Eucharistic Congress (1897). Membership in the association, *Réparatrices des Billettes*, was primarily Christian women and priests who rejoiced in the work of adoration and reparation because their chapel was centered on the site of the miracle itself. The sacrilege was initiated by a woman who carried the host to the Jew and the reparation was begun by the woman who carried it to the church after the Jew had exhausted himself. Women under the direction of priests participated in the ceremonial calendar for the sanctuary, which consisted of an adoration of the Blessed Sacrament exposed from Thursday evening to Friday evening, "and the solemn Exercise is performed at the likely hour of day or night at which occurred the mystery being honored."

The gender of the participants, the place and the time of the religious exercise were precisely coordinated with the miracle's persons, place and time, as close to ritual reenactment as possible. The twenty-five Thursdays culminating in Holy Thursday (Thursday before Easter Sunday) were each an adoration dedicated to a mystery of the Passion of Christ; the other Thursdays of the year were to honor the Passion in general. The miracle and its reenactment were incorporated into the annual cycle of Lent and Easter.

Current lives of Paris Christians and service to the poor were connected to the miracle through "the Easter dress," a subscription taken up by the members of the association to purchase a dress for an impoverished woman each Easter. This curtailed in real time the legendary corruption of the woman who traded the host for her Easter finery.

In ending his recitation Delinotte evoked the "the churches forced open, the door of tabernacles broken, the sanctified vessels stolen, and the blessed species profaned stories of which fill the newspapers. The Jew of the Billettes has all too many imitators. The work to which his crime gave birth has been reborn at the opportune moment." Delinotte fixes the Jew in a wider category of violent transgressors against the sanctity of the host, which can be addressed by "adoration! love! reparation!" Like the miracle itself, the Jew is an instance of a type that is repeated in time and addressed by the work of the association.

The absence of Catholic control over the chapel of the Billettes was countered by reparation in the immediate vicinity that expanded to address contemporary assaults on religion. Yet this arrangement must have been fragile. The only further mention of the miracle of the Billettes in the record of the Eucharistic congresses is in an incident by incident "history of the Eucharist across the centuries" gathered by an anonymous author for the 1904 congress held in Angoulême, France.[312]

The compiler gets the year wrong in which the Jew directed his satanic rage against the consecrated host (1290, not 1230, though it might be a typo), before he quotes a 16th century authority: it is as if the miracle happened yesterday. The chapel of the Billettes was built on the site of the Jew's house, but the surrogate for the chapel is not part of the story. Today the expiatory ceremonies in reparation for the crime of the Jew take place annually at St. Jean-St. François. "Touched and enlightened by the miracle" the wife and children of the Jew converted to Christianity. The fate of the Jew is not part of the story.

The long agony of the Dreyfus affair, a political and cultural crisis in France's Third Republic, also refracted the remnants of the Paris miracle during the same period that the restoration of the miracle's ritual proceeded and collapsed. Army captain Alfred Dreyfus, of Jewish descent and identity, was unjustly accused of espionage for the ever threatening German empire, tried and convicted of treason in 1894, imprisoned on Devil's Island, and eventually released and still more eventually reinstated in the Army. Those opposed to Dreyfus and his supporters included a roster of nativists, clericalists, anti-republicans, monarchists and anti-Semites.

No less an anti-Semite than Edouard Drumont entered a comment broadly alluding to the circumstances of the miracle. He addressed the outcry of other commentators of the same bent at the time of Dreyfus' conviction. Dreyfus is not French, they said. Writing in his newspaper *Libre Parole (Free Speech)*, Drumont refined the slur:[313] "All these accusations have the effect on me of people who would accuse a man who is a stranger to the mysteries of our faith of having stolen the host."

In betraying his country, Drumont implies, Dreyfus is (like) the Jew who stole the host, not knowing its deep spiritual significance. His actions can only have been as unfeeling as they appear due to a lack of connection to the mystic body of the faith and nation, worse than the simple malice of an enemy foreigner. This judgment is more severe in temper than condemning the Jew to be burned after he refuses to be converted. That burning was absent.

Dreyfus was not a convert, but he was a trained artillery officer, one among several Jewish officers in the army. That a Jew could achieve this status without conversion placed him in a perilous position, like the economic status of Jews in the time of Jonathas, holding the purse strings (or artillery shells) and yet vulnerable to confiscation and condemnation. Billette's using the relic of the True Cross forfeited by a Christian debtor to her father to try to influence the queen to procure her father's release reflects the same circumstances.

Dreyfus was released from imprisonment on Devil's Island by a presidential pardon in 1899, but he remained under house arrest and the dishonor of his discharge clung to him until his rehabilitation in 1906. The imagery of the miracle was not the most intense source of the anti-Semitic imagery marshalled polemically against him during the decade of his induced disrepute, but it was utilized to fake the past and the present against him.

The art historian Michael Camille identified a miniature in a 16th century book of hours that seemed to be a forgery inserted among the authentic pages.[314] An image of a hook-nosed Jew running a spear point into a bleeding host is not to be found in any other books of hours. Camille suggested that this was an "anti-Dreyfus" book of hours concocted during the late 19th century to legitimize historically the anti-Christian perfidy of Jews. It resembles Ragot's engraving of the Jew's spear thrust, colored in a medievalizing style. This piece is a minor example of anachronistic forgery projecting into the past a present bias like "the protocols of the elders of Zion" or the blood libel testimony of Desportes' convert monk.

A *bande dessinée* (sequential graphic) broadsheet of the Miracle des Billettes was issued by a Liège, Belgium press around 1900.[315] It was not a unique production; Gordinne published colored lithographs of saints' lives, other miracles and historic events. The images of the graphic marked a transition. They do strongly resemble the Ragot prints, sometimes published as a black and white *bande dessinée* (see earlier this chapter) or the illuminated sequence that had long been on view at St. Martin des Champs (transferred to a museum after 1790). The miracle had been redrawn in the style of the *images d'Épinal* that set the standard for popular sequential art in France and Belgium.[316]

The Gordinne broadsheet was an ephemeral publication, unlike the Ragot prints published in books or the St. Martin illumination, a singular and unique museum piece. It survived due to the zeal of a collector-critic, Didier Pasamonik. Both the Ragot prints and the illumination have three frames devoted to the judgment and punishment of the Jew, the broadsheet has only one: a crowd stands gazing at a fiery pile across an urban square. Only the long caption tells the reader about the Jew's arrest, condemnation, burning and the conversion of his family. The Jew is never seen dragged in a cart as in the illumination and other drawn representations, nor is he shown tied to a post about to be burned, as in the Ragot prints.

1.He thinks to get rid of it this way and calm his frightened wife. But what was his terror when the miraculous Host rose intact from the middle of the flames and flitted here and there about the room.

2. More and more furious, he attaches it to a stake and strikes it with a flail, thinking to cut it into pieces. Vain efforts, it remains whole. Worthy son of his fathers, vowing not to spare it any outrage, the Jew places it on a wall and pierces it with a lance.

3. Driven by a satanic horror, the criminal seizes the white host and throws it into a cauldron of boiling water. O wonder! this water becomes blood, and the figure of the crucified Savior appears to the Jew, to his wife, to his children. The Host really is God. The miserable man went to hide.

4.At this notice the people invaded the house of the Jew. Taken prisoner with his family, Jonathas admitted all the details of the crime. He was condemned by the king to be burned alive. The unhappy man did not utter a word of repentance, but his wife and children, being converted, received baptism.

Entering the currency of mass publication, the miracle is returned to the old sequential scene form and loses detailed representation of the judgment and punishment section.[317] This new form is consistent with the miracle of the Eucharistic congresses and anti-Semitic billingsgate. With this, however, the entire miracle became absent.

Notes

[299] Gaultier de Claubry (1894: 637-43)
[300] JAB (1888); Caron (2014: 44)
[301] Desportes (1889: 113-21)
[302] Gottschalk (1989)
[303] Costello (1842: 337-38)
[304] *Catalogue du Musée Départmental d'Antiquités de Rouen.* Rouen: Imprimerie de Nicétas Periaux, 1836: 17-19.

[305] Viewable on line in the Medieval Stained Glass Photo Archive.
http://www.therosewindow.com/pilot/Rouen-Musee-Antiquites/table-Frame.htm
On the left side of the first window the woman pawns her robe with Jew, on the right she and the Jew make the agreement. The second juxtaposes the woman handing the host to the Jew with the Jew standing knife posed over the host on a table, three spurts of blood leaping from it. In the third a different woman is about to remove the host from where the sleeping Jew has left it, and on the other side she hands it to a priest while others look on.

[306] Cochet (1868: 33) "These precious windows, which date to the 16th century, originate in the church of St. Eloi in Rouen. It is likely that a seventh and an eighth panel, representing the condemnation and punishment of the Jew, completed the sequence. They no longer exist today."

[307] Tougard (1915: 417). Contains the first photographs of the windows to be published. The presenter told the audience that the Photo Club of Rouen had succeeded in projecting color slides of the windows at a recent meeting.

[308] Licquet (1843: 118-19)

[309] Gaultier de Claubry (1889: 447) "Around two years ago, in the course of some restoration work on the façade, was made to disappear the image of the host which had decorated the center of the pediment in the edifice." Repeated by Bernard (1897: 66), who says it was "around twelve years ago."

[310] Coullié (1897: 351)

[311] Delinotte (1898: 615)

[312] Anonymous (1904: 479)

[313] Quoted by Reinach (1901: 469-70) from *Libre Parole*, December 26, 1894: L'âme de Dreyfus.

[314] Camille (2009 131-32). Smith-Lesouëf 317 fol.13v in the Bibliotheque Nationale Français manuscript collection. Camille includes a black and white photo in his text.

[315] Kotek and Kotek (2003: 27)

[316] Blanchard (1974: 65)

[317] Kunzle (1970: 134) makes the same excision from the exemplary graphic of another Eucharistic miracle.

20.

Presence

As the miracle surged once more ritually and narratively, then faded, a beat that had originated some time earlier remained, largely unheard as such, which probably is why it remained. It tracked forces not directly related to the miracle or its medium, forces that left impressions that can be read apart from the miracle's own plastic history, yet which are illuminated by that history.

A number of churches in France outside of Paris and Rouen acquired stained glass lights of the miracle centuries after its alleged occurrence. Most of these windows have survived to the present day, though the degree to which they are intact, and how they are intact, is a matter of individual churches and their histories.

The miracle of the Billettes windows, with one exception, were completed between 1500 and 1563. There always are other-themed windows in the same church, some of them Eucharistic in subject, most thematically unrelated to the miracle. Besides the temporal clustering, there is a spatial concentration. Eight of the ten churches with these windows are located in Champagne-Ardenne, the agricultural region to the northeast of Paris, bordering Belgium in the north. Seven of them are within a fifty kilometer radius of Troyes, in the Aube department, and slightly to the west, both north and south.

Distribution of Miracle of the Billettes stained glass windows
in churches in the Champagne-Ardenne region, 1500-1563

All these churches acquiring stained glass windows with the same subject in the same narrow time period seemed to 19th century antiquaries to be a reaction to the invasion of Calvinism into France from the east.[318] The 16th century wars of religion between Catholics and Calvinists proceeded with singular violence in the area. Visual imagery often was put forward as an instructional device for a population of limited literacy and access to written materials. The Calvinist denial of the real presence of Christ in the host was countered by the vividly translucent colors fixed in the church walls. The churches themselves were arrayed like a defensive phalanx from north to south against the attacking denial of Catholic doctrine.

An inscription in Gothic letters over three windows of the miracle in the church of St. Nizier, Troyes, read that the named patron had caused them to be made "to serve as a catechism and instruction to the peoples."[319] When an antiquary sought out the inscription in 1837, however, he had to copy it from "an ancient manuscript" kept in a local library.[320] Inscription and windows had been covered by the installation of an organ in the church choir in 1737. At present the windows are in "a state of debris."[321]

This brief history of the St. Nizier windows registers a process parallel to the written miracle over the same period of time: presence, absence, and revival as a curiosity in their enrollment among the churches that contained such windows. The scenes of the miracle shown in these windows is unknown. A single window in the church of Montsuzain dedicated to the Jew's purchase of the host was listed as in fragments in a 1971 tourist guide[322] and as "disappeared" twenty years later.[323] These windows are blank spaces where the miracle once was, the presence of an absence. Shifts in the church fabric, decay and lack of conservation have disposed of these windows, leaving only the written record to place the churches with the others in the same line.

Tall windows held together by strips of lead came are especially susceptible to damage by weather. After three centuries two Champagne churches containing miracle stained glass were the victims of severe storms within a decade of each other. The response revealed how the miracle stood in the minds of at least some in the local communities.

For the antiquary and bibliophile Alexis Socard the destruction wrought on the windows of the church of Bar-sur-Seine by the hailstorm of July 16, 1865 compounded injuries by tempests in 1706 and 1711 and rendered windows in the south and southeast exposure irreparable.[324] Socard was especially concerned about the window painted in *grisaille*, a medium giving sculpture-like effects in tones of gray, with scenes of the miracle of the Billettes. Its relation to the wars of religion between Catholics and Huguenots in the 16th century no longer mattered; the fine rendition of the figures in the window, and its influence on artists in his own time, called for attention.

Its artistry was superior to a colored window of the same subject in the church of Ricey-Bas also in Champagne, on another tributary of the Seine. Socard wanted to place the glasswork entirely within the realm of esthetic judgment, and to leave aside the religious considerations..

Bar-sur-Seine had been long contested between the Burgundians allied with the English and the French crown prior to the tumult of the 16th century, which pitted Roman Catholics against the Calvinist Huguenots. It had been the site of attacks, counterattacks and massacres, and the particularly gruesome execution of an intransigent Protestant.[325] At the apex of the religious war in 1598 a castle built by the Burgundians was torn down by the Catholics. The church and its windows, constructed earlier in the century, survived this human storm nearly to succumb to the wind and ice storm hundreds of years later. Socard aimed to displace the history of violence into the view of art.

Socard's project for the window was to describe it for the reader from a photograph that had been translated into a line drawing for clearer reproduction.

Socard just as finely delineates the boundary between history and legend in sight when viewing the window. The better to enable readers to reconstruct

in thought, the dramatic episodes of the legend, which the artist had neglected to paint on our window, and even to revive those which are missing as the result of mutilations, in order to form a judgment of this legend with awareness of its origins, such as is reported by an old author, after an eyewitness, I am going to transcribe the passage in which Jacques Dubreul…

There follows a long quotation from a major 17th century source on the miracle legend, which includes all the episodes of the model narrative from the host procurement to the Jew's execution and the enshrinement of the host. Socard includes Dubreul's note on his own sources in the 1604 Léon publication, the Billettes and St. Jean-en-Grève archives.

Like many other authors on the miracle Socard distances himself from belief in the truth of the events without adopting outright skepticism. He allows for the formation of an independent judgment while affirming the existence of *eyewitness* testimony about the miracle. This approach is enhanced by the disjointed convergence of narrative streams when the window's pictorial and verbal stories are mentally compared with each other and with Dubreul's account. Omission and mutilation, deliberate and accidental, combine with the strict historical record to yield a Paris miracle contemporary to Socard and his readers, a consciousness of the battles taking place around it.

The panels are briefly described in order, each one followed by a transcription of the lettering (*légende*) beneath the panel.

1er Panneau supérieur à gauche. — Une femme assise, et placée entre son ange gardien et le diable, semble écouter les avis de ce dernier; car elle se bouche l'oreille du côté de l'ange. Plus loin, elle quitte la maison et va trouver le juif.

LÉGENDE :

Comēt en la ciste de paris auint que une fēme teptee du diable de enprūtez a usure a.....
luy presta sur son abit par mauuais.....

First upper panel on left. A woman seated, and placed between her guardian angel and the devil, seems to hear the advice of this latter, because she covers her ear on the side of the angel. Farther on, she leaves the house and goes to find the Jew.
Legend:
How in the city of Paris there was a woman
tempted by the devil to borrow at usurious rate…
loaned to her on her dress for evil…

This panel of the window in the line drawing does not contain the details presented in Socard's summary.[326] From the words of legend and what was visible in the window Socard inferred that the artist prefaced the woman's vile bargain with the immemorial contest for the soul between angel and demon. The well-known iconography of visual representations rather than the history of the miracle was the source of this interpretation. Dubreul and his sources do not mention it.

From the beginning, Socard remakes the miracle within the antiquarian cosmology he shares with his readers. His references to "our counties" and "our windows," to the artists' marks which "we" cannot read today, the paintings the artists have bequeathed to "us" all circumscribe the community of observers and inquirers striving with him to preserve and interpret what their forbears erected in the church. Within this "we" is still a nation and a faith.

The successive panels are reconstructed according to the same strategy. Socard reads both the image and the legend beneath to follow the course of the miracle projected from the windows and legend into a space that includes Dubreul's words. The figures and objects in each frame of the line drawing correspond to the words of Socard's descriptions with some differences. The photographs of the contemporary windows in the digital photograph archive online today resemble the line drawings.

For instance in panel five : "Interior of a chamber. Armchair with backing, bed. A cauldron on the fire. The Jew jabs at the host with a long knife. Two children and a woman manifest their astonishment. Another woman looks in by the frame of a door."

The legend is effaced, and "one divines rather than reads the following words":

"How the Jew jabs the body of Our Lord with his long knife and the blood runs out the wife of the Jew and his children are quite mournful."

The furniture is just visible upper right in both the line drawing and the photo, as is the woman looking in, apparently the good Christian about to rescue the host. The blood is known by a few dark marks and explicitly in the legend, which Socard recreated by supposition.

In the sixth panel the Jew strikes the host rising above the cauldron with a fork while the cross appears, the woman and children gaze on in horror and the Jew exits in the description and the modern photograph but not Socard's line drawing. The legend is too incomplete even for supposition.

The twentieth century reconstruction of this frame seems to have taken Socard's description as the key.

All in all the five components of Socard's miracle (line drawing,description,legend,Dubreul, and the contemporary photographs) complement each other to create a self-realizing mental picture at least through the eighth panel. On the bottom course the correspondence breaks down. The line drawing frames nine and twelve are blank. In the verbal description nine is composed of disparate colored pieces unrelated to each other. Ten, eleven and twelve, all seriously mutilated successively contain the enthroned bishop interrogating the Jew, a martyr with a halo holding a palm (the patron?) and a person kneeling at a prie-dieu. No legends are visible.

The modern stained glass restorations reassembled the pieces of the ninth into a kneeling figure and a looming face. The bishop interrogating the Jew has been retained in the tenth, but in the eleventh the martyr has been transformed into the Jew being led away from the Bishop apparently to his punishment, and twelve does have a kneeling figure with another woman looming over her. Possibly it is a picture of the Jew's wife's conversion, or a patron with a saint.

The punishment of the Jew is absent from the Bar-sur-Seine series in Socard's version, and never was restored, if it was there in the first place. The row was filled in where he described frames as empty which weren't empty according to the drawing. This also is the completion of his vision of the miracle, only it is a completion of the absence that had developed.

At the end of his essay Socard explained that "he would have liked to show this masterpiece as the unknown artist left it to us, but he could only describe it mutilated by intemperate weather and made unknowable by the carelessness of men."

He did describe an art work decaying away from its subject, a process completed by the restoration that followed. Thanks to Socard we have the whole picture.

Socard's brother Emile, a cultural officer in local government, wrote in Alexis' obituary that in later years he became convinced that the air in Troyes was unbreathable, and that he must pack his library and move to a small town in Champagne.[327] A month after his arrival, before he could put his books in order, he was found lifeless, kneeling in his bed, his head on the wooden frame, which was the only way he could get any sleep.

On July 11, 1874, nine years to the day after the Bar-sur-Seine hailstorm, lightning struck another champaignois church with a Miracle of the Billettes stained glass window. The fire it kindled burned the wooden steeple and attic, and marred the interior of the church of Ste. Tanche in Lhuitre.[328]

The Miracle of the Billettes was one of five windows added to the church in the early 16th century. Since it was constructed in the 12th century on the site of a memorial to the virgin and martyr of Syrian origin Ste. Tanche, the church had been increased in size by additions that did not disrupt its symmetry. The other windows were an Old Testament subject- Joseph sold by his brothers-, the eight beatitudes, and the Passion and Resurrection of Christ.

Lhuitre had not seen clashes between the Huguenots and the Roman Catholics as severe as in Troyes and Bar-sur-Seine. Until the 12th century there had been a Jewish population and a synagogue in Lhuitre, and in Troyes, where the rabbi and commentator on the Talmud, Rashi, was born and spent part of his career.[329] The Joseph story was also the subject of a stained glass window series in Troyes Cathedral (and in St. Merri, Paris, the source of the host). The two churches in towns with Jewish history exhibiting the Genesis story of betrayal by kin and triumph in a foreign land is not coincidental.

The miracle window of Lhuitre, like the others, is organized in two contiguous columns of four panels, read from the bottom left to right back to left and up. The motion is toward the victory of the faith over small human dealings. The uppermost panel on the right is a rendition of the conversion of the Jew's family (now missing its upper half). By converting, the Jews could remain in the towns, as the entire story implies. The Jew being drawn off in the cart to his punishment, as in the miracle play, is directly below.

The curé of the Lhuitre church at the end of the century, Ulysse Bernard, wrote that while the previous curé with the help of donors had made remarkable progress in the restoration of the church, reconstructed the steeple and attic, and made many other improvements, the church as a whole still appeared to be in ruins.[330] In addition to work that needed to be done on a major support pillar of the choir, the five windows were badly in need of restoration.

Bernard published a brochure soliciting funds for a full restoration of the windows. Following very high contrast photograph prints of the windows, he gave a verbal description of them focusing on their content not so much as works of art, as Socard did with the Bar-sur-Seine windows, but on their representational significance from appearance to symbol. If Socard was a symbolist in his reading of the windows, making even the decayed condition of the paint and glass into a symbol of the tempestuous and negligent times, Bernard was a realist, framing the entire enterprise of description with the state of the church fabric, deplorable but part remedied and with a prospect for betterment.

He comments at the beginning on the information provided by the panels on the dress and furnishings of the time they were painted. The distinctive clothing and headgear of the Jew and his wife are notable. At the outset of his description Bernard verbalizes in detail occasioned by the painting the dress and accoutrements of the Jew, the poor woman and the Jew's wife as the transaction is made.

At the apex of the window is a four lobe arrangment in which a seated personnage seems to be delivering a discourse on the host (Bernard supposes once was shown) descending from heaven. The eight panels below are surrounded by and separated by decorative frames. None of this is apparent from the photograph reproduced before the text.

7. The Triumph of the Host	8. The Conversion of the Jew's Wife and Children
5. The Collecting of the Host	6. The Punishment of the Jew
3. The Delivery of the Stolen Host	4. The Profanation of the Host
1.The Sacrilegious Trade	2. The Communion

Bernard in some passages medievalizes his description by quoting passages in 13th century French spelling and grammar, taken from the archival text of the miracle narrative. For instance the Christian woman *"n'aïant le moïen de le païer"* (*"ne pas avant les moyens de lui payer"*), "not having the means to pay him." (the Jew) to release her dress, agrees to bring him the host.

The language joins the costume of the characters in forming a constrast drawing a viewer into the past of the window. Of perhaps greater importance for Bernard are the gestures and expressions of the characters which reveal that this is not a simple agreement. While the Jew explains to the woman the conditions of the exchange, she looks aside toward the Jew's wife, who remonstrates with her. Just the same, the woman reaches to receive the coins that fall from the Jew's hand.

> The wife of the Jew wears a round coiffure with a swollen cap streaked with yellow, a cape fastened at the neck with a gilded button, loose sides and sleeves cut at the level of the shoulders, a long dress beneath. One sees from her face and the gesture of her left hand that she is far from approving this shameful trade. Her right hand reaches toward the money on the counting table, to seize it.

Nearby the Jew's son is sharing a secret he has heard with a young man who has come to play a game of handball with him. The balls are visible in a fold in his cape.

The furnishings of the room, a bed on a platform beneath a blue ceiling, a fireplace where at the moment there is no fire, and a yellow door, are repeated in the other scenes with variations. These variations are not due, Bernard remarks, to any lack of taste; they are meant to keep interest from one scene to another necessarily resembling each other.

The priest of St. Merri parish gives communion to the congregation kneeling before the altar. A young man has preceded the woman, who is slipping the host into her mantle. The expression on the face of the priest betrays a sadness. Has he noticed the furtive gesture of his parishioner corrupted by her misery? The young man receiving communion at the moment will appear again twice in the house of the Jew. His face is sorrowful like that of the priest.

Bernard contrasts the facial expressions of the people gathered at the Jew's house. The woman, now dressed in her festive gown retrieved from the Jew, and the Jew himself wear happy expressions as she passes the host to him on a plate. The Jew's wife looks upon it tenderly, her right hand resting on the head of her infant son, who is vexed that he cannot see what the adults do. The young boy, friend of the infant, stands near the fireplace which has been repositioned and altered for variety's sake. From his stance and expression he is ready to flee if noticed.

Jonathas, long teeth showing in his open mouth a sign of his rage, has stabbed the host twice and two droplets of blood have appeared. He has raised his arm for a third thrust as his wife looks on in horror and his infant son gazes, having lifted himself to eye level at the edge of the counter. The young man who received Communion and who evidently has been in the Jew's house since the host was delivered and witnessed the horrifying attack is about to leave and sound the alarm. He will not reappear.

The bed and chimney have vanished from the room, replaced by a large window admitting light. Through the part-open door a woman is seen conducting two children to Mass at the church of Ste. Croix de la Bretonnerie nearby (again a detail not evident from the painting but supplied by Bernard).

Bernard resorts to the archaic language of the archival record to list the profanations made upon the host but not appearing in the next frame, which is divided into two scenes. The crucifixion over the cauldron attests to the act of tossing the host into the boiling water. Seeing this the Jew "could not do but flee," and in fact he has fled to his bed where he sits knees raised, tongue stilled between chattering teeth, his right hand raised toward the platform, fending off the host flying about the room, his left hand hanging impotently behind him. "Below his wife is seated. In the fright the prodigy has inspired is mingled a sentiment of admiration."

Neither is aware of what is happening around them. Their infant son, part hidden behind the fireplace, looks upon the scene. The woman, named "Martine" in the Bar-sur-Seine windows, kneels at the fireplace her right arm flung out in amazement as the host miraculously settles itself on the plate she holds. She beams in heavenly joy at the sight that terrified the Jew: the crucifixion with Mary and disciple permanently fixed on the surface of the host.

A cart carries the Jew tied up in a rope that encircles his neck, shoulders and hands (6). He looks "more cynical than intimidated," but the clouds of smoke that swathe him anticipate his burning and his eternity in Hell. Bernard perceived many details in this frame that are no longer visible in the glass today, for instance the figure of a monk beside the Jew, the provost of Paris and another personage on horseback beside the cart.

He also makes out the figure of the driver of the cart, who is bending back to receive orders from the executioner riding behind. This rider, accompanied by an assistant, reaches out to receive a book. Bernard repeats the Jew's request for the volume which he says will protect him from the flames. The execution window at another Champagne church, Longpré, features a copy of this book, its pages open to reveal a text he quotes.

The role of the Jew's two sons, the younger one, who tells the congregants arriving for mass that his father has killed their god, not knowing that this will be lethal for his father, and the elder one announcing his father's deed to a friend, who spread the word, also is not directly represented in this window.

The good Christian woman's bringing of the host to the curé at St. Jean-en-Grève is recalled rather than seen in the next window. Instead a procession, described in detail, bears the ostensoir containing the host to the doors of the church (7). This recalls the Eucharistic processions that traveled the streets of Paris at the time the window was made.

The final panel, the highest on the right, Bernard introduces with a quote from Dubreul on the subject, the conversion of the Jew's wife and children (8). The upper half of the panel is missing, he clarifies, and then proceeds to interpret the parts visible for the entire scene.

> The baptismal fonts are visible in the center. To the left of the fonts a priest, no doubt the Bishop of Paris Simon Matifas, called Simon de Bucy from his birthplace, in the Soissonais, with a stole in gold cloth of equal width along its length, without fringes and scattered with black crosses. He holds a container in his hand that a thick layer of cement obscures. On the other side a priest in surplice, followed by a cleric with folded hands.

To the left of the tableau the wife of the Jew is on her knees, hands joined together. She has left her obligatory dress as a Jewish woman and now wears a Christian woman's costume. Nearby, her children stand erect.

This photograph of the panel as it is today hints at the visual information Bernard drew upon for his description, not as rich today as it was when he reported it in a brochure intended to raise funds for its restoration. At no time were there facial expressions in the panel to be read for subtleties of mood and intention. This is the only panel with that portion, and that alone, entirely missing. He does not comment on the extreme selectiveness of the weather in destroying those faces alone.

In the next section, on "historical information," Bernard wants his readers to be sure not to confound the act of the miracle portrayed in the window with "more or less proven legends." The wonder of the events supporting the real presence in the Eucharist spread throughout France and congregations were drawn to embellish their churches with many windows of the miraculous host. "The piety of the faithful asked that one put the moving and dramatic scenes of the miracle before the eyes." These are not to be taken for historic truths, for what is written. The windows in this state have persisted to our day.

Several of the other Champagne windows of the miracle are named, and Socard's analysis of the Bar-sur-Seine panels is given its due. Bernard was taken with the panel of the woman between the angel and the devil, closing her ear to the angel. The fact of the miracle had become fact about the miracle, not to be confused with the miracle itself. The Jew still was present.

Notes

318 "protestations painted on glass" Socard (1866: 97)
319 Langlois (1832: 13-14)
320 Bareste (1837: 74)
321 Inventaire Générale (1992: 27)
322 Parisot and Bonnard-Folliot (1971: 200)
323 Inventaire Générale (1992: 126)
324 Socard (1866)
325 Coutant (1846: 68-71)

326 The color photograph of the window in the Medieval Stained Glass Photographic Archive, a clearer image than what is obtained standing in the church, shows a restored panel but still without a demon present.

327 E. Socard (1877)
328 Boulanger (1875)
329 Thévenot (1903: 108)
330 Bernard (1897)

21.
The Last Miracle

The last reference to reparation services at St. Jean-St. François was in 1950.[331] The eight tapestry paintings of the miracle were on exhibit in the church in 1970.[332] That year St. Jean-St. François was reconsecrated as Ste. Croix des Arméniens, the cathedral of Armenian Catholics in Paris.[333] Apart from quotations from sources on the miracle and reproductions of imprints in books like this one, its only tangible remains are the stained glass windows in St. Etienne-du-Mont in Paris, the Champagne churches and two others in Normandy and the Loire Valley. I do not know of any specialty tours visiting them.

In 1990 Gilbert Dahan wrote a brief article for *Communauté Nouvelle* on the 700th anniversary of the *"affaire des Billettes."*[334] No longer "the miracle," as it had been for the revivalists at its 600th anniversary in 1890, nor even "the legend," as it was for Wogue, Lazard and others around the same time: it was an *affaire,* a scandalous historical matter.

If anyone chooses to recall it at its 2090 anniversary any title given to it will reflect the historical context and nothing more. "Sacrilege mutated into miracle" was how the program of the 1965 *Festival du Marais* referred to the event that had eventually given birth to the Billettes and the extant medieval cloisters that was one of the Festival venues.[335] Both sacrilege and miracle were just words describing how it was viewed at various times.

The miracle has been perpetuated as a matter of belief, an investment, an object of study and regret. Each of these phases has dimensions: degrees of belief and incredulity; amount of commitment to the consequences of belief from "it really happened" to the question of whether it all happened that way and why it was described happening that way and if any miracle of this sort or of any other sort can happen.

Its history can be measured by gradations of remove from the miracle to a vanishing point always somewhere in the future. The perspective of the miracle depends upon that point. The first remove came not when the ontology or verifiability of the miracle was questioned, but when comparable events were not miraculous in nature.

A pamphlet published in 1765 some years after the young Jean-François de la Barre was judicially tortured and burned for his alleged mutilation of a cross in the town of Abbeville cited such a comparison.[336] "The convent of the Billettes, in Paris, is an authentic proof that this horror belongs to the receding centuries." S. René earlier that century named the convent as a proof of the miracle's veracity, but here it is proof that the barbarous punishment of the supposedly enlightened present is that of an earlier era. No Jews are mentioned in the pamphlet, published in London as the revolutionary fervor built in France. The Jew and de la Barre were equally victims of a savage system about to be overthrown.

Focusing on the punishment all out of proportion to the events that preceded it places the reader at a uniform distance from both prosecutions. The acts of blasphemy and profanation attributed to the Jew and to de la Barre were sufficient to warrant the punishment only from the viewpoint of those promoting and carrying out the punishment. No degree of accuracy of reporting would be sufficient to justify torture and burning. From this viewpoint the injustice and barbarity of treatment, which could be generalized to the injustices of the regime in power, place in doubt the validity of the testimony that led to this outcome.

Belief in the miracle, or in miracles, could then be separated from reportage of a particular case, and subordinated to the interests of the parties. The consequent absence of any attempt to obtain an unimpeachable source for what actually occurred in the work of even the most skeptical historians leads to examining the logic and psychology of the actors to test credibility. Why did the Jew want the host? Would he have continued to stab the host if it actually bled?

The punishment equation that emerged on the verge of the Revolution also included for those so oriented seeing anyone executed for profanation as a martyr, which reverses and maintains the old formula of sainthood. As the relics, buildings and personnel of the miracle vanished, and all that remained was a cyclically repeated liturgy the punishment section vanished as well. The miracle was supported by other miracles only as a historic belief, an example of what preceded the treatment of those who did not conform to the imposed standards whatever their reasons. Most particularly when they were Jews in a Christian city.

Establishing the critical distance needed to write about the miracle while taking into account the beliefs of those concerned requires a consensus, and that comes from a reaction to the punishment, which itself has nothing to do with whether marvels occurred or can occur. The vanishing point is justice, not sanctity.

The bleeding yet indestructible host, documented elsewhere, was an imported special effect to lend emphasis, and a fantastical credibility, to the entire proceeding. When de la Barre allegedly mutilated the Abbeville cross it did not bleed or move. Jews and flagrant disbelievers, or those who were accused of disbelief, were burned without supernatural antecedents. Their sacrifice gave us the distance from the mob, including the judicial mob, surrounding us at the present moment. Until someone profanes what is dearest while seriously threatening a livelihood.

The Paris miracle was remarkable in the degree of institutionalization that followed the lead events. Driven by the wish to cover the violation of sanctity with a continual act of reparation, the bilateral structure of the Billettes and St. Jean-en-Grève was assured of patrons craving the benefits of making up for violation of the divine. The amount of time it took for that institutionalization to become established, to work itself into the religious economy of Paris, predicted the amount of time it lasted as its custodians consolidated their tenure and found sidelines.

The critical distance and active proximity gained during the Revolution also ended those institutions and made them into a sought-after memory. That memory was perpetuated in the reparation services continued in a church rededicated for that purpose until it was rededicated again. All that remained of the miracle was the cumulative record and the fact of its distance from the present.

On March 19, 2015 in Kabul, Afghanistan a 27 year-old woman named Farkhunda Malikzada was murdered and burned by a mob a number of whose members photographed the scenes of her demise and posted them on social media.[337] She had been accused by the custodian of the shrine she was visiting on women's day of burning the Quran, and the accusation, rapidly spread, brought a large number of men to confront her, lethally, as it turned out. Not all of her attackers identifiable from testimony and videos were charged, and of those who were, a few given the death penalty, the shrine's custodian and others, had their sentences commuted. Her family fled the country. At Farkhunda's part-finished grave reporter Alissa J. Rubin heard a 6 year-old child name Farkhunda and say that she had burned the Quran and so was punished and lynched.

This was a lie concocted by the shrine's fortuneteller, who prospered writing paper charms he sold mostly to women vistors, condoms and Viagra to male visitors. Farkhunda, a theology student, voiced her objections to the traffic in superstition at a holy site, and threatened the fortuneteller's business, the full extent of which she did not know.

The shrine's custodian, an illiterate, recovered some charms that Farkhunda burned, added some pieces of an old Quran, and showed the mixture to men who answered the call put out by the fortuneteller, who managed not to be at the shrine on the day Farkhunda was attacked. The lie that best served the status quo became the truth as far as anyone wanted to know, and despite the ghastly punishment of Farkhunda and the prosecution of some of the attackers many in the population embraced the lie.

The Jew, young de la Barre, Farkhunda each was accused of a profanation and punished judicially or extrajudicially with burning annihilation. The progressively greater accuracy of documentation of the supposed profaner's acts did not forestall levying the ultimate penalty. The burning was among the horrors recorded by Farkhunda's attackers, yet like the burning of the Jew and de la Barre it began to vanish from the record while the alleged profanation remained. And those who were present as established by the documentation were left without blame.

The three alleged profaners and many others treated the same way with similar justification differed in culture, social setting, historical moment, gender, and age and came to the same final image: self-justified violent ejection of the presumed transgressor amid the expectation of a miracle. The potential to repeat this has only grown.

Notes

---

[331] *Vingtième Siècle* 103-4 (2009): 211
[332] Momarché and Bonnard-Folliot (1972: 284)
[333] Pérouse de Montclos (1994: 458)
[334] Dahan (1990)
[335] *"sacrilège moué en miracle,"Festival du Marais* 1965: 118
[336] *Recueil intéressant sur la mutilation du crucifix d'Abbeville, arrivée le 9 août 1765.* London: 1776: 49-50.
[337] Rubin (2015)

Appendix

A-1.

De miraculo hostiae a Judaeo Parisiis anno Domini M. CC. XC multis ignominis affectae, *Recueuil des historiens des Gaules et de la France* 22(1865): 32-33 and Lenoir (1893: 217-18n1). Also in S. René (1725: 2,148).

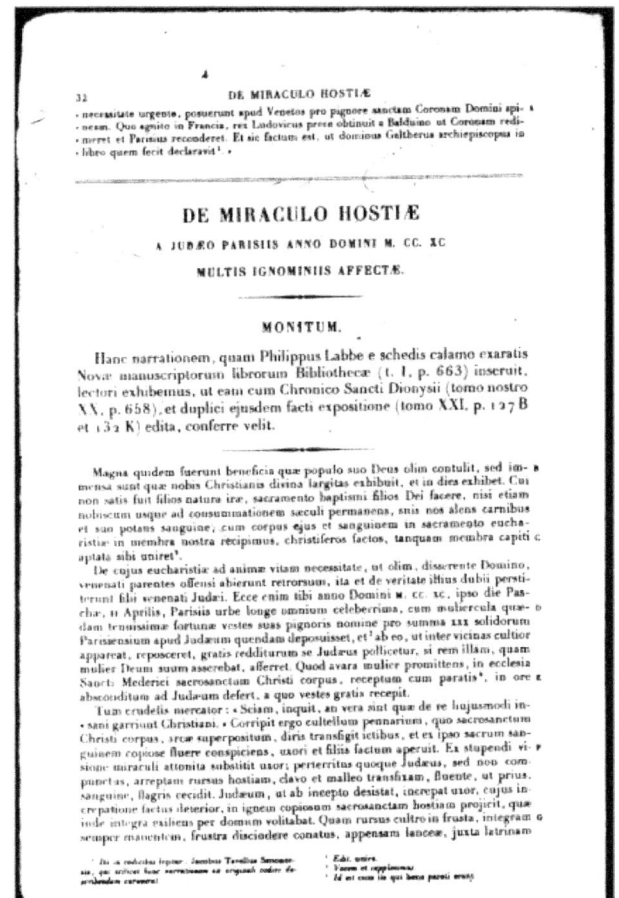

a totis viribus percutit. Unde, ut et prius, abunde rursus fluente sanguine, in bullientis aquæ caldariam projecta', aqua sanguinea facta, suæ majestatis virtute sursum elevata, in corporis Domini crucifixi specie Judæo se videndam præbuit: cujus aspectu uxore cum filiis flentibus ex eventu prodigioso contritis, totus amens fugiensque cubiculum suum intravit.

b Hæc qui secum perpenderit, divinam mirabundus laudabit pietatem, aliamque Domini (licet a mortuis resurgens jam non moriatur) quasi resurrectionem dicet. Sacrosanctam enim illam hostiam, post punctionem, transfixionem, flagella, flammarum ardorem, discidium, lancinationem, et in bullientis aquæ caldariam projectionem, illibatam et integram in ecclesia Sancti Joannis in Gravia, honorifice

c reconditam, portiuncula vestis Domini involutam, et ad majorem gratiam Crucis dominicæ portiuncula ornatam; cultellum quoque pennarium prædictum, sanguinem qui mire ex punctione profluxit et vasculum ligneum in quod insilivit, in ecclesia fratrum Charitatis Beatæ Mariæ, in eadem vicinia, corporalibus oculis fideles possunt intueri.

d Hæc autem domi facta sic ad populi notitiam prodierunt. Cum, hora majoris missæ, in ecclesia Crucesignatorum nola signum daretur, ut eo conveniens populus sacrosanctum Christi corpus adoraret, filius Judæi, foras progrediens, prætereuntes, quo currerent, interrogat. — Ad Mysteria sacrosancti corporis Christi adoranda dicentibus : — Frustra in ecclesia illa Christianos Deum suum quærere

e ait, quem flagellatum, injurius affectum et male tractatum, modo pater suus occidisset. Quod audiens, mulier quædam, resciendi avida, Judæi domum, horrore plenam, signo Crucis armata ingrediens, dominicæ carnis iteratum intuetur martyrium; statimque in ligneum vasculum, quod quasi ad suos usus ignem mulier petitura portaverat, sacrosancta hostia sacra et incolumis insilit. Quam magna

f cum reverentia sub gremio recondens, sacerdoti Sancti Joannis in Gravia conservandam detulit. Mulier autem illa, quasi vinculis constricta fuisset, ecclesiam prædictam licet egredi tentaret, non potuit, quousque præfato sacerdoti [hostiam]² quam ferebat, videntibus multis qui jam eo facti rumore convenerant, obtulisset. Quibus mulier factum, ut viderat, enarravit. Sacerdos autem episcopo Parisiensi

g nunciandum curavit. Ad spectaculum tota ruit civitas; Judæus cum uxore et filiis in vincula conjiciuntur. Accersitus coram episcopo et viris ecclesiastica dignitate insignitis, Judæus de delicto fatetur monetur ut pœniteat, scriptum esse. Nolo mortem peccatoris, sed magis convertatur et vivat, veniam speret quando pro crucifigentibus se Deus olim oraverat. Uxore et filiis ad christianam fidem conversis,

h pertinax quoque Judæus igni cremandus condemnatus, ductusque ad locum supplicii, cum ignem supponere vellet carnifex : « O me infelicem, exclamat, qui tam « subito deprehensus, arma mecum assumere non potui! « Quæ hæc essent arma inquirenti præposito Judæus respondet : « Habeo librum in domo mea, quem si « mecum haberem, Deus vester non posset me facere comburi. » Jusso præposito ab

i apparitoribus allatus libellus, Judæo alligatus, igne supposito tam facile uterque est in cineres redactus quam difficile ab infelicitate sua converti Judæus potuit. Tum populi astante corona, Parisiensis episcopus, ob miraculum, ut gestum fuerat, recensuit, Judæi uxorem, filium et filiam, baptismate ablutos, sacri chrismatis unctione signavit. Multi quoque Judæorum, tam manifesto moti miraculo, ad fidem conversi, baptismi sacramentum perceperunt. Quo autem in loco tam immane facinus patratum est, Raynerius Flamingus, civis Parisiensis, capellam quæ Miraculorum nomine nuncupata est, suis sumptibus anno Domini M. CC. XCIII ædificandam curavit; deinde, procurante Guidone de Joinvilla, fratribus Charitatis B. Mariæ Catalaunensis diœcesis attribuit; Philippus autem, Francorum rex,

k dictus Pulcher, domo quadam prædictæ' capellæ vicina anno Domini M. CC. XCIX auxit. Fratres vero prædicti ordinis tanti miraculi commemorationem Dominica in Albis solemniter quotannis celebrari statuerunt.

---

¹ Edit. projectam. — ² Voces horum supplevimus. — ³ Edit. prædicta.

On the Miracle of the Host Afflicted with Many Ignominies by the Jew of Paris in the Year of the Lord 1290

Great were the benefits that God often bestowed upon his people, but immense are those divine largesse exhibits to us Christians. To whom it was not enough to make "children by the nature of wrath," with the sacrament of baptism to make them children of God, even unto the end of time, by eating his flesh and drinking his blood, with his body and blood into our members we receive the Eucharist, made Chirst-bearers, as members fitted to the head unite.

From the necessity which the Eucharist is to the life of the soul, often, disserving God, poisonous relations turn back upon offenses, as when poisonous Jews attach doubts to the children concerning the truth of that. Thus to you in the year of the Lord 1290 on the day itself of Easter, April 11, in the city of Paris long celebrated by all when a poor woman of tenuous fortune gave her clothing in pledge with a Jew for the sum of 30 Parisian solidi, and from this so she might appear better dressed among the neighbors, as she asked, the Jew would take it upon himself to return it for free if the woman brought to him the thing that she assured him was her god. Which the greedy woman promising, having received with the communicants the most sacred body of Christ in the church of St. Mederic, in her mouth having carried it off she passed it to the Jew, from whom she received her clothing for free.

Then the cruel merchant, "I will know," he said, "if what the insane Christians gabble about a thing of this sort is true." Then he gripped a bread knife with which he transfixed the most sacred body of Christ laid upon an ark with dire blows, and seeing the sacred blood copiously flow from it, the deed appeared to his wife and children. His wife stood dumbfounded at the stupendous vision of the miracle, the Jew terrified as well, but not repentant, having seized the host again, and transfixed it with hammer and nail, the blood fluidly as before, he fell upon it with whips. The wife chides the Jew from the beginning that he stop, her rebuke having become more severe, he throws the most sacred host into a full flame from which it immediately exits intact and flits about the room. Once more the knife in vain, always remaining whole, trying to shred it in vain, setting upon it with a lance, beside the latrine/he attacked it with all his strength. Thereupon as before blood flowed freely released into the cauldron of boiling water, by virtue of his majesty having risen above in the form of the body of the Lord crucified he offered himself to be seen by the Jew. At his aspect the wife with children fleeing from the event contrite, out of his mind he entered his closet.

This which was considered, surprise celebrated divine piety, and like another resurrection of the Lord (like rising from the dead yet not dead) that most sacred host after piercing, transfixing, flagellation, heat of flames, cleaving, lanceing, and tossing into boiling water of the cauldron, whole and complete in the church of St. Jean-en-Grève, honorably concealed, enclosed in a portion of the garment of the Lord, and in the highest grace ornamented with a portion of the Lord's Cross. The aforesaid bread knife that caused blood to flow wondrously from the stab, and the wooden vessel into which it entered, in the church of the Charity of the Blessed Mary, in the same vicinity, with fleshly eyes can be beheld.

This in the house they brought thus to the notice of the people. When at the hour of high mass in the church of the Ste. Croix de la Bretonnerie the bell was rung so the people gathering there might adore the most sacred body of Christ, the son of the Jew, going out, asks the passers-by where they are going. -To adoring the Mysteries of the most sacred body of Christ, they say.-In vain, he says, do you seek, Christians, in that church your god, whom having flagellated, afflicted with injuries and treated badly our father killed. A certain woman eager to find out, full of horror, arming herself with the sign of the cross, entered the house of the Jew. She saw the repeated martyrdom of the Lord's flesh, and immediately the most sacred host jumped safely into a wooden vessel the woman carried to seek fire for her uses. With what great reverence guarding upon her lap she passed it to the priest of St. Jean-en-Grève for safekeeping. However that woman might try to leave the church she was unable to, as if bound by chains, until what time that the aforementioned priest, seeing many who already gathered at the rumor of the deed, might show the host he carried. To them the woman told about the deed as she saw it. The priest delivered the announcement to the bishop of Paris.The entire city rushed to the spectacle. The Jew with wife and children were bound fastened together in chains. Called before the bishop and men charged with church dignity, the Jew admits the offense, is advised to repent, as it is written, *I do not want the death of a sinner, but more that he convert and live,* that he might hope pardon as when before his crucifiers God once prayed. The wife and children converted to Christianity, the unyielding Jew condemned to be burned by fire, and led to the place of punishment, when the executioner wishes to set the fire,"O unhappy me," he exclaims, "who was so quickly apprehended I couldn't take up my arms!" To the inquiry, what might these arms be, the Jew responds, "I have a book in my house, which if I have it by me, your God cannot make me burn." At an order of the officer the book having been brought by the attendants, the Jew fastened to the stake, was easily burned by the fire set there until reduced to ashes with such difficulty was the Jew converted from his faithlessness. Then standing at the head of the people the Paris bishop reviewed where and how miracle was done, the wife, son and daughter of the Jew, having been abluted by baptism, he signed with the unction of blessed chrism. Many of the Jews, moved by the manifest miracle, converted to the faith, received the sacrament of baptism. In the very place where the severe crime was committed, Raynier Flaming, Paris citizen, at his own expense founded in the year of the Lord 1294 a chapel designated by the name of Miracles. Then under the guidance of Guy de Joinville was entrusted to the brothers of the Charity of the Blessed Mary of Chalons diocese. Philip, king of the French, called le Bel, added a house near the aforementioned chapel in the year of the Lord 1299. The Brothers of the stated order instituted a commemoration of such miracle to be solemnly celebrated each year on Dominica in Albis [the Sunday after Easter].

A-2.

Extrait d'une chronique anonyme finissant en M.CCC.LXXX, *Recueil des historiens des Gaules et de la France* 21(1855): 127B.

B   L'an mil ıı. c̃. ııı. xx. ıx.[3] avint à Paris, en la parroisse Saint-Jehan en Grève, que ung juif fist tant pardevers une femme chrestienne qu'elle luy apporta le corps Jhesu Christ en une hostie sacrée, laquelle elle avoit receue à Pasques, et le bailla au juif. Lequel juif mist la sainte ostie en une chaudière de eaue bouillant, et la poigny d'un coustel; et l'eaue devint vermeille. Et avint que une aultre
C femme chrestienne aloit quérir du feu sieux[4] le juif; et l'ostie sailly en une escuelle que la femme tenoit, laquelle la porta incontinent à l'évesque. Et fut pris le juif, qui confessa le cas, et fut condempné à mort. Et de ce miracle est fondée une église à Paris que on dit les Billettes; et est ou lieu là où le juif demouroit.....

The year 1290 happened at Paris, in the parish of St. Jean-en-Grève, that a Jew so manipulated a Christian woman that she brought him the body of Jesus Christ in a blessed host, which she received at Easter and gave it to the Jew. Which Jew put the host in a cauldron of boiling water and pierced it with a knife and the water became vermillion. And it happened that another Christian woman went in search of fire at the Jew's house and the host entered a vessel the woman had, who carried it contained to the bishop. And the Jew was taken, and confessed the crime and was condemned to death. And from this miracle was founded a church in Paris that is called the Billettes and it is the place where the Jew lived...

A-3.

Extraits d'une chronique anonyme française finissant en M.CCC.VIII, *Recueil des historiens des Gaules et de la France* 21 (1855): 132-33.

En ce meisme an, advint à Paris une chose merveilleuse, selon le record de ceux qui à ce point y estoient. En celle cité avoit une femme à qui un juif avoit presté argent par usure, sur ses draps. Celle vint au juif le jour de la sainte Pasque, et dist

A qu'elle vouloit ses draps rachater; et cellui lui respondi que se elle lui vouloit apporter son Dieu qu'elle aouroit, et qu'elle devoit en ce jour recepvoir, il lui rendroit ses draps seus rien prendre de son argent. Celle, qui de convoitise estoit embrasée, vint au monstiers et receupt sans dévotion le précieux corps de Jhesu Crist, et l'apporta au juif, qui ses draps lui rendi, et prinst la digne personne, et le jetta en une paielle
B d'eaue qui sur le feu bouloit. Et quand il vey qu'il ne le pourroit par celle manière destruire, si traist son coustel et le commença l'eaue à férir; et l'eaue, qui clère estoit, devint vermeille comme meslée avecques sang. Après ce, entra en la maison du juif une autre femme chrestienne, qui bien s'aperceut de la desloyauté que le juif faisoit; si le commença à laidengier durement, et manacier que elle le
C feroit savoir à l'évesque. Cil, qui eult paour, lui promist à donner xx. sols se elle se vouloit taire et lui aidier à son Dieu destruire; mais celle, qui ne fut mie si convoiteuse que la première avoit esté, respondi que elle mieulx ameroit qu'il fust art en ung feu. Dont yssi de la maison bien courrouciée, et le nonça à deux sergens, qui tantost vindrent à l'ostel le juif, et trouvèrent que riens n'estoit
D son cuer changié de despit faire à Nostre Sauveur, pour chose qu'il eust veue; ains l'avoit puis féru par plusieurs fois du coustel et remis en l'eaue froide, qui, en telle manière comme la première, estoit devenue toute vermeille. Mais quant il perceut que ceulx venoient pour lui prendre, il respandi l'eaue en tel lieu que oncques ceulx n'en peulrent une seule goutte recevoir; et trouvèrent la digne
E personne sur une table, où elle estoit si soubtillement saillie que le juif ne autre ne s'en estoient perceux. Dont fut le juif prins et mis en prison; si recongneut tout le fait, sans avoir repentance; et pour ce il fut art à Paris, en la place aux pourceaulx, comme tirant de dur cuer et de mauvais couraige.

In this same year there happened in Paris a marvelous event, according to the record of those who were there at that time. In that city there was a woman to whom a Jew loaned money at interest, on her clothing. That woman went to the Jew on the day of holy Easter and said that she wanted to buy back her clothing. And he responded to her that if she was willing to bring her God that she would have and that she ought to receive this day he would return her clothing without taking any of her money. That woman, taken up with greed, went to the communion rail and received without devotion the precious body of Jesus Christ, and brought it to the Jew, who returned her clothing to her, and took "the worthy person" and tossed it into a pot of water boiling on the fire. And when he saw that he could not destroy it in that way, he took counsel and began to agitate the water, and the water, which was clear, became vermillion as mixed with blood. After that another woman entered the house of the Jew who well noticed the disrespect that the Jew practiced. She began to chastise him harshly, and threatened to make it known to the bishop. That one, who was afraid, promised to give her twenty sols if kept quiet and helped him destroy her God. But that woman, not as greedy as the first one had been, said that she would like it better if he was burned in a fire. Then she left the corrupted house and told two sergeants who soon went to the house of the Jew and found that nothing in his heart had changed to treat Our Savior differently, as a result of the thing he had seen. Thus he had jabbed it several times with a knife and put it back in cold water which in the same way as the first had become all vermillion. But when he noticed that they came to take him he threw it out in a place so they would never find a drop, and they found "the worthy person" on a table where it had secretly come to rest so neither the Jew nor anyone else noticed it. Thus the Jew was taken and put in prison, the whole deed was confessed, without repentance, and for that he was burned in Paris, at the pig market, as being hard hearted and ill-tempered.

References

Academie des Inscriptions et de Belles Lettres. 1897. *Histoire literaire de la France: Suppléments, Tome XXI.* Paris: Chez Firmin Didot.

d'Arbaumont, Jules. 1863. *Essai historique sur la Sainte-Chapelle de Dijon.* Paris: Lamarche.

d'Argens, Jean-Baptiste de Boyer. 1738. *Lettres juives, tome 3.* Lausanne and Geneva: Marc Michel Bousquet.

d'Argens, Jean-Baptiste de Boyer. 1769. *Lettres chinoises, tome 5.* The Hague: Pierre Paupie.

d'Auton, Jean. 1834. *Chroniques,* ed. by P.L. Jacob, *tome troisieme.* Paris: Silvestre.

Baloche, Constant. 1911. *Église Saint-Merry de Paris: histoire de la paroisse et de la collegiale, tome premier.* Paris: Oudin.

Bareste, Eugène. 1837. Histoire de la peinture sur verre: depuis son origine jusqu'à nos jours, III, *l'Artiste* 13: 72-78.

Barluzzi, J. 1862. *De la procession solennelle au Vatican dans la Fête-Dieu commentaire.* Rome: Imprimerie de la Chamber Apostolique.

Baron, Salo Wittmayer. 1967. *A social and religious history of the Jews.* New York: Columbia University Press.

Basnage de Beauval, Jacques. 1707. *Histoire des juifs depuis Jesus Christ jusqu'á present, tome cinq.* Rotterdam: Reinier Looy.

Bates, William. 1876. *George Cruickshank.* London: Houlston and Sons.

Belin, Jules-Leonard and A. Pujol. 1843. *Histoire civile, morale et monumentale de Paris.* Paris: Le Prieur.

de Belleforest, François. 1882. *L'ancienne et grande cite de Paris, introduction et notes par l'Abbé Valentin Dufour.* Paris: A. Quantin.

Béraud, A.-N. and P.-J.-S. Dufey. 1828. *Dictionnaire historique de Paris, tome II.* Paris: Chez J.N. Barba.

Berault-Bercastel, Antoine-Henri. 1809. *Histoire de l'église, tome VII.* Toulouse: Chez Desclassan et Navarre.

Berger, Elie. 1884-1911. *Les registres d'Innocent IV.* 4 tomes. Paris: Ernest Thorin; Albert Fontemoine.

Bério, Nicole. 1999. Entre sottises et blasphèmes: echos de la dénunciation du Talmud dans quelques sermons du XIIIe siècle, 211-37 IN Colloque sur le brûlement du Talmud à Paris en 1242-1244, ed. by Gilbert Dahan. Paris: Cerf.

Bernard, Ulysse. 1897. *Notice descriptive et historique sur les vitraux de l'église de Lhuitre.* Lhuitre: Chez l'Abbé Bernard.

Bertholet, Jean. 1746. *Histoire de l'institution de la Fête-Dieu.* Liège: F.A. Barchon and J.Jacob.

Bertholet, Jean. 1846. *Histoire de l'institution de la Fête-Dieu.* Liège: Felix Oudart.

Bicknell, Ethel B. 1911. *Paris and her treasures.* New York: Charles Scribner's Sons.

Bins de Saint-Victoire, J.-M.-B. 1809. *Tableau historique et pittoresque de Paris depuis les Gaulois jusqu'à nos jours, tome second.* Paris: H. Nicolle.

Blanchard, Gérard. 1974. *Histoire de la bande dessinée.* Verviers: Marabout Université.

Bonfons, Pierre and Jacques Dubreul. 1608. *Les antiquitez et choses plus remarquables de Paris*. Paris: Nicolas Bonfons.

Bonnardot, Alfred. 1851. *Études archéologiques sur les anciens plans de Paris*...Paris: Deflorenne.

Bonnardot, François, et al., eds. 1886. *Registres des délibérations du Bureau de la Ville de Paris, t. 2 (1527-1539); t. 4 (1552-1558)*. Paris: Imprimerie Nationale.

Bordier, Henri-Leonard, ed.1856. *Les églises et monastères de Paris, pièces en prose et en vers des IXe,XIIIe et XIVe siècles*. Paris: Chez Aug. Aubry.

Boulanger, Henri. 1875. Note de l'église de Lhuitre et sur l'incendie de 10 juillet 1874, 67-70 IN *Annuaire administratif et statistique du Departement de l'Aube 1875*.

Boulier, Philibert. 1646. *Remarques historiques et chrestiennes sur la saincte et miraculeuse hostie de Dijon*. Dijon: Pierre Palliot.

Boulier, Philibert, 1649. *Recueil de quelques pieces pour servir à l'histoire ecclésiastique et sacrée de la ville de Dijon*. Dijon: Palliot.

Boutaric, Edouard, editor. 1863. *Actes du Parlement de Paris, tome premier: de l'an 1254 à l'an 1328*. Paris: Henri Plon.

Bruyn, P.-J. 1820. *Histoire de l'église collégiale et paroissiale des SS. Michel et Gudule*. Brussels.

Cachau, Philippe. 2004. *Jacques Hardouin-Mansart de Sagonne, dernier des Mansart (1711-1778)*, thèse d'histoire de l'art soutenue à Paris, t. II.

Caesarius of Heisterbach. 1851. *Dialogus miraculorum*, ed. by Joseph Strange. Cologne: J.M.

de Cafmeyer, Petrus. 1720. *Hooghweirdighe historie van het alder-heylighste sacrament van mirakel Brussels*. Brussels: Georgius de Backer.

Calvin, Jean. 1817. Advertissement très utile...[Traité des reliques], 405-52 IN *Ioannis Calvini Quae Opera Supersunt Omnia, Volumen VI*, ed. by Gulielmus Baum. Brunschwig: apud A. Schwetske et filium.

Calvin, Jean. 1921. *Traité des reliques* (1521). Paris: Editions Bossaru.

Camille, Michael. 2009. *The gargoyles of Notre-Dame: medievalism and the monsters of modernity*. Chicago: University of Chicago Press.

Caron, Vicki. 2014. Catholics and the rhetoric of anti-Semitic violence in fin-de-siècle France, 36-60 IN *Sites of European anti-Semitism in the age of mass politics, 1880-1918*, ed. by Robert Nemes and Daniel Unowsky. Lebanon, New Hampshire: Brandeis University Press.

Cartuyvels, Charles, et al. 1898. *Les voies de dieu: un jubilé Eucharistique dans l'église expiatoire du Très Saint Sacrement de miracle à Bruxelles, 1848-1898*. Brussels: Desclée, de Brouwer.

Chiffoleau, Jacques. 1990. Les processions parisiens de 1412: analyse d'un rituel flamboyant, *Revue historique* 284: 37-76.

Claretie, Jules. 1881. *La vie à Paris, 1880-1885: Année 4*. Paris: Havard.

Clarke, George. 1832. *Pompei, v.2*. London: Charles Knight.

Cochet, Jean-Benoit-Desiré. 1868. *Catalogue du Musée d'Antiquités de Rouen*. Rouen: Chez tous les Libraires.

Collette, Charles Hastings. 1880. *The Roman Breviary: a critical and historical review*. London: W.H. Allen.

Collin de Plancy, J.-A.-S. 1818. *Voyage de Paul Bérenger dans Paris après quarante-cinq ans d'absence*. 2v.

Paris: Le Rouge.

Collin de Plancy, J.-A.-S. 1821. *Dictionnaire critique des reliques et des images, tome premier*. Paris: Guien et Co.

Collin de Plancy, J.-A.-S. 1844. *Dictionnaire infernale*. Paris: Paul Mellier.

Commission du Vieux Paris. 1899. *Procès verbaux-année 1898*. Paris: Imprimerie Nationale.

Commission du Vieux Paris. 1901. *Procès verbaux-année 1900*. Paris: Imprimerie Nationale.

Commission du Vieux Paris. 1903. *Procès verbaux-année 1902*. Paris: Imprimerie Nationale.

Corblet, Jules. 1885. *Histoire dogmatique, liturgique et archeologique du sacrement de l'Eucharistie, tome premier*. Paris: Société Générale de Librairie Catholique.

Corrozet, Gilles. 1874. *La fleur des antiquitez de la noble et triumphante ville et cité de Paris par Gilles Corrozet (1532), publiée par le bibliophile Jacob*. Paris: L. Willem.

Corrozet, Gilles. 1550. *Les antiquitez, histoires et singularitez de Paris, ville capitale de la royaume de France*. Paris: Au Palais, en la boutique de Gilles Corrozet.

Corrozet, Gilles. 1581. *Antiquitez, chroniques et singularitez de Paris*. Paris: Nicolas Bonfons.

Costello, Louisa Stuart. 1842. *A Voyage to Auvergne, v.2*. London: Richard Bentley.

Coullié, Pierre. 1899. Instruction pastorale de S.E. le Cardinal-Archeveque de Lyon sur la Sainte Euchariste, *Semaine religieuse du diocese de Lyon* 17 February: 345-54.

Coutant, Lucien. 1846. *Fragments historiques sur la ville et l'ancien comté de Bar-sur-Seine*. Bar-sur-Seine: Imprimerie et Librairie de Saillard.

Coyecque, Ernest. 1893. *Catalogue general des manuscrits des bibliothèques publiques de France, Departments, Tome XIX: Amiens*. Paris: E. Plon, Nourrit et Cie.

Dahan, Gilbert. 1991. Il y a sept cents ans à Paris (1291): l'Affaire des Billettes, *Communautè nouveau* 58: 72-84.

Dahan, Gilbert. 1999. *Le brulement du Talmud à Paris, 1242-1244*. Paris: Editions du Cerf.

Davis, Adam J. 2013. The economic power of a hospital in thirteenth-century Provins, 121-34 IN *Center and periphery: Studies on power in the medieval world*. Leiden: Koninklijke Brill.

Delinotte, Charles-Bernard-Augustin, 1898. L'oeuvre de reparation Eucharistique des Billettes, 613-20 IN *Dixième Congrès Eucharistique International tenu à Paray-le-Monial du 20 au 24 septembre 1897*. Autun: Imprimerie Dujussieu.

Delisle, Leopold, editor. 1885. *Testament de Blanche de Navarre*. Paris.

Deneev, J. 1922. Le miracle de la sainte hostie, *La Cité: Bulletin trimestriel de la Société Historique et Archeologique du IVe Arrondissement de Paris* 22: 169-91.

Descimon, Robert. 1998. Le corps de ville et le système ceremoniel au début de l'age moderne, 73-128 IN *Statuts individuels, status corporatifs et statuts judiciaires dans les villes européennes*. Leuven-Kessel-Lo: Garant.

Desportes, Henri. 1889. *Le mystère du sang chez les juifs de tous les temps*. Paris: A. Savine.

Drumont, Edouard. 1886. *La France juive: essai d'histoire contemporaine*. Paris: Librairie Blériot.

Dubreul, Jacques. 1612. *Le theatre des antiquitez de Paris*. Paris: Claude de Latour.

Dubu, M. 1854. *Histoire, description et annales de la basilisque de Notre Dame de Paris*. Paris: Ancienne Maison Saignier et Bray.

Dulaure, Jacques-Antoine. 1787. *Nouvelle description des curiosités de Paris, tome premier, première partie*.

Paris: Chez Lejay.

Dulaure, Jacques-Antoine. 1789. *Description des principaux lieux de France, tome seconde: Languedoc.* Paris: Chez Lejay.

Dulaure, Jacques-Antoine. 1829. *Histoire physique, civile et morale des environs de Paris, tome troisième.* Paris: Guillaume et Compagnie.

Dulaure, Jacques-Antoine and J.L. Belin. 1857. *Histoire physique, civile et morale des environs de Paris, tome premier.* Paris: Furne et Cie.

Du Moulin, Pierre. 1609. *Apologie pour la sainte cène du Seigneur.* La Rochelle.

Duplessy, Eugene. 1900. *Paris religieux: guide artistique, historique et pratique.* Paris: A. Roger et F. Chernovitz.

Einbinder, Susan L. 2002. *Beautiful Death: Jewish Poetry and Martyrdom in Medieval France.* Princeton: Princeton University Press.

Eisner, Will. 2013. *Fagin the Jew.* Milwaukee, Oregon: Dark Horse Books.

Estienne, Henri. 1735. *Apologie pour Hérodote, ou traité de la conformité des merveilles anciennes avec les modernes, tome second.* The Hague: Henri Scheurleer.

Farin, François. 1738. *Histoire de la ville de Rouen, sixième partie.* Rouen: Le Balouen.

Favre, Marie-Joseph. 1837. *Le ciel ouvert par la confession sincère et par la communion fréquente.* Lyon and Paris: Librairie Catholique de Perisse frères.

Félibien, Michel. 1725. *Histoire de la ville de Paris, tome second, tome troisième.* Paris: Guillaume des Prez.

Flacius, Mathias, et al. 1574. *Ecclesiastica historia, integram ecclesiae Christi ideam, quantum ad locum…* Basel.

Foa, Eugénie. 1843. Billette, ou la fille du juif, *La Macédoine Litteraire* 3: 355-57 and passim.

Foa, Eugénie. 1845. *Alexandrine, tome 1.* Paris: Passard.

Ford, Caroline. 2005. *Divided Houses: Religion and Gender in Modern France.* Ithaca: Cornell University Press.

Forgeais, Arthur. 1858. *Notice sur les plombs historiés trouvés dans la Seine.* Paris: l'auteur.

Fuchs, Rachel G. 2008. *Contested paternity: constructing families in modern France.* Baltimore: Johns Hopkins University Press.

Gabourd, Amédée. 1864. *Histoire de Paris, tome 2.* Paris: Gaume Frères et J. Duprey.

Gallagher, Caroline and Stephen Greenblatt. 2000. *Practicing New Historicism.* Chicago: University of Chicago Press.

de Gaulle, Julien and Charles Nodier. 1839. *Nouvelle histoire de Paris et de ses environs.* Paris: J.M. Pourrat Frères.

Gaultier de Claubry, Charles-Emmanuel-Simon. 1889. Le miracle de la sainte hostie de 1290, 441-49 IN *Le Congrès Eucharistique de 1888 tenu à Paris du 2 au 6 juillet.* Paris: Imprimerie de D. Dumoulin et Cie.

Gaultier de Claubry, Charles-Emmanuel-Simon. 1891. Les fêtes du sixième centenaire du miracle de la sainte hostie de 1290, à Paris, 453-58 IN *Le Congrès Eucharistique de 1890 tenu à Anvers du 16 au 21 août.* Anvers: Typographie Bellemans Frères.

Gaultier de Claubry, Charles-Emmanuel-Simon. 1894. Miracle de la sainte hostie de 1290, à

Paris 637-43 IN *Congrès des oeuvres Eucharistiques tenu à Jerusalem les 28, 29 et 30 de juin 1893.* Paris: Imprimerie Paul Foron-Vrau.

Géraud, Hercule. 1837. *Paris sous Philippe le Bel.* Paris: Crapelet.

Géraud, Hercule. 1843. *Chronique Latine de Guillaume de Nangis de 1113 à 1300…Tome premier.* Paris: Jules Renouard.

Giani, Arcangelo. 1618. *Annali sacri ordinis fratrum Servorum B. Mariae Virginis.* Florence: Cosmus Junta.

Gottschalk, Alfred. 1989. The German-Jewish Legacy: A Question of Fate, 81-86 IN *The German-Jewish Legacy in America, 1938-1988,* ed. by Abraham Peck. Detroit: Wayne State University Press.

Gourdon de Genouillac, Henri. 1881. *Paris à travers les siècles, tome premier.* Paris: F. Roy.

Graetz, Michael. 1996. *The Jews in nineteenth-century France: From the French Revolution to the Alliance Israélite Universelle,* trans. by Jane Marie Todd. Stanford; Stanford University Press.

Grente, Joseph. 1903. *La culte catholique à Paris de la Terreur au Concordat.* Paris: P. Lhetielleux.

Griffet, Henri, et al. 1770. *Histoire des hosties miraculeuses qu'on nomme le très saint sacrement du miracle.* Brussels: Chez B. Le Franq.

Guérin, Paul. 1878. *Les petites Bollandistes vies des saints, tome seizième.* Paris: Bloud et Barral.

Guiffrey, Georges, ed. 1860. *Cronique du Roy Françoys, premier de ce nom.* Paris: Chez Mme. Ve. Jules Renouard.

Guillot. 1875. *Le dit des rues de Paris (1300),* ed. by Edgar Marouse. Paris: Librairie Générale.

Helyot, Pierre. 1714-15. *Histoire des ordres monastiques, religieux et militaires, tome premier, tome troisième.* Paris: Jean-Baptiste Coignard.

Hanasse, Charles. 1890. Eglise de Reims: vie diocesane, *Bulletin du Diocèse de Reims* 28: 200-01.

Hurtaut, P.T.N. and Magny.1779. *Dictionnaire historique de la ville de Paris et de ses environs, tome 2.* Paris: Chez Moutard.

Inventaire Générale des Mouvements et Richesses Artistiques de la France. 1992. *Les vitraux de Champagne-Ardenne.* Paris: Editions de Centre National de la Recherche Scientifique.

Izbicki, Thomas. 2010. The Bleeding Host of Dijon: its place in the history of Eucharistic devotion, 227-46 IN *Saluting Aaron Gurevitch: Essays in history, literature and other related subjects,* ed. by Elena Mazur-Matusevic. London: Koninklijke Brill.

JAB. 1888. *Le sang chrétien dans les rites de la synagogue moderne.* Paris: H. Gautier.

Jacob, P.L. 1864. Addenda aux oeuvres des grands écrivains, *Bulletin du bouquiniste* 188: 555-62; 189: 587-91.

Jacquemart, Nicolas-François. 1792. *Remarques historiques et critiques sur les abbayes, collégiales et paroisses supprimées dans la ville et les faubourgs de Paris d'après le décret de l'assemblé constituante du 11 fevrier 1791.* Paris: Bureau de l'Imprimerie de la Société Bibliographique.

Joanne, Adolphe Laurent. 1863. *Paris illustré: nouveau guide de l'étranger et du Parisien.* Paris: Librairie Hachette.

Juvenal des Ursins, Jean. 1653. *Histoire de Charles VI.* Paris: Imprimerie Royale.

Katz, Dana. 2008. *The Jew in the art of the Italian Renaissance.* Philadelphia: University of Pennsylvania Press.

Kotek, Joel and Dan. 2003. *Au nom de l'antisionisme: l'image des juifs et d'Israel dans la caricature depuis la seconde intifada.* Editions Complexe.

Kumler, Aden. 2011. The multiplication of the species: Eucharistic morphology during the Middle Ages, *Res/Anthropology and Aesthetics* 59/60: 179-206.

Kunzle, David. 1970. The Comic Strip. 133-45 IN *Narrative Art: Art News Annual XXXVI*,ed. by Thomas B. Hess and John Ashbery. New York: Macmillan.

de L. 1926. L'initiatrice des congrès Eucharistiques: Mlle. Tamisier, *Semaine réligieuse du Diocèse de Lyon* 27, tome deuxième: 373-76; 389-91.

Lacroix, Sigismond, ed.. 1897. *Actes de la Commune de Paris pendant la Revolution, 2e serie, tome V.* Paris: L. Cerf.

Lacroix, Sigismond, ed. 1905. *Actes de la Commune de Paris pendant la Revolution, 2e serie, tome IV.* Paris: L. Cerf.

Lalanne, Ludovic, ed. 1854. *Journal d'un bourgeois de Paris sous le règne de François premier (1515-1536)* Paris: Chez Jules Renouard.

Langlois, Eustache-Hyacinthe. 1832. *Essai historique et descriptif sur la peinture sur verre ancienne et moderne.* Rouen: Edouard Frère.

de Lanzac de Laborie, Léon. 1907. *Paris sous Napoleon: la Religion.* Paris: Librairie Plon.

Lavin, Marilyn Aronberg. 1967. The Altar of Corpus Domini in Urbino: Paolo Uccello, Joos van Ghent, Piero della Francesca, *Art Bulletin* 49: 1-24.

Le Fèvre, Placide F. and O. Praem. 1953. Le thème du miracle des hosties poignardées par les Juifs à Bruxelles en 1370, *Le moyen âge: revue d'histoire et de philologie* 60: 373-98.

Le Fèvre, Placide F. 1931. Het oudste verhaal der "legende" van het H. Sacrament van Mirakel van Brussel, *Eigen schoon en de Brabander* 14: 241-50.

Le Maire, Charles. 1685. *Paris ancien et nouveau, tome premier.* Paris: Michel Vougon.

Le Rebours, Pierre-Almir. 1886. Rapport verbal de M. Le Rebours, curé de Sainte Madeleine à Paris, sur l'adoration perpétuelle à Paris, avant la Révolution, 462-66 IN *Congrès des oeuvres Eucharistiques tenu à Fribourg du 9 au 13 septembre, 1885.* Lille: Imprimerie de J. Leforet.

Le Rouge, Georges-Louis. 1742. *Les curiositez de Paris, tome premier.* Paris: Chez Saugrain.

Leber, M.C. 1839. *Catalogue des livres imprimés, manuscrits, estampes, desseins et cartes de jouer composant le bibliothèque de M.C. Leber avec des notes par le collecteur, tome second.* Paris: Chez Techener.

Lebeuf, Jean and Hippolyte Cocheris.1863. *Histoire de la ville et de tout le diocese de Paris, tome premier.* Paris: Auguste Durand.

Lecanu, Auguste François. 1866. *Dictionnaire des prophéties et des miracles, tome premier.* Paris: J.-P. Migne.

Lecomte, Matthieu. 1884. "oeuvre sacerdotale à Jerusalem," 609-25 IN *Congrès des oeuvres Eucharistiques tenu à Liège du 5 au 10 juin, 1883.* Lille: Imprimerie de J. Lefort.

Lenoir, Alexandre. 1893. *Epitaphier du vieux Paris, tome II.* Paris: Imprimerie Nationale.

Lipton, Sara. 2014. *Dark mirror: the medieval origins of anti-Jewish iconography.* New York: Henry Holt.

Licquet, Théodore. 1843. *Rouen: son histoire, ses monuments, son commerce, ses grands hommes: guide necessaire.* Rouen: A. Lebrument.

Loeb, Isidore. 1881. *La controverse sur le Talmud sous Saint Louis.* Paris: Baer.

Loth, Arthur. 1894. *Le miracle en France.* Desclée, de Brouwer et Cie.

Léon de St. Jean. 1664. *L'histoire de l'hostie miraculeuze arrivée au couvent des religieuses Carmes du Saint-Sacrement des Billettes.* Paris: Chez la veuve Denys Thierry.

Liber, Dom (Charles Potvin). 1874. *Le faux miracle du Saint-Sacrement à Bruxelles.* Brussels: Adrian Campan.

Lombard-Jourdan, Anne. 1973. La naissance d'une légende parisienne: le miracle du Lendit, *Annales E.S.C.* 28: 981-96.

Lombard-Jourdan, Anne. 1976. Fiefs et justices Parisiens au quartier des Halles, *Bibliotheque des Chartres Revue d'Érudition* 134: 301-88.

Lombard-Jourdan, Anne. 1987. Les foires de l'abbaye de Saint-Denis, *Bibliotheque de l'école des Chartres* 145: 273-338.

Lonergan, Walter F. 1896. *Historic churches of Paris.* New York: Thomas Whittaker.

Lubiniecki, Stanislaus. 1685. *Historia reformationis Polonicae.* Freistadt: Johannes Aconius.

Lucas, Alphonse. 1851. *Les clubs et les clubistes.* Paris: E. Dentu.

Maioli, Simone. 1609. *Dies caniculares, continuatio, sive tomus tertius.* Frankfort: Johann Theobald Schönvetter.

Marcus, Ivar. 2014. Why Did Medieval French Jewry (Ṣarfat) Disappear, 99-117 IN *Jews, Muslims and Christians in early modern times.* Leiden: Koninlkjke Brill.

de Marlès, Jean. 1838. *Paris Ancien et Moderne ou Histoire de France.* Paris: Parent-Desbarres.

McGuire, Brian Patrick. 2005. *Jean Gerson and the last medieval reformation.* University Park: Pennsylvania State University Press.

Macy, Gary. 2012. Theology of the Eucharist in the High Middle Ages, 365-98 IN *A Companion to the Eucharist in the Middle Ages,* ed. by Ian Levy, et al. Leiden: Koninljke Brill.

Marmursztejn, Elsa.2001. Du recit exemplaire au *casus* universitaire: une variation théologique sur la thème de la profanation des hosties par les Juifs, *Médiévales* 20,41: 37-64.

Maupoint, Jean. 1878. *Journal Parisien de Jean Maupoint, prieur de Sainte Catherine de-la-Couture,* ed. by Gustave Fagniez. Paris: H. Champion.

Maurel, V. 1895. Histoire sommaire des Congrès Eucharistiques, 291-300 IN *Congrès Eucharistique tenu à Reims du 25 au 29 juillet, 1894.* Reims: Imprimerie de l'Archévêché.

Meister, Aloys. 1901. Die Fragmente der Liber VIII Miraculorum des Caesarius von Heisterbach, *Römische Quartalschrift für Christliche Altertumskunde und für Kirchengeschichte, Vierzehntes Supplement.*

Meindre, A.J. *1855.* Histoire de Paris et de son influence en l'Europe. Paris: E. Dentu.

Merback, Mitchell B. 2012. *Pilgrimage and pogrom: violence, memory and visual culture at the host-miracle shrines of Germany and Austria.* Chicago: University of Chicago Press.

Mercier, Louis-Sebastien. 1782. *Tableau de Paris, tome troisième.* Paris.

Michaux, Lucien. 1901. Temple des Billettes (Paris le 15 février 1888), 94-99 IN *Inventaire general des richesses d'art de la France. Paris: Monuments religieux, tome troisième.* Paris: Librairie Plon.

Milon, P. 1633. *Le sacrifice de la croix representé en l'Eucharistie par l'hostie miraculeuse de Paris.* Paris: Pierre Bilaine.

Monmarché, Georges and Denise Bonnard-Folliot. 1972. *Paris: Haut-de-Seine, Seine St. Denis, Val de Marne*. Paris: Librairie Hachette.

de Morande, Charles Theveneau. 1777. *Gazetier cuirassé*. Imprimé à cent lieues de la Bastille, à l'enseigne de la Liberté.

Musset, Yves. 2000. *Le Christ du Père Chevrier*. Paris: Desclée.

Nauclerus, Johannes. 1614. *Chronica*. Cologne: Apud Arnoldum Quentellum.

Navez, J.J. 1790. *Dissertation historique sur les hosties miraculeuses*. Brussels: Chez Lemaire.

Newbigin, Nerida. 2009. Dieci sacre rappresentazioni dei Quattro e Cinquecento, *Letteratura italiana antica* 10: 21-397.

Nonnotte, Claude-François. 1772. *Dictionnaire philosophique de la religion, tome troisième*.

Offices propres de l'église paroissiale de Saint Jean-en-Grève, premiere partie, seconde partie. 1747. Paris: Le Mercier and Boudet.

d'Ormesson, Olivier. 1861. *Journal d'Olivier LeFèvre d'Ormesson et extraits des Memoirs*, ed. by M. Cheruel, *tome première, tome seconde*. Paris: Imprimerie Imperiale.

Paget, V. 1912. Le miracle des Billettes à Paris, *L'Eucharistie* 3.

Pagniol de la Force, Jean-Aymar. 1742. *Description de Paris, tome troisième, tome quatrième*. Paris: Charles Nicolas Poirion.

Paris, Paulin, ed. 1837. *Grandes Chroniques de France, selon que elles sont conservées en l'église de Saint-Denis en France, tome cinquième*. Paris: Techener.

Patin, Gui. 1856. *Lettres de Gui Patin, tome troisième*. Paris: J.-B. Baillière.

Peltier. 1797. *Tableau du massacre des ministres Catholiques et des martyres de l'honneur, executés dans le couvent des Carmes et à l'abbaye Saint-Germain, etc. les 2,3,4 de septembre, à Paris, par les infâmes suppôts de l'anarchie*. Paris.

Pérouse de Montclos, Jean-Marie. 1994. *Le guide de patrimoine: Paris*. Paris: Hachette.

Petit de Julleville, Louis. 1880. *Histoire de théâtre en France: les mystères, tome second*. Paris: Librairie Hachette.

Petryszcze, Camille Salatko. *Le mistere de la saincte hostie, introduction, edition du texte, et notes*. Mémoire de Master sous la direction de D. Hüe, Université de Rennes 2. http://www.sites.univrennes2.fr/celam/cetm/Edition%20Hostie/ostie.html

Pisani, Paul. 1891. *La maison des Carmes, 1610-1875*. Paris: Librairie Ch. Possielgue.

du Pleix, Scipion. 1624. *Histoire générale de France avec l'état de l'église et de l'empire, tome II*. Paris: Lavron Sonnius.

de Pratz de Pressy, François-Joseph. 1767. *Instruction pastorale de Monsieur l'Évêque de Boulogne* Boulogne: Chez Ch. Batiut.

Prod'homme, Jacques-Gabriel. 1911. *Niccolo Paganini: A Biography*, trans. by Alice Mattullath. New York: Carl Fischer.

Rahlenbeek, Charles. 1870. *Le jubilé d'un faux miracle: dissertation sur l'histoire du Saint-Sacrement du miracle de l'église des SS. Michel et Gudule*. Brussels: Le Revue Belgique.

Raunié, Emile. 1893. *Epitaphier du vieux Paris, tome II*. Paris: Imprimerie Nationale.

Raynal, Jean. 1759. *Histoire de la ville de Toulouse*. Toulouse: Jean-François Forest.

Reinach, Joseph. 1901. *Histoire de l'affaire Dreyfus: le procès de 1894*. Paris: Editions de la Revue

Blanche.

Rémi, Joseph-Honoré, et al. 1782. *Encyclopédie méthodique de jurisprudence, tome 10 (police et municipalités, tome 2; danse-voiture)* Paris: Chez Pancoucke.

Renou de Chevigné, Jean-Baptiste. 1773. *Recherches critiques, historiques et topographiques sur la ville de Paris, onzième quartier: La Gréve.* Paris: chez l'auteur.

Richard, François-Marie-Benjamin. 1889. Lettre pastorale, 11-23 IN *Le Congrès Eucharistique tenu à Paris de 2 au 6 juillet 1888.* Paris: Imprimerie de D. Dumoulin et Cie.

Rodríguez Barral, Paulino. 2008. *La imagen del judío en la España medieval: El conflicto entre cristianismo y judaísmo en las artes visuales góticas.* Barcelona: Universitat Autónoma de Barcelona.

Robert, Ulysse. 1881. Catalogue d'Actes relatifs au juifs pendant le moyen age, *Revue des Études Juives* 3: 211-24.

Roche, Daniel. 1987. *The people of Paris: An essay in popular culture in the 18th century.* Berkeley: University of California Press.

Roy, Emile. 1903. *Le mystère de la Passion en France du XIVe au XVe siècle.* Dijon: Damidot Frères.

Rubin, Alissa J. 2015. A mob killing and flawed justice, *New York Times* December 27: 1;10-12.

Rubin, Miri. 1999. *Gentile tales: the narrative assault on late medieval Jews.* New Haven: Yale University Press.

Rubin, Miri. 2006. Jewish Women: Latin and European Vernacular Literature. 429-30 IN *Women and gender in medieval Europe: An Encyclopedia.* New York: Routledge.

de S. René, Theodoric. 1725. *Remarques historiques données à l'occasion de la sainte hostie miraculeuse, tome premier, tome second.* Paris: Antonin des Hayes.

de Salamon, Louis Sifrein Joseph Foncrosé, 1896.*Unpublished memoirs of the Internuncio at Paris during the Revolution, 1790-1801.* Boston: Little, Brown and Co.

de Sales, François. 1758. *Lettres de S. François de Sales, tome premier.* Paris: Claude Herrisaint.

Samuels, Maurice. 2010. *Inventing the Israelite: Jewish fiction in nineteenth-century France.* Stanford: Stanford University Press.

Sauval, Henri. 1724. *Histoire et recherches des antiquités de la ville de Paris, tome premier.* Paris: Jacques Chardon.

Sebastian, John T., editor. 2012. *Croxton Play of the Sacrament.* Kalamazoo: Medieval Institute Publications.

Séguier, Jérôme. 1604. *Histoire miraculeuse de la saincte hostie gardée en l'Eglise de S. Iean en Greue.* Paris.

de Segur, Louis-Gaston. 1886. *La France au pied du Saint Sacrement.* Paris: Librairie St. Joseph.

Smet, Cornelis. 1839. *Histoire de la religion Catholique en Brabant.* Brussels: La Société Nationale pour Propagation des Bons Livres.

de Sommerard, Edmond. 1861. *Musée des Thermes et de l'Hôtel de Cluny: Catalogue et description des objets d'art de l'antiquité, du moyen âge et de la Renaissance..* Paris: Hotel de Cluny.

Sellier, Charles. 1910. *Anciens hôtels de Paris: nouvelles recherches historiques, topographiques et artistiques.* Paris: H. Champion.

Socard, Alexis. 1866. Un mot sur quelques verrières de l'église de Bar-sur-Seine et en particulier sur la grisaille de l'hostie miraculeuse, *Annuaire de l'Aube* 93-102.

Socard, Emile. 1877. Necrologie: Alexis Socard, 146-49 IN *Nouvelle Revue de Champagne et de Brie.*

Paris: H. Menu.

Sorel, Alexandre. 1864. *Le couvent des Carmes et le seminaire de Saint-Sulpice pendant la Terreur*. Paris: Didier et Cie.

Stow, Kenneth. 2006. *Jewish dogs: An image and its interpreters*. Stanford University Press.

Suenens, Kristien. 2014. Jésuites et congregations feminines en Belgique (ca. 1850-ca. 1880): rencontres, influences et conflits 249-70 IN *Les échelles de pouvoir. rapports de genre: femmes, Jésuites et modèle ignatien dans le long 19eme siècle*, ed. by Silvia Mostaccio, et al. Louvain-la-Neuve: Presses Universitaires de Louvain.

Thévenot, Arsène. 1903. *Monographie de la commune de Lhuitre (Aube)*. Arcis-sur-Aube: Imprimerie Léon Frémont.

de Thilrode, Jean. 1835. *Chronique de S. Bavon à Gand (1298)*. Ghent: Chez Vassas.

Thiéry, Luc-Vincent. 1795. *Paris tel qu'il étoit avant la Révolution, tome premier*. Paris: Delaplace.

Tomita, Soko, comp. 2009. *A bibliographical catalogue of Italian books printed in England, 1558-1603*. Farnham: Ashgate.

Tougard, A. 1915. Les verrières du "Miracle des Billettes" au Musée d'Antiquités, *Bulletin de la Commission des Antiquités de la Seine-Inférieure* 16: 415-18.

Toussenel, Alphonse. 1845. *Les juifs, rois de l'époque: histoire de la féodalité sociétaire*. Paris: La Librairie de l'École Sociétaire.

Tuety, Alexandre, ed. 1881. *Journal d'un bourgeois de Paris, 1405-1440*. Paris: Chez H. Champion.

Tuety, Alexandre. 1902. *Répertoire general des sources manuscrites de l'histoire de Paris pendant la Revolution Française, tome sixième*. Paris: Imprimerie Nouvelle.

Valois, Noel. 1901. Gerson curé de Saint Jean-en-Grève, *Bulletin de la société de l'histoire de Paris et de l'Île de France* 28: 49-57.

de Vigneulles, Philippe. 1852. *Gedenkbuch des Metzger Bürgers Philippe von Vigneulles aus den Jahren 1471 bis 1522*. ed. by Heinrich Michelant. Stuttgart: Bibliothek des Literarischen Vereins.

Villani, Giovanni. 1537. *Chroniche de Messer Giovanni Villani, cittadino Fiorentino*. Florence: Bartolomeo Zanetti.

Vloberg, Maurice. 1946. *L'Eucharistie dans l'art*. 2t. Grenoble: B. Arthaud.

Voillery, [Abbé]. 1898. Les miracles Eucharistiques de Saint-Victor-sur-Ouche et de la Sainte Hostie de Dijon. 393-96 IN *Dixième Congrès Eucharistique International tenu à Paray-le-Monial 1897*. Autun: Imprimerie Dejussieu.

Voltaire. 1769. *Essai sur les moeurs et l'esprit des nations, tome troisième*. Geneva.

Voltaire. 1832. Commentaire historique 1776, 315-402 IN *Oeuvres de Voltaire, tome 48,* ed. by M. Beuchot., Paris: Chez Lefèvre.

Walker, James Bernard. 1933. *The "Chronicles" of Saint Antoninus: a study in historiography*. Catholic University of America Studies in Medieval History, v. 6.

Weber, Auguste. 1908. *Un centenaire: l'église evangelique Lutherienne de Paris, 1808-1908*. Paris: l'Agence du Consistoire.

Wieck, Roger S. 2007a. The Sacred Bleeding Host of Dijon in choir books and on posters, 385-96 IN *Manuscripten en miniaturen: Studies aangeboden aan Anne S. Korteweg…*Zutphen: Walburg Pers.

Wieck, Roger S. 2007b. The Sacred Bleeding Host of Dijon in Books of Hours, 393-404 IN *Quand la peinture était dans les livres: Melanges en honneur de François Avril...*, ed. by M. Hoffman and C. Zöhl. Paris: Brepols.

Wogue, Lazare. 1885. Une fête intempestive, *L'univers israélite* 16: 499-503.

Wolff, Jetta Sophia. 1921. *Historic Paris*. London: John Lane The Bodley Head.

Ydens, Steven. 1605. *Histoire du sacrament du miracle gardé à Bruxelles en l'église collegiale de S. Gudule*. Brussels: Rutger Velpius.

Index

www.ingramcontent.com/pod-product-compliance
Lightning Source LLC
Chambersburg PA
CBHW061959280526
45787CB00005B/1926